Thinking About Peace:

The Conceptualization and Conduct of U.S.-Soviet Detente

Paul F. Herman, Jr.

LANHAM • NEW YORK • LONDON

Copyright © 1987 by

University Press of America,® Inc.

4720 Boston Way
Lanham, MD 20706

3 Henrietta Street
London WC2E 8LU England

Printed in the United States of America

British Cataloging in Publication Information Available

Library of Congress Cataloging-in-Publication Data

Herman, Paul F., 1956-
   Thinking about peace.

   Bibliography: p.
   Includes index.
   1. United States—Foreign relations—Soviet Union.
2. Soviet Union—Foreign relations—United States.
3. Detente.   I. Title.
E183.8.S65H45   1987   327.73047   86.32520
ISBN 0-8191-6105-5 (alk. paper)
ISBN 0-8191-6106-3 (pbk. : alk. paper)

All University Press of America books are produced on acid-free
paper which exceeds the minimum standards set by the National
Historical Publication and Records Commission.

Acknowledgements

I would like to begin by thanking members of the University of Pittsburgh faculty who had a hand in shaping this book -- William Dunn, Donald Goldstein and Robert Gromoll of the Graduate School of Public and International Affairs (GSPIA), and Jonathan Harris of the Department of Political Science. Each person brought to the project unique areas of expertise from which I could draw. I would also like to thank Professor Emeritus Michael Flack, former-Dean John Funari, and Paul Y. Hammond, all of GSPIA, for making valuable contributions at various points in the book's preparation.

Lending valuable advice and assistance since the very inception of this project has been my friend Russell Moses. A greal deal of useful support was also rendered by Melissa Neofes. Also responsible for a much appreciated input was Pete Lehmann. Many productive (although perhaps not satisfying to all) revisions have been fostered by the suggestions of several anonymous reviewers. Here in Washington, I would like to thank Douglas Brisson and George Clarke for helping me to get the book in final form. A debt of gratitude also goes to Raymond Garthoff of the Brookings Institution, who graciously took time from a busy schedule to comment on the manuscript.

It is usually perfunctory to thank the person responsible for a manuscript's physical preparation; however, in my case this acknowledgement is most sincere. Many thanks to Estelle Cantwell of Kind Words for the rendering of a truly professional and conscientious service.

I have saved the bulk of my praise for Richard Cottam, University Professor of Political Science at the University of Pittsburgh. This book is so suffused with the thoughts, perspectives and inspiration of Professor Cottam, that to do justice to his contribution via miscellaneous footnotes is impossible. Professor Cottam is as impressive and admirable a man as I have ever met, both in his capacities as a scholar and as a human being. I am very grateful for his collaboration.

TABLE OF CONTENTS

LIST OF TABLES

LIST OF FIGURES

INTRODUCTION

I remember one Saturday morning when I was about five or six years old. This particular Saturday occurred during the early 1960s; a time which had produced U.S.-Soviet confrontations over Berlin and Cuba, although I doubt I was consciously aware of these two specific settings. Yet from the ambiance of that time as I perceived it-- drawing from overheard adult conversations and news-casts, and even television sitcoms -- I was imbued with a sense of disquiet about the Russians, their motives, and about war between their country and mine. So on that particular Saturday morning I took a dusty globe of the world from a bedroom shelf and fretted over how large the USSR was compared to the U.S. I reasoned that like big boys and little boys who get in a fight, the big boy is likely to prevail. With some anxiety I carried the globe to my father who was having coffee in the kitchen and asked him, "are the Russians going to get us?" My father explained that although our country was smaller than the USSR, it was militarily very strong and that the Russians would not succeed in "getting us." With some immediate relief I carried the globe back to its bedroom shelf, yet I knew that quarrels sometime erupt which are desired by none of the parties involved, and I suspected that our enemy, the Russians, were probably intent on building a military force eventually capable of overwhelming our current level of strength; my relief was therefore short-lived, and my anxiety returned. It was almost two decades later that as a college student I realized one need not be fatalistic about the Soviet-American relationship, and began to think creatively about a concept called detente.

As the title of this text suggests, the following pages concern themselves with the notion of U.S.-Soviet detente. For the moment, detente may be considered in shorthand as a process of accommodation and transformation. It seems safe to say that the word detente must certainly be one of the most contentious and controversial to be found in the American foreign-policy lexicon of the last three decades. There are many reasons for such contention, including the problems of trying to discern what is meant by the word detente as it is used in other political systems, of drawing from 19th century European diplomacy an inappropriate definition which is intrinsically bound up in a multipolar balance-of-power international system, and of Americans' propensity to define detente in ways that are compatible with their own individual beliefs and interests. It is certainly anomolous that a concept as important as detente has received such sloppy and ad hoc treatment. There is the added complication that even if one wanted to be precise in his usage or investigation of the term, it may still be conceptualized in very different ways, such as a desirable state of affairs, a policy, or a view about causal relations between means and ends.[1] Other conceptualizations are of course possible. Since my approach to detente will be process-oriented, I am largely concerned with the above notion of causal relations between means and ends; however, my mind's eye is always looking for policy relevance, and I assume that there is a short -- but traversed all too infrequently and clumsily -- distance between policy-relevant theory and actual policies. It is clear that, for example, Alexander George feels there is a role for theory in policymaking, and I can fully empathize with his lament as he begins Chapter 16 of <u>Deterrence in American Foreign Policy: Theory and Practice</u> with a section entitled "The Gap Between Deterrence Theory and Deterrence Policy."[2]

One can categorize the irregularities found in the treatment of detente into two general problems -- one "policymaking" and the other "scholarly." Looking first at the policymaking problem, one dimension involves the absolute lack of consensus in the American setting on the fundamental nature of the Soviet system and its foreign policy. The loss of our cold-war consensus on Soviet foreign-policy motivation has not been replaced with a realistic, comprehensive assessment of the course and state of, as well as potentialities for Soviet-American relations. In the absence of such a thoughtfully derived core consensus, decisionmakers' assumptions tend to be so divergent as to result in a situation where policy prescriptions are incommensurate, and talk tends to be past, rather than to one another. This produces a rather dangerous recipe for policy incoherence, if not immobility. One also gets the perverse situation where policymakers may support (or oppose) detente for absolutely different, and in many cases antithetical reasons, with confusion sure to be the inevitable end result. For example, on a general level, one might support detente as a means of finally imposing some constraints on the insidious Russians' quest for expansion, while another might support detente as the logical outcome of the U.S. having discarded erroneous stereotypes about the USSR's implacable hostility. To use a more specific example, one might favor trade with the USSR because the enhancement of Soviet consumerism is seen as the best way to soften the underbelly of Soviet society and thus render that state less truculent, whereas another might support U.S.-Soviet trade as the logical manifestation of two states seeking a constructive relationship with each other.

A second dimension to the policymaking problem is the omission to date of an attempt by decisionmakers to systematically come to grips with the breadth and interconnectedness of the complex range of detente-related issues and their particular dynamics; to the extent that academics can or should provide such information, this is partially a scholarly problem. Without answers to such questions as the following -- What are the main policy areas or interactional genre which are encompassed by or contribute to detente? Does the early pursuit of any particular policy area or genre facilitate the subsequent undertaking of other types of interactions? Do undertakings in different policy areas produce results contemporaneously or asynchronously? -- the likelihood of a state being able to pursue a consistent and effective policy of detente is almost nil. I will cite an example of two simultaneous Amercian foreign policy initiatives toward the USSR taking place in 1974 in different fields or policy areas which worked absolutely at cross-purposes with each other -- namely, the Jackson-Vanik amendment to the Trade Reform Bill which linked Most-Favored Nation status for the USSR to their policy on Jewish emigration, and the Ford-Brezhnev agreement at Vladivostok limiting strategic nuclear weapons -- one reflecting disgust and confrontation, and the other a certain amount of trust and cooperation. Of course one can argue that it makes sense to negotiate arms limitations even with, or especially with a dreaded enemy; the point, however, is that the Vladivostok agreement was launched and perceived as a cooperative venture, the Jackson-Vanik amendment as a confrontational one. Neither the terms "linkage" nor "carrot and stick" can account for this type of discrepancy. In general, a policy strategy for the pursuit of detente vis-a-vis another actor must be an intricate and multi-faceted endeavor. To exclude a careful deliberation of the components of a detente strategy, their sequencing and interrelationship, is to start the detente process with a glaring handicap.

I would like to begin my discussion of the scholarly problem with a colorful passage from Frei and Ruloff..

...when talking about the "progress" or "stagnation," the "crisis" or even the "end," or about the "irreversibility" and "reversibility," of the process of "detente," the situation and development trends are usually assessed by a rule-of-thumb interpretation, that is, by pure intuition. References, for example, to a "typical" statement of politician X or politician Y or to arbitrary events (meetings, contracts, protests, incidents, and so on) are used as more or less "significant" proofs for one's theory.[3]

Although I have some methodological disagreements with the authors of the above passage, and we focus our work somewhat differently, the indictment found in the passage is right on target. However, I might even be a bit less kind in my indictment of detente scholarship. I do not think most scholars writing on detente even have a "theory" to work from, only gut feelings as to whether or not detente is progressing, regressing or moribund; and their intuitive proofs seek to validate only these impressions or gut feelings. The number of journal articles which follow the stock "demise of detente" formula are a vivid embodiment of this problem.

By and large, we have a situation where in the absence of good theorizing on detente, authors cannot know what types of data to look for, and where; and key concepts -- often insightfully conceptualized -- are left unoperationalized (if not unoperationalizable), making any sort of rigorous attempt at measurement impossible. Despite the travail of producing it, rigorous research on detente stands to yield rich rewards. Discussing the applications of their self-admittedly "descriptive" or "evaluative" framework, Frei and Ruloff propose that

...by developing indicators of East-West relations, it would become possible to monitor the East-West interaction process in Europe and elsewhere and provide useful information; such information is the most crucial requirement for deciding on future courses of action...[4]

I would submit that beyond this, an explanatory framework which is prescriptive in the (minimal) sense that it identifies key variables, and stipulates their functions as well as their combined net effect or impact does more than just help to choose among alternative courses of action, but can also act as a guide to action in designing that future course: this is a fitting introduction to my own research.

A. Research Design

First, a theoretical framework will be deduced concerning how states improve relations with one another (e.g. pursue detente); this framework will facilitate the meaningful selection of components for a measuring device of the state of Soviet-American detente (or its absence) over time. I might add, that I will use the word detente in connection with periods of time which one might intuitively feel were less than cordial, and thus question the usage; however, due to my normative assumption that the superpowers' foreign policies should pursue a detente or cooperative course (rather than one of exclusion or confrontation), and have often had a rationale for doing so, I will use the word detente frequently if only to note its nonexistence or inchoate nature. On the basis of the deductive theoretical underlay, two measures of the state of U.S.-Soviet detente will be devised; the first measure will have an "events" orientation, whereas the second will be of a "perceptual" or inferential nature. I hasten to point out that everything previewed in this Introduction will be explicated in great detail in the next two chapters. The use of two measurement techniques is an attempt to utilize "between-method triangulation" in guarding against findings which are artifacts of a particular method.[5] It is expected that the two different measures of detente will corroborate each other so that when the measurement techniques are applied per annum to the post-war period, high and low points in U.S.-Soviet relations will be similarly identified. This in itself would be no mean achievement, as an objective and widely accepted charting or interpretation of the course of U.S.-Soviet post-war relations would tend to foster that proximate consensus or base of discourse which is so important to policymaking and academic tasks.

After applying the detente-measuring devices historically, the results may be employed prescriptively by combing the actual interactions and acts of policy occurring during the most cooperative years for patterns and commonalities from which one could generalize. The specific occurrences in periods of reversing or deteriorating relations will also be examined so as to enable us to prescribe preventive measures for anticipated negative influences. By considering both types of patterns, one should be able to go a long way towards extracting or inducing a refined and sequenced political strategy for initiating and conducting a policy of detente. A fair question that could be raised at this point concerns whether or not the post-war period is homogeneous enough so that lessons or patterns drawn from its early years are still applicable today. Specifically, has the Soviet-American relationship been transformed by the advent of nuclear parity in the 1970s? The implication here is that the USSR as a nuclear equal will be more confident and risk acceptant in its dealings with the U.S. and the West. A review of the recent literature on Soviet foreign/national security decisionmaking, however, finds a conspicuous recurrence of such words as "cautious" and "risk averse."[6] You would have been hard pressed to have found this appraisal so widely held in the 1940s (witness the Soviet "betrayal" of Yalta), the 1950s (the instigation of the Korean War), or the 1960s (the Cuban missile crisis). The majority view seems to be that a swaggering USSR has yet to arrive on the scene. Another reason for looking at the full post-war record draws upon the cybernetic decisionmaking perspective, which posits that in a highly bureaucratized political system such as the USSR's, emphasis is given to official reliance on past behavior and learned routines. In any case, those most resistant to the notion of U.S.-Soviet accommodation often trace their line of reasoning back to the expansionist tendencies of Kievan Rus; investigating the prospects of accommodation in the forty years since WWII seems, in comparison, like current history.

Although the above version of the text's research design is drastically abridged, this design was consciously planned as a multi-stage procedure -- which should become clear in the following chapters -- in order to capitalize on the strengths of one approach while tempering its draw-backs by linking it to another. Specifically, I am talking about the problem of relying exclusively on either a deductive or inductive method. A model of detente based purely on deductive logic, while capable of producing insightful and elegant concepts, runs the risk of empirical irrelevance. The traditional inductive approach of amassing data, then spinning it out into a handful of basic dimensions via factor analysis runs the risk of producing concepts which are counterintuitive if not artifactual, and since these dimensions are so closely tied to the nature of one's collected data, research findings tend to be non-additive across different data sets.[7] I seek to use a deductive approach to structure an inductive approach, with the ultimate aim being a narrative on detente built from and incorporating the best elements of both approaches.

Despite only a table of contents and sketchy introduction thus far, I will not preview at this time the chapters which are to follow. This is due to the fear of playing my trump cards too soon, or doing violence to the cards themselves because of oversimplification.

Notes

[1] Erich Weede, "Detente-Related Policies: An Evaluation," in Definitions and Measurements of Detente, ed. Daniel Frei (Cambridge, Mass.: Oelgeschlager, Gunn and Hain, Publishers, Inc., 1981), pp. 141-151.

[2] Alexander George and Richard Smoke, Deterrence in American Foreign Policy: Theory and Practice (New York: Columbia University Press, 1974), p. 503.

[3] Daniel Frei and Dieter Ruloff, East-West Relations, 2 Vols. (Cambridge, Mass.: Oelgeschlager, Gunn and Hain, Publishers, Inc., 1983), Vol. 1: A Systematic Survey, pp. 1-2.

[4] Ibid., p. 2.

[5] H. W. Smith, Strategies of Social Research (Englewood Cliffs: Prentice-Hall, Inc., 1981), p. 380.

[6] For example, see Dennis Ross in Valenta and Potter, eds. (1984); Thomas Hammond (1976); and Hannes Adomeit (1982).

[7] Patrick Callahan, Linda Brady and Margaret Hermann, eds., Describing Foreign Policy Behavior (Beverly Hills: Sage Publications, 1982), see Part I.

CHAPTER 1

THE ANALYTICAL FRAMEWORK

This chapter will set the broad theoretical context from which the more mechanical measurement techniques of Chapter 2 will be drawn. I define detente as: the "process whereby each of two sides-- both committed to improving relations with the other -- responds favorably to the other side's conciliatory actions, so that tensions and distrust increasingly wane, cooperation is made possible and indeed undertaken across an increasingly broad and salient range of issues, and rising levels of mutual reward impel each side to become increasingly attentive to accommodating the other." My analysis will focus almost exclusively on the U.S.-Soviet dyad; the NATO and WTO (Warsaw Treaty Organization) blocs are important, but not determining, and I do make conceptual room for alliance politics in a discussion of "background factors" later in this chapter.

It should be clear from my definition of detente that the aim of detente is "relational change" between the superpowers. It is not an attempt to enact a static modus vivendi, where underlying sources of hostility are ignored, and the threat of either side defecting from a type of behavior that is marginally acceptable to the other remains ever present. The aim of detente is to transform the superpowers' relationship with one another from "enemy" to something which might be called "collaborative peer." The competitive aspects of the collaborative peer are seen by each side as limited and legitimate (even if sometimes irritating or unhelpful). This focus on change in relational-type is absolutely necessary, because the competitive aspects of the enemy relationship transcend any specific acts or endeavors: for example, in 1978 when the U.S. ratified the new Panama Canal Treaty, this should have been an act which the Soviets truly hailed (and from which perhaps even drew lessons about the reasonableness of American foreign policy), for they had decried the previous treaty for many years as an outrageous and anachronistic vestige of old-world colonialism; however, I suspect that -- perfunctory rhetoric aside -- they hated to see the new treaty, which would be widely interpreted as a popular and progressive decision, thus elevating American foreign policy in the world's eyes and robbing themselves of an effective propaganda point.

The simple notion of relational change harbors a major conceptual switch from the mainstream perspective on detente. To date, there seems to have been an analytical fixation with "definitions of detente," "codes of conduct," etc.; and oftentimes the highly expected yet marginally informative conclusion that detente broke down in the mid and late 1970s due to differing definitions of detente on both sides is offered. This is a perfect example of putting the cart before the horse. Should we expect the USSR and the U.S. to have differing conceptions of detente at the start, or even in the early years

1

of such a process? The answer is "yes, of course." I see this point as almost truistic. The logic of detente is not to shun it until the other side somehow comes to adopt or assimilate perceptions and attitudes similar to one's own, but to embark on such a policy expecting full well that there will be divergencies in viewpoint, and to seek to somehow co-evolve through mutual endeavor to more compatible and sustainable orientations.

I assume that not all periods of history are capable of spawning and nurturing a detente process. The ground was fertile for detente in the late 60s and early 70s, and could be fertile again today with some adjustments; this leads into my discussion of background factors. Background factors are perceived conditions in the policymaking environment of each superpower which prompt or suggest a policy of detente. These conditions tend to do one of two things, or both; namely, induce perception of resource finiteness, or induce perception of mutual interest. Background factors can manifest themselves in either the domestic or international policymaking environments of a superpower, and may either be an extant state of affairs, or a policy need which compels a pro-detente posture for realization. Looking first at the Soviet Union, background factors which would tend to warrant the USSR pursuing a policy of East-West detente include economic problems (and thus the need to obtain technology, to conserve resources via arms control, etc.), a desire to codify the European status quo, the need to free up and divert military resources and attention toward China, the achievement of an appropriate military balance (e.g., rough parity), etc. Background factors which would serve this same function for the U.S. might include the seeking of relief from the burden of arms spending, a post-Vietnam social reluctance to support an activist or global foreign policy, a desire to cultivate export markets in the USSR, fear of unilateral West European pursuit of detente, etc. Of course, some background factors obtain for both superpowers, such as centrifugal forces in the international system which act against the preservation of a tight bipolar world. Graphically, we can picture detente as being possible when an inventory of objective conditions reveals a relative preponderance of them to be located in the second quadrant of Figure 1.

2

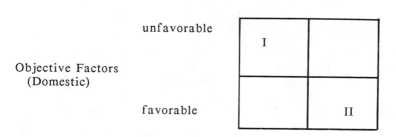

Figure 1

Detente and Environmental Background Factors

A. The Trust/Benefit Equation

A simple theoretical framework will now be presented; this framework must explain the essential function or functions a state's detente-designated policy behavior must fulfill if it wishes to sustain an effective detente policy. In thinking about the manifestations of detente -- e.g., relaxed tensions, nonstereotyped perceptions of the other, lowered threat of war, etc. -- it appears that they are all dependent on heightened levels of mutual trust; therefore, I assume that increasing levels of mutual trust is the sine qua non of detente, and actions by each side which facilitate a detente process are those which "engender trust." For working purposes we can use Pruitt's definition of trust -- "the expectation that another nation will usually be helpful and avoid being harmful."[1] This definition includes two elements which tend to be common to most definitions of trust; the first element is "predictability," and the second is that prediction usually augurs "favorable outcomes" as a result of engagement.

However, the phenomenon of trust is unstable, and we can envision various circumstances under which it may be destroyed. For example, mutual trust is highly unstable if a trusted party is superfluous to one's core interests (e.g., the U.S. trusts Papua New Guinea but there would be little cost in initiating actions which would change this); however, if both sides act to provide the other with benefit, this condition of superfluousness is removed. Another example, involving at least two variants, occurs when the payoffs from enmity simply outweigh those from amity. According to the first variant, an opportunity to substantially gain by the invasion or domination of another country may induce the aggressor to negatively valuate a state of mutual trust between themselves and their target (e.g., trust

3

precludes preemptive attack, not acquisitive attack). The second variant holds that a state may stand to gain more from allies and potential allies by manipulating tensions than by reconciling with the traditional enemy (there is certainly some significance in this second variant for the U.S.-Soviet example). For both variants, mutual provision of benefit creates a disincentive to break an amicable, utilitarian relationship. Therefore, in addition to "engender trust," "provide benefit" is the second element in a formula for identifying actions which tend to generate forward movement in a detente process. We can define provision of benefit in the context of detente as being the contribution of one side towards the partial or complete realization of a policy goal stated by the other side; it may take the form of a commodity as well as a certain mode of behavior. I must add, however, that provision of benefit cannot stand on its own as the engine of detente. For such provision may in some instances be warranted or compelled by the situation or environment, much as a cowboy in an old western movie might be amenable to dancing when bullets from a patron's sixshooter are ricocheting about his feet. There must be a volitional element, and this is the role played by the trust concept. Influence strategies characterized by toughness or bullying will not induce an opponent to lower his hostile objectives.[2] In summation, I assume that actions undertaken by both sides which seek to enhance a detente process must "engender trust" and/or "provide benefit." It should be pointed out that this simple formula applies equally, without alteration, to both the U.S. and USSR. Of course, when one moves to the level of detail necessary for policy prescription, differences in each side's policy process and expressed needs would mandate a varied application of the trust/benefit guideline.

The trust/benefit formulation is not just a casual insight, but rather one which is strongly supported by empirical research; I will now briefly look at some of that research. I would like to say that whereas much of the experimental research on such concepts as trust, responsiveness and cooperation is based on two-person game situations such as prisoners' dilemma, I feel that, much as parents of high school football players live vicariously through the fate of the team, rather than through only the offense or defense, or even more finely delimited, the offense's or defense's respective lines or backfields, policymakers in both the U.S. and USSR, despite their bureaucratic interests live a vicarious life through the fate of their nation; and in this sense policy choices can actually be viewed as part of a two-person or two-actor game. The relation of individual-level analogies to complex international situations is an unresolved (and perhaps unresolvable) question. There is, however, an influential group of researchers which feel that the best way to attain a logical and theoretical understanding of interstate behavior is to focus on a stripped-down microcosmic level (e.g. dyadic interpersonal relations).[3] If this is the case, then much of the experimental research mentioned above may be extended in application to U.S.-Soviet interactions.

Morton Deutsch says "there are social situations which, in a sense, do not allow the possibility of 'rational' individual behavior as long as the conditions for mutual trust do not exist."[4] I believe that detente is an example of rational behavior, in that it involves adapting to environmental realities, and discarding certain stereotyped patterns of thought and behavior; and that it, unlike the situation described by Deutsch, is dependent on the condition of mutual trust. The security dilemma -- representing the near converse of the logic of a detente process -- illustrates the irrationality (e.g., lack of contribution toward realizing a primary goal) produced in conditions where mutual trust is largely absent: both sides seek safety in thinking the worst about the other, both amass armaments defensively, see the other's arming as confirmation of their worst suspicions, and arm themselves further; the end result being not an addition to, but a diminution in real security, all at colossal material and spiritual costs. Although rarely acknowledged explicitly, most authors looking at East-West relations flirt with, if not focus on trust as a key concept. There have been a number of efforts to empirically test Osgood's Graduated Reciprocation in Tension-reduction (GRIT) strategy, which seeks to ameliorate the Soviet-American conflict through a "trust-building" process involving a unilateral (and presumably reciprocated) sequence of increasingly important policy initiatives. To the extent that Osgood focuses on trust, his diagnosis of and prescription for U.S.-Soviet relations are basically compatible with my own. Such techniques as historical scrutiny (Etzioni - 1970), two-person experimental game situations (Pilisuk and Skolnik - 1968; Tedeschi, Bonoma and Lindskold - 1970) and multi-person simulations (Crow - 1963) -- all more or less creating the conditions stipulated by Osgood as necessary for GRIT -- have produced results which moderately-to-strongly substantiate the conflict lessening properties of a graduated trust-building process.

The research on provision of benefit -- usually involving different but synonymous terms -- is quite rich and extensive. The branch or school of sociological thought known as "exchange theory" contains a potential wealth of insights into the concept of benefit provision. Prominent exchange theorist Peter Blau says that whereas the influence derived from coercion is more absolute, the influence derived from met needs (benefit) is wider in scope.[5] A detente policy which must obviously direct superpower relations into untried or previously unsuccessful modes of cooperative behavior cannot be realized via coercion, but requires a type of noncoercive leverage such as that associated with met needs. A paraphrase of the work of Georg Simmel relating to met needs or benefit states that "service" leads to a sense of "gratitude" in a recipient which consequently leads to "return service."[6] The receipt of return service helps to counteract those conditions which were previously identified as destabilizing to an existing or incipient trusting relationship; namely, superfluousness and potential loss of pay-offs from accommodation. The Simmel paraphrase suggests a linkage of benefit provision to the concept of responsiveness; this linkage is spelled out in the following passage by Dean Pruitt.

> One nation's responsiveness toward another is a joint function of the other nation's apparent level of fate-control (positive fate-control = provision of benefit; P.H.) and its apparent flexibility in the use of this fate-control (flexibility = the volitional point made earlier; P.H.).[7]

This means that if one side cooperates with and rewards another (in an uncoerced manner), then a sympathetic and cooperative orientation will be induced from the other in return. Thus, Pruitt's formulation reflects much of the logic found in my deduction that provision of benefit functions in a detente-enhancing capacity. I would also like to point out, in reference to Pruitt's formulation, that I consider responsiveness to be a key manifestation of a detente process, and remind the reader that my definition of detente includes the phrase "each side (becomes) increasingly attentive to accommodating the other." I disagree with persons such as Kjell Goldman (1982) who treat responsiveness as undesirable, equating it with hyper-sensitivity to shocks which threaten the stability of detente, and thus requiring cognitive and bureaucratic tricks to counter this hyper-sensitivity. As extensive as the superpowers' interests are at present, conscious and continuous attention to the avoidance of stepping on each others' toes is a necessity; whereas the psychological withdrawal involved in the mere monitoring of key variables to keep them within acceptable value ranges is a poor prescription for crisis prevention.

Although already implicit in his above statement, Pruitt then draws out the iterative or interactive consequences of responsiveness by stating that "levels of responsiveness in the interaction of two nations tend to be reciprocal."[8] This means that provision of benefit by either side to the other is not likely to be all give or all take. What is more, reciprocity seems to be the greatest at high levels of cooperation. Alan Alexandroff in his book The Logic of Diplomacy (1981) finds historical evidence to substantiate the hypothesis that the more cooperative the aggregate level of behavior between A and B, the higher the symmetry of cooperation and the lower the symmetry of conflict. This means that the more cooperative the relationship between two states, the more assured either of them can be that a cooperative initiative made on their part will be reciprocated, and that an isolated or incongruous conflictual act will be ignored or at least allowed to go unretaliated.

We have seen that various research findings argue for a policy of gratifying the other side via provision of benefit; while on this topic I would like to introduce a particular guideline to be followed as part of such a policy. This guideline concerns the notion of equity. Two sociologists, Marwell and Schmidt, have recently conducted experimental research on the effects of inequity in the benefits received from cooperation on the continuation of cooperation in two-person interactions; they found that inequity had significant effects in destroying cooperation.[9] I argue that equity is crucial within each detente-related issue-area and even for each specific agreement. Ex-Secretary of State Kissinger felt that the U.S. and USSR would benefit from different measures, and that a balance could only be struck over time and across a whole range of issues. I feel that this is an incorrect approach, for there is no objective balancing mechanism with which to gauge the balance of benefits Kissinger mentions; the balance will look different to different persons, and even for the same person, a balance perceived at one point in time may appear as an imbalance in retrospect. To illustrate the problems of balancing disparate goods and services, look at the interminable discussions on theatre nuclear force reductions in Europe regarding how arsenals that mix bombers, missiles and cruise missiles can be equilibrated; and this is "within" the arms control issue-area. Therefore, the terms of an agreement should be made to stand or fall on their own merit to the extent possible, at least in the early stages of a detente policy.

The following proposition will seek to put the trust/benefit formula into a dynamic cast, as well as to highlight the two processes' interrelationship. "By discharging their obligations for services rendered, if only to provide inducements for the supply of more assistance, individuals demonstrate their trustworthiness, and the parallel expansion of mutual service is accompanied by a parallel growth of mutual trust."[10] In general, within the context of a relationship characterized by mutual trust, and in situations where the conditions of mutual comparative advantage and/or mutual benefit obtain, there are "no" reasons why a request made to the other side for assistance or cooperation (benefit) should be refused. Any such refusal would impact negatively on the original level of mutual trust. This line of reasoning raises the notion of expectational realization/nonrealization. Dashed expectations lead to feelings of frustration, if not of having been double-crossed. Frei and Ruloff state that "...disappointment and frustrations are hardly conducive to reaffirm the willingness to engage in additional and more decisive steps forward."[11] Such an eventuality would tend to foster perceptions of stagnation or break-down, and would most likely embolden those opposed to the original detente policy, thus facilitating its further reversal or dismantling. This is the antithesis of a perception of policy momentum (the result of expectational realization), which seems to be crucial for the development of a detente process; this consideration will come prominently into play later in the manuscript as part of the discussion on policy prescription. Therefore, the trust and benefit processes can be seen to act and change very much in tandem.

For purposes of conceptual completeness I have discussed both the "engender trust" and "provide benefit" stipulations, as well as shown their interrelationship; however, for the purposes of measurement, this interrelationship translates into covariance. The logic behind the covariance is that one is willing to assist another when he does not fear misuses or aggressive applications of transferred goods and services; whereas when dealing with an unremitting enemy one's security is best protected by trying to limit the enemy's capabilities and advantages. Therefore, without a significant loss of anticipated evaluative power, I will focus only on "trust" as my key concept, using it as the basis for operational definitions and spinoff concepts. In any case, the operationalization of benefit would have been most complex due to the necessity of having to infer benefit according to a state's value system (the explication of which would have been most contentious).

In summary, this chapter has put forth the proposition that actions which enhance detente are those which "engender trust" and/or "provide benefit." Using the word cooperation as shorthand for the trust/benefit formula, this chapter has also sought to establish that cooperative behavior toward another state tends to be reciprocated, and that as the cooperative nature of a relationship increases, so does its stability or resistance to reversal. The relevance of these two patterns to detente -- which seeks to transform a dyadic relationship into a mutually satisfying, stable and cooperative mode -- is clear. "Trust" has been singled out as the key concept, and in fact, I assume that trust is the basic underlying dimension which differentiates allies from enemies (as well as all mixed or ambivalent relational-types falling in-between the ally/enemy extremes). The notion of "relational type" will be important to my image-based or perceptual approach to measuring detente. With this last statement having foreshadowed Chapter 2, I will remind the reader that the next chapter seeks to measure the relative favorableness of orientation between the U.S. and USSR per annum for the post-war period utilizing two different perspectives or points of attack -- the first being an historical or events-data approach (disciplined by an interpretative framework), and the second is a perceptual approach. It is hoped that the two approaches will evaluate the years I examine similarly, and that such a corroboration will validate my concepts and measures.

Notes

[1] Dean G. Pruitt, "Definition of the Situation as a Determinant of International Action," in *International Behavior*, ed. Herbert Kelman (New York: Holt, Rinehart and Winston, 1965), p. 397.

[2] Russell Leng and Hugh Wheeler, "Influence Strategies, Success, and War," *Journal of Conflict Resolution*, 23 (December 1979), p. 680.

[3] Barry Schlenker and T. V. Bonoma, "Fun and Games: The Validity of Games for the Study of Conflict," *Journal of Conflict Resolution*, 22 (March 1978), p. 34.

[4] Morton Deutsch, "Trust and Suspicion," *Journal of Conflict Resolution*, 2 (December 1958), pp. 265-279.

[5] Peter Blau, *Exchange and Power in Social Life* (New York: John Wiley and Sons, Inc., 1967), p. 22.

[6] Ibid., p. 1.

[7] Dean G. Pruitt, op. cit., p. 418.

[8] Ibid., p. 419.

[9] Richard Bilder, *Managing the Risks of International Agreements* (Madison: The University of Wisconsin Press, 1981), p. 79.

[10] Peter Blau, op. cit., p. 94.

[11] Daniel Frei and Dieter Ruloff, *East-West Relations*, 2 Vols. (Cambridge: Oelgeschlager, Gunn and Hain, Publishers, Inc., 1983), Vol. 1: *A Systematic Survey*, p. 282.

CHAPTER 2

CHARTING THE COURSE OF U.S.-SOVIET
POST-WAR RELATIONS

A. The Detente Index

The first measure of detente, drawn from the historical record, is comprised of per annum (1949-1981) compilations of all policy acts relevant to Soviet and American positions vis-a-vis one another; with each act being assigned an individual numerical value that reflects the act's influence and relative impact in defining the character of a particular stream of events or segment in time. A policy act's numerical value is derived from two components; each of the two components yield coefficients, which in turn are multipled together to produce the policy act's numerical value. The first coefficient is ascribed according to an act's membership in an issue-area or genre of activities (e.g., arms control, trade, cultural exchanges, etc.); issue-areas with a greater potential for contributing to a change in the U.S.-Soviet relationship -- either for the better or worse -- carry more weighty (e.g., larger) coefficients (method of weighting to be discussed). The second coefficient simply reflects an act's relative magnitude within its particular issue-area or genre; for example, even though both come under the rubric of "cultural exhange," a three-city visit to the U.S. by an obscure Ukranian folk singer is certainly less magnitudinous by anyone's reckoning than the establishment of a U.S.-Soviet bilateral musical exchange program with various avenues and opportunities for individuals and troupes from both sides to perform and study in each other's country. Cooperative policy acts bear positive (+) magnitude coefficients, conflictual acts bear negative (-) magnitude coefficients. The magnitude scale (to be discussed in detail), having a more-or-less natural zero-point, runs from .25 to -.25; and when each act's issue-area coefficient is multipled by its magnitude coefficient, the product is a positive or negative numerical value for the act itself. When these values are summated across all acts per any one year, the resulting "Detente Index" annual scale score will be positive or negative -- a positive score connoting relatively cooperative U.S.-Soviet intercourse, a negative score connoting relatively conflictual intercourse. The larger the absolute value of the scale score, the more intense is either the accommodation or antagonism. Although seemingly complicated, I will now walk through each stage of this procedure, taking special care to persuasively explicate the conceptual underpinnings of my measuring device.

Obviously, the first step to be attended to is to define "policy act," so that one may gauge how inclusive or exclusive the body of data to be worked with is. I define policy act as "any purposive action which either states, authorizes or executes an official stance or initiative, and which directly or indirectly affects the other side's

11

domestic and/or international pursuits." (This definition is elaborated upon at length in Appendix A.) The above definition has proved to be accommodating to both broad, general lines of policy, e.g., the declaration of the Truman Doctrine, as well as particularistic instances of policy-relevant behavior, e.g., the expulsion from one's country of a diplomat representing the other side. Facts on File served as the data collection source, and when scoured for policy acts according to the definition above, the result is a data set of some 4,800 entries.* This is a sizable number, compared even with the respected CREON data set, which contains only 2,922 Soviet or U.S. actor-initiated events. Each year represented in my data set has an average of 151 policy acts, with a mean deviation across all years of 42. Given the structure of my scaling technique, the number of entries per year is immaterial to arriving at a Detente Index scale score of zero or thereabouts; and given the average of 151 entries with a mean deviation of 42, any of the 33 years sampled should more-or-less be capable (e.g., have enough entries) of producing a scale score that would place it at either extreme of a continuum that characterizes the relative amity or enmity of the U.S.-Soviet relationship. This means that my sampling technique has not overly biased the possible value for any one particular year's Detente Index scale score. Source bias is, of course, usually associated with the representativeness of the universe of events that is captured by a data source, rather than with the size of the (per annum) sample(s) per se. Careful comparison of Facts on File with rival reference works (e.g., Keesing's Contemporary Archive) showed it to highlight developments in Soviet-American relations more prominently, and to draw its press accounts from a wide variety of international publications. Should a systematic bias actually be present in Facts on File, its influence should more or less be uniformly felt over time.

As was implied in the opening paragraph of this chapter, the Detente Index can be conceived of as constituted by issue-areas or interactional genre. The classificatory genre I have chosen to use are:

Political Cooperation/Noncooperation: High Politics
Arms Control
Trade
Political Cooperation/Noncooperation: Routinized
Political Cooperation/Noncooperation: Facilitative
Scientific-Technical Cooperation
Cultural Exchanges

----

*Due to space limitations, the 33 years worth of policy acts cannot be reproduced in this study. Two of the years, however, are provided in Appendix B. The two selected years are 1972 and 1973, which as the historical highpoints of detente (as our measuring exercise will soon indicate) should be of the most interest to readers. The entire data set is available through the Inter-University Consortium for Political and Social Research.

12

The meanings of the three types of "Political Cooperation /Noncooperation" are not self-evident, and require elaboration. "High Politics" refers to the traditional stuff of diplomacy -- actions which are couched in the national interest, which draw a state closer to or farther away from another state, and which always involve the, at least latent, prospects of open conflict either erupting or being resolved. "Routinized" simply means that action takes place in an established multilateral forum, such as the U.N., ILO, Geneva 18-nation Disarmament Committee, etc. "Facilitative" implies that a preliminary, although often very important action -- usually involving infrastructure -- has been carried out for the purpose of initiating, enhancing, or interrupting further interchange; e.g., the U.S.-Soviet "Hotline" is installed, additional consulates are opened, etc. The interactional genre are listed above in order of decreasing importance for salience to the ultimate fate of a detente policy; I will now explain my method for ordering them.

If we want to order these genre according to their propensity for spurring (or reversing) detente, and if detente is essentially spurred by the fostering of mutual trust, then we might ask how these seven interactional genre differentially contribute to mutual trust. What operational feature of a type of activity determines how much trust or distrust that activity sows? I reason that this feature is "risk." For example, a state may engage in joint military planning (high risk) with a trusted ally, yet spend billions of dollars on counterintelligence activities to prevent the untrusted enemy from learning these same military plans. An analogy on the level of the individual illustrates well this point of "risk" having a trust fostering capacity. If I stop an acquaintance leaving the office for lunch, hand him a nickel, and ask him to stop at the store while he is out and get me a piece of bubble gum, this has little effect on our relationship. I have demonstrated little trust in my colleague by assuming such a negligible risk -- e.g., it is tolerable to me should he decide to pocket my nickel; therefore, he is unlikely to reevaluate his perception of our mutual intimacy and trust. Likewise, should he execute my request faithfully, there is little reason for me to elevate my feelings of trust toward him, since he had practically no incentive (5¢) for being untoward. However, given the same situation, should I hand my life's savings over to this person, and ask him to make a down payment on a new car for me, he would most likely return the trust I have placed in him, seeing how vulnerable I had made myself; and should he execute my request faithfully, I would elevate the feelings of trust I had toward him, knowing that despite a considerable incentive to betray my good faith, he had acted in an honest and trustworthy fashion.

My reasoning which treats risk as the major operationalizable aspect of trust has similarly occurred to others. Such a parallel treatment by Morton Deutsch has been paraphrased as "a trusting response may be defined as one by which the responder risks a possible loss, depending upon the behavior of another party."[1] Therefore, we see the importance of such notions as "vulnerability" and "exposure." Taking the above considerations into account, I define risk as "the amount of damage suffered by one's own side should worst-case abuses of having cooperatively engaged the other side occur." I will now move beyond the identification of risk as the key concept for ranking the potency of various detente-relevant genre or categories of interactions, and give the term operational meaning.

I reason that if one takes an analytical framework for looking at a state's power or capability, and if this framework itemizes and "prioritizes" the components of power, then detente-related initiatives which affect a high-priority component of national power are riskier than those affecting a lower-priority component. Richard Cottam has devised an analytical framework for looking at national capability or power which suits my purposes well.[2] In order of increasing importance, he schematizes power as consisting of: (1) resource base, (2) mobilization base, and (3) power instrument base. The meanings of these terms are fairly self-evident; resource base being closely identified with a state's natural resources, mobilization base being those skills and institutions which translate resources into something which is usable, and power instrument base simply comprising those usable end-products with which a state can act upon its environment. The logic behind these three power components' order of priority hinges on the notion of "immediacy." If what a state ultimately risks by virtue of interacting in the international system is its own viability as a sovereign entity, then this loss of sovereign viability can only be threatened by another state's instruments of power. Only available instrumentalities can inflict harm; a state's mobilizing capabilities are one step removed from this ability, and its resource base yet another step removed. Likewise, a state's self-defense can only be mustered through power instruments; the other two power bases are one and two steps, respectively, removed from being employable in a self-defense capacity. Therefore, if we wished to weight these three components according to the above logic, we might do the following:

Power Instrument Base (PIB)   = .3
Mobilization Base (MB)   = .2
Resource Base (RB)   = .1

I will now carry through with my previously discussed intention of matching the seven categories of the Detente Index to the power component(s) which would be the direct target(s) of a worst-case abuse by the other side of activities falling within each category. A Detente Index category which involves or affects only, for example, the Power Instrument Base (one's own and/or the other side's) will take a risk coefficient of .3 (derived from the Power Instrument's Base's component value of .3); categories affecting more than one power component will have those component values summated in order to calculate risk coefficients. The matching procedure in tabular form would look like the following:

14

Table 1

Risk Coefficients Per Categories of the Detente Index

Category	Capability Component(s) Affected	Risk Coefficient
Political Coop./ Noncoop.: High Politics	MB, PIB	.5
Arms Control	RB, PIB	.4
Trade	RB, PIB	.4
Political Coop./ Noncoop.: Routinized	PIB	.3
Political Coop./ Noncoop.: Facilitative	PIB	.3
Scientific-Technical Coop.	RB, MB	.3
Cultural Exchange	MB	.2

Random examples of policy acts which would be assigned the various risk coefficients found in Table 1 might be: a U.S.-Soviet declaration calling for a halt to the current Iran-Iraq war = .5; U.S.-Soviet START talks are not reconvened = .4; an agreement for the U.S. to sell wheat to USSR is signed = .4; the U.S. introduces a U.N. resolution which denounces the USSR for downing KAL flight 007 = .3; a joint Apollo-Soyuz space flight takes place = .3; the Bolshoi Ballet books a U.S. tour = .2. Of course, within their respective categories, these policy acts represent occurrences of varying magnitudes; this introduces the second coefficient which will be assigned to each policy act used in the data set, and which will measure this very dimension-- namely, magnitude. I remind the reader that risk times (x) magnitude coefficients per each policy act will yield that act's particular numerical value -- this value capturing an act's gravity, or potential for influencing the subsequent course of events.

The magnitude scale I set out to devise was to be parsimonious for ease of application, and couched in general terms so as to accommodate all types of actions which might occur across each of Detente Index's seven categories; thus ensuring standardization and comparability. I also desired a scale with a more-or-less natural zero-point, and symmetrical terms on both sides of this zero-point, so that when the risk and magnitude coefficients are multiplied together for each policy act per annum, and the resulting products are summated across all acts, the positive or negative value of the resulting score will have interpretational significance in and of itself. The magnitude scale I devised and applied per each policy act in my chronology appears as follows:

Table 2

Magnitude Scale

.25: Action explicitly hailed as a major accretion to detente/improved relations
.20: Act or agreement: sweeping - positive
.15: Act or agreement: narrow - positive
.10: Acceptance or offer of engagement (e.g., negotiations): offer of information or approbation (e.g., diplomatic notes)
.05: Unilateral verbal expression of policy preference or orientation: entreaty/cooperation

-.05: Unilateral verbal expression of policy preference or orientation: admonition/conflictual
-.10: Rejection of engagement (e.g., negotiations): refusal to provide information or approbation (e.g., diplomatic notes)
-.15: Act or agreement: narrow - negative
-.20: Act or agreement: sweeping - negative
-.25: Action explicitly treated as a threat, or threatening military confrontation

Although the magnitude scale's terms are fairly self-evident, I will say a word of elaboration about the terms "act or agreement: narrow (+ or -)" and "act or agreement: sweeping (+ or -)." The difference between the two is simply one of scope. Although judgmental, the intent here is to differentiate between, e.g., a ban on the importation of Soviet crabmeat, and a ban on all Soviet exports. In retrospect, having already used this scale for coding my chronological data, it can be said that the scale's application -- like that of the risk coefficients -- worked very conveniently. If it were

16

to be redone, I think I would break the .15 (+ or -) level out into two levels. As it now stands, sometimes one would get a situation where both a "proposed" action (or a "rejected" action) and its "adoption" (or a "disavowal" of a previously agreed upon action) would both get scores of .15 (or -.15). Since I feel that the adoption/disavowal actions are usually more momentous than the proposal/rejection actions, perhaps they should be appreciated in value to .20 (or -.20), leaving the proposal/rejection actions at .15 or (-.15); with the remaining terms at either end of the scale getting pushed to .25, .30 and -.25, -.30, respectively.

Having now introduced and discussed the measurements for both risk and magnitude, I enjoin the reader to peruse Appendix B. This appendix contains a subset of the 4,800 policy acts comprising my events data set -- each act having its own risk and magnitude coefficients. It is important for the reader to review the materials in Appendix B so as to judge whether or not the concepts I have settled on (risk and magnitude) are the most relevant and informative, and whether my measurements of these concepts are inaccurate and distorting or intuitively pleasing and agreeable. The author's coding of events has been replicated by two political science graduate students; the results of intercoder reliability tests can be found in Appendix C.

Now that the reader has become fully versed with the mechanics of the Detente Index, I will plot in Table 3 the Detente Index scale scores for the years of the post-war period, 1949-81.

The next matter at hand is to perform a duplicate measuring exercise covering the same span of years; only this time to employ an alternate method of measurement. The hoped-for result of this second set of measurements is that it will support or corroborate the rank orderings listed above, and in this way lend greater confidence to the treatment of certain years in the U.S.-Soviet relationship as being either relatively friendly or frosty.

B. The Hierarchy of Criticisms Scheme

The approach to measuring detente which is presented at this point is perceptually oriented in the sense that it deals with actors' interpretations of events, rather than the events themselves. It too revolves around the concept of trust, which as I mentioned earlier is so central as to practically define the relation-type which obtains between two parties. Before presenting the mechanics of this approach -- called the Hierarchy of Criticisms (HOC) scheme -- I would like to briefly provide the underlying logic of the approach. We can visualize trust as being measured on a continuum ranging from "treachery" (enemy relationship) to "loyalty" (allied relationship). I assume that per varying levels of trust, or various dyadic relational-types, there is a unique modal range of predominant interactional concerns; for example:

17

Table 3

Detente Index Scale Scores, 1949-81

Year	Detente Index: Raw Score	Detente Index: Rank Order	Year	Detente Index: Raw Score	Detente Index: Rank Order
1949	- .93	14	1966	- .6	12
1950	-1.31	18	1967	.32	7
1951	-2.61	26	1968	-1.92	23
1952	-2.50	25	1969	1.50	3
1953	-1.03	16.5	1970	0.0	9
1954	-1.61	22	1971	.82	6
1955	1.20	5	1972	2.72	2
1956	-1.00	15	1973	4.86	1
1957	-1.36	19	1974	1.35	4
1958	- .83	13	1975	- .28	10
1959	-1.03	16.5	1976	-2.25	24
1960	-4.03	31	1977	- .43	11
1961	-3.30	29.5	1978	-3.30	29.5
1962	-1.50	20	1979	-2.79	27
1963	.29	8	1980	-5.87	32
1964	-1.55	21	1981	-6.50	33
1965	-3.10	28			

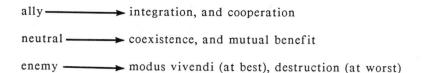

ally ——————▶ integration, and cooperation

neutral ——————▶ coexistence, and mutual benefit

enemy ——————▶ modus vivendi (at best), destruction (at worst)

It is therefore logical to assume that when disputes or disagreements erupt between partners over one of these modal ranges of concerns, that the resulting criticism-types will also be of a generic or modal nature, for example:

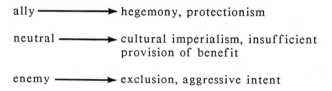

ally ——————▶ hegemony, protectionism

neutral ——————▶ cultural imperialism, insufficient provision of benefit

enemy ——————▶ exclusion, aggressive intent

Let me quickly illustrate this same point with an individual-level analogue. A personal enemy trying to gain at my expense (e.g., steal or vandalize my property, spread rumors about me, etc.) would be expected, however regretably, given our relationship. For a good friend to do these same things, the strongest expressions of disillusionment and reproach would be elicited. For a good friend, a scolding might even be called for if he were, e.g., late for an appointment, preoccupied and neglectful of me, etc. -- from an enemy these minor transgressions would be imperceptible. The point is, that the types of criticisms one actor makes of another depends on the type of relationship which obtains between them, which in turn depends on the level of mutual trust. Therefore, I propose that one can measure trust with a scheme which monitors and categorizes types of criticisms per unit of time. Tables 4 and 5 present the specific catalogues of Soviet criticisms of American foreign policy, and U.S. criticisms of Soviet foreign policy, respectively, that I use in putting this approach into practice. The criticisms deal only with the other's foreign policy behavior; criticisms of the other side's domestic policy would require an entirely separate and distinct catalogue. The types of criticisms listed in the HOC scheme have been selected according to the intuition and experience of the researcher, as well as according to a moderate pre-testing. Please see Tables 4 and 5 on the following pages.

At the top of the hierarchies, representing the treacherous end of the trust continuum, we have such criticisms as "aggressive military intent," whereas at the bottom, representing somewhat misguided good faith, we see such criticisms as "detente policy is subject to loss of central direction...." Using the Current Digest of the Soviet Press for Soviet criticisms of American foreign policy (appearing in Pravda or

Table 4

Hierarchy of Criticisms Scheme: Soviet Criticisms
of the U.S.

		Coefficient Value
I.	Aggressive military intent*	.466
II.	Political or economic subversion: sabotage*	.466
III.	General interest in the outbreak of war	.433
IV.	Aggressive Third World imperialism or domination of allies: militarism	.433
V.	General malevolence or intransigence of the other's foreign policy leadership	.433
VI.	General misinformation, propaganda, or slander*	.366
VII.	Perpetration of a provocative act	.300
VIII.	Aggression by proxy: support of an aggressor	.300
IX.	Neocolonialism	.300
X.	Meddling in the other's internal affairs*	.233
XI.	Breaking bilateral agreements*	.233
XII.	A bilateral agreement's terms are not carried out sufficiently, due to, e.g., stinginess, tardiness*	.233
XIII.	Official foreign policy seeks to reverse improving bilateral relations*	.233

*Against one's own state and/or attendant bloc.

Table 4 (Cont'd)

		Coefficient Value
XIV.	A tacit bilateral understanding is construed or miscomprehended*	.233
XV.	Refusal to admit mutual equality and the need for reciprocity in bilateral agreements*	.233
XVI.	Breaking, or inadequate adherence to international law	.200
XVII.	An act is anachronistic given an improved bilateral relationship/ international environment	.200
XVIII.	Detente policy is subject to loss of central direction due to the influence of irresponsible domestic or international third parties*	.133
XIX.	Failure to foresee the negative connotation which would be attached to certain actions	.100
XX.	Some circles: major malevolence	.075
XXI.	Some circles: malevolence	.050

---

*Against one's own state and/or attendant bloc.

Table 5

Hierarchy of Criticisms Scheme: U.S. Criticisms
of the USSR

		Coefficient Value
I.	Aggressive military intent*	.466
II.	Political or economic subservsion: sabotage*	.466
III.	Aggressive Third World imperialism or domination of allies: militarism	.433
IV.	General malevolence or intransigence of the other's foreign policy or foreign policy leadership	.433
V.	General misinformation, propaganda, or slander.*	.366
VI.	Use of military pressure for political gains	.333
VII.	Perpetration of a provocative act	.300
VIII.	Aggression by proxy: support of an aggressor	.300
IX.	Probing Western resolve*	.266
X.	Meddling in the other's internal affairs*	.233
XI.	Breaking bilateral agreements*	.233
XII.	A bilateral agreement's terms are not carried out sufficiently, due to, e.g., stinginess, tardiness*	.233
XIII.	Official foreign policy seeks to reverse improving bilateral relations*	.233

---

*Against one's own state and/or attendant bloc.

Table 5 (Cont'd)

		Coefficient Value
XIV.	A tacit bilateral understanding is construed or miscomprehended*	.233
XV.	Refusal to admit mutual equality and the need for reciprocity in bilateral agreements or relations in general*	.233
XVI.	Forwarding an unreasonable or counterproductive proposal*	.233
XVII.	Easing tensions for short-term tactical reasons*	.233
XVIII.	Breaking or inadequate adherence to international law or norms	.200
XIX.	An act or policy is anachronistic given an improved bilateral relationship/ international environment	.200
XX.	Fishing in troubled waters; unconstructive mischief-or trouble-making	.200
XXI.	Detente policy is subject to loss of central direction due to the influence of irresponsible domestic or international third parties*	.133
XXII.	Extant bilateral agreements are peripheral, and do not address crucial issues and problems*	.133
XXIII.	Problems with inadequate or erroneous information preclude correct/cooperative policy choices	.100
XXIV.	The other side's proposals are duopolistic (between the Superpowers) at the expense of other states	.100
XXV.	By not bringing an unsavory domestic policy into line with improving bilateral relations, the other side refuses to support a constructive foreign policy	.100

<u>Izvestia</u>), and the <u>New York Times Index</u> to find American criticisms of Soviet foreign policy (written by or quoted from all sources-- journalistic, governmental, and private*), I thematically analyze all articles per annum concerning the other's foreign policy. When a specific criticism is made, I record its incidence by finding the analogous criticism on my hierarchy of criticisms coding sheet, and then logging it with a single mark. (Note: There is some slight overlap between my criticism-types, and the meaning of some of them is not self-evident; so as to help ensure systematization and reliability, I have formulated a codebook sufficient for differentiating the location in the hierarchy of somewhat ambiguous real-world criticisms. The codebooks for both Soviet and U.S. criticisms of the other have been reproduced in Appendix D.) Each criticism-type, or level, in the hierarchy bears a coefficient value (the derivation of which will be discussed in detail following this methodological overview) -- high values reflecting an absence of trust, low values the relative presence of trust. <u>I contend that by multiplying the frequency of recorded criticisms per each criticism-type for one year, times the coefficient value accorded to that criticism-type, and then summating across all levels of the scheme, you come up with an interval-level scale score measuring trust</u> -- which can be calculated for one side or the other, or treated as mutual by adding each side's rank-ordered results. These scale scores have good sensitivity to changes in both volume and types of criticisms made. The raw data used in the above method of calculation, as well as the resulting HOC scale scores can be found on the HOC coding sheets in Appendix E. Due to space constraints, only the coding sheets for "Soviet criticisms of U.S. foreign policy" are provided. I suggest the reader scan Appendix E at this time, as well as Appendix D if one has not done so already. I also need to call attention to the fact that due to the inordinate number of hours it takes to apply this scheme, as well as due to its main function being simply the corroboration of the Detente Index presented earlier in this chapter, I have only calculated HOC scale scores (for each side) for

---

*Although all such sources are certainly not directly involved in foreign policy decisionmaking, images held by the mainstream of society do set the bounds beyond which policy initiatives are not likely to venture (hence the rationale for the broad spectrum of opinions incorporated into the HOC measure).

for eleven yeear of the post-war period*; each of the eleven years was chosen randomly from three-year blocks.

Before addressing the resulting HOC scale scores, I would like to present the reasoning and methodology behind my assignment of coefficient values to each criticism-type of the HOC schemes. I assumed earlier that there was a modal range of criticisms one state has for another, depending on the relational-type which they perceive as obtaining between them (e.g., enemy, neutral, ally, etc.). I now assume that perceived relational-type is synonymous with "image." This allows us to utilize the research on imagery, such as that of Richard Cottam, in <u>Foreign Policy Motivation</u>. The point is that image can serve as an ordering device for the relative severity or degree of equivocation present in types of criticisms of another state's foreign policy.

Since I assume that the image both the USSR and the U.S. have had of one another in the post-war period is basically adversarial, we need only deal with the "enemy" image, with one extreme representing the stereotyped "dire enemy," and the other a much milder version which we could call the "complex competitor."** The extremes or poles would line up on my criticism scheme as follows:

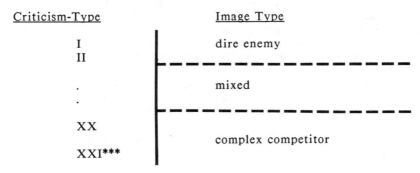

Criticism-Type	Image Type
I	dire enemy
II	
.	mixed
.	
XX	
XXI***	complex competitor

Figure 2

The Relationship of Criticism-Type to Imagery

---

*Note: both statistics I would use in comparing the rank-ordered results (years) of the Detente Index and the HOC scheme -- namely, Spearman's rho and Kendall's tau -- have more-or-less normal distributions with a sample of ten or more.

**"Complex" meaning perceptually based on a detached and highly differentiated appraisal of factual evidence, rather than on a simplification of reality.

***This would have been no. XXV if the "HOC scheme: U.S. Criticisms of the USSR" had been used here.

25

Therefore, we need indicators which would allow us to discern the location between the two extremes of the enemy image of each criticism-type, or in other words, which variant of the enemy image best captures the thrust and relevance of each criticism-type. I use four indicators for this, based on Cottam's work in Foreign Policy Motivation; they are: (1) motivation: simplicity of ascribed goal(s); (2) motivation: aggressiveness/evil; (3) decisional style; and (4) locus of decisionmaking. It would be ideal if each indicator could be converted into a numerical scale, and then each criticism-type could be evaluated per indicator, and the four scale values summated; however, each criticism-type, e.g., neocolonialism, just simply does not convey enough information to make these types of evaluations. What I have done instead, is to basically scale the indicators, but then to take the coterminous segments of each scale, and by representing these segments with verbal descriptions, to lash the descriptions together into composite "profiles" of hypothetical states' foreign policy motivation-- I have four such profiles (see Table 6). At one extreme is a profile of the "dire enemy," carrying a coefficient value of .4; at the other extreme is a profile of the "complex competitor," carrying a coefficient value of .1: falling between these two extremes are two more middling, and approximately equidistant profiles, carrying coefficient values of .3 and .2, respectively. I make a decision as to which profile best equates with each criticism-type. This means I evaluate which of the four states described in the profiles would be the most likely, and the most logical, target of each particular type of criticism. For example, taking the criticism "aggressive military intent (against one's own state and/or its attendant bloc)," which of the four states described in the profiles would be most expected to warrant such a criticism? In other words, which state profile most closely reflects the thrust of each criticism-type? Each criticism-type assumes the coefficient value of its most compatible state profile.

Since there are a number of ties among criticism-types' scores using this method, which diminish the potential sensitivity of the hierarchy of criticisms scheme, I have introduced two decision-rules that will foster further differentiation; they are:

1. If the criticized act involves one's home state as the target, a coefficient value is jacked up by .33.

2. If the criticized act reflects or implies an absence of agreement or overall accommodation (pre-agreement or -- accommodation), then a coefficient value is also jacked up by .33 -- (.66) if the first rule also obtains).

This means that the possible range of values for the coefficients per each criticism-type is from .1 to .466. Actual calculation of coefficient values, using the "HOC Scheme: Soviet Criticisms of the U.S." as the example, is presented in Table 7.

26

Table 6

State Profiles

coefficient value: .4

This state is seen as driven by a single goal, namely to spread its system throughout the entire world, by whatever means necessary. This goal is independent of the welfare of others, and its underlying motivation is basically evil, malignant, and highly aggressive. Because of the state's unbridled aggressiveness, we can be sure it has forged all the necessary means for its offensive, irrespective of the sacrifices and privations of its own citizenry. Appeasing this state is fruitless, for its goal is inexorable. Its leadership is monolithic and disciplined, and its decisions are diabolically rational, changing only for tactical reasons.

coefficient value: .3

This state is by nature expansionist; however, it is possible that some of its military preparations are a reaction to other states' armaments. The state's foreign policy seeks easy advances, through whatever unsavory means necessary, although it has an interest in avoiding the outbreak of war. Containment of this state is very difficult; therefore, one must constantly seek to infer its high priority targets for expansion, and to study and evaluate the readiness and potence of its foreign-policy/military arsenal. On certain foreign policy matters, a hawk/dove split in this state's leadership can be seen to induce a certain vacillation in its actions. On balance though, its decisions are rational, and responsive to the changing international environment.

coefficient value: .2

In addition to defense, various vested interests may be reflected in this state's foreign policy decisions. Due to a self-image as avant garde, although beleaguered, this state's foreign policy orientation is one of agitation or troublemaking, and a refusal to act responsibly. Presuming it has the correct foreign policy or military instrument available, it will embark on any foreign policy adventure, even if it is difficult to see how such an adventure augments its stature or resources. Cooperation with this state is imaginable, but confidence in its reliability is marginal. Not only is a hawk/dove split evident on some issues, but a general hard- and soft-line split tends to define most political debates. Due to the assertion of certain vested interests and factional claims, an irrational element enters into foreign policy decisionmaking, an element that may alter foreign policy's congruence with international reality.

Table 6 (cont'd)

coefficient value: .1

The formulation of this state's foreign policy takes into account a number of complex considerations. The state's leaders pursue their state's own national interests as best as they can discern them, even if this pursuit outrages other members of the international community. Where international cooperation and state interest converge, this state can be expected to act responsibly with respect to international agreements. Some cognizance and support for international law underlay this orientation. Although certain general foreign policy goals are subscribed to, foreign policy decisionmaking is fractionated, with various interest groups vying for foreign policy authority. Due to shifts in interest group coalitions and loyalties, foreign policy decisions sometimes appear disjointed or ad hoc.

Table 7

Calculation of Criticism-Types' Coefficient Values
(Soviet Criticisms of U.S. Foreign Policy)

	Profile Number	Rule 1	Rule 2	Total
I.	.4	.33	.33	.466
II.	.4	.33	.33	.466
III.	.4	not nec.	.33	.433
IV.	.4		.33	.433
V.	.4		.33	.433
VI.	.3	.33	.33	.366
VII.	.3	not nec.	not nec.	.3
VIII.	.3		not nec.	.3
IX.	.3			.3
X.	.2	.33	not nec.	.233
XI.	.2	.33		.233
XII.	.2	.33		.233
XIII.	.2	.33		.233
XIV.	.2	.33		.233
XV.	.2	.33		.233
XVI.	.2			.2
XVII.	.2	not nec.		.2
XVIII.	.1	.33		.133
XIX.	.1			.1
XX.				.075*
XXI.				.05*

a. Please see Table 4 for verbal descriptions of criticism-types I-XXI.

b. "not nec." = not necessary.

*Because these criticisms do not even apply to official foreign policy, they are the two least serious criticisms, differentiated one from the other according to the rule set forth in Appendix C.

I contend that even if one were prone to haggling over the soundness of my method for hierarchically ordering criticism-types according to how extreme an enemy image they reflect, or even over my method for ranking the issue-areas or interactional genre of the Detente Index according to how much risk they embody, skepticism on these matters should not be overly emphasized as threatening the validity of the findings they yield, as both ordering methods square easily with what might just as well have been an intuitive or off-the-top-of-the-head effort by an informed person. We therefore get the dual benefits of systematic methodology, and results which do not elicit an immediate tendency toward rejection or repudiation. At this point in the treatment of the HOC scheme, both its mechanics and underlying logic have been laid out; however, before finally reviewing and summarizing the HOC scale scores, an important digression is in order. This digression anticipates and addresses a key issue; namely that the logic of the entire HOC approach which I have presented thus far stands or falls on the reliability of the public press as an outlet for the expression of official policy preferences. Naturally, someone who claims that the communists (or the imperialists) can be trusted only inasmuch as we can trust them to lie, and that, for example, Soviet newspapers are only propaganda vehicles which bear little connection to actual policy preferences, would not be overly enthralled with the HOC approach. I personally feel that there are important constraints on not using a state's press for strictly deceptive reasons, and incentives to use it for accurately reflecting foreign policy views. In general, a state is compelled to accurately broadcast its impressions of another because a state's leadership needs to depict the other side as either responsible in its international contacts and commitments (e.g., if it were pursuing a policy of rapprochement toward that state) or dangerous and deceitful (e.g., if it were pursuing a policy of exclusion or confrontation), in order to legitimate or rationalize the logic of their own foreign policy. You cannot logically pursue a policy of peaceful coexistence vis-a-vis another state if you attribute destructionist or aggressive goals to that state. However, a state can pursue a foreign policy of peaceful coexistence, attribute reliability to the other, yet criticize the other's domestic system in order to guard against one's own society being beguiled or attracted to the other as the two states come into more intimate contact. In this instance, policy and verbal behavior diverge, but only regarding criticisms of the other's domestic situation; my scheme only examines foreign policy criticisms, and I therefore do not anticipate such a divergence.

Knowing the target of a communication also helps us to evaluate its veracity. We can envision three main targets and functions for official published critiques of another actor: (1) to inform or indoctrinate one's own society; (2) to try to persuade the other side's society; and (3) to inform the world community of one's stands on issues. Since the newspapers I am looking at -- Pravda, Izvestia, and The New York Times -- all function as both national and international newspapers, with very large circulations, and to a great extent reach

30

all three of the targets identified above, it is therefore very difficult to perpetrate a lie through them that will be effective in all three contexts, which in a backhanded way produces a compulsion to tell the truth. In addition to my reasoning presented above, Axelrod and Zimmerman in a recent study have argued that the Soviet leadership uses Pravda and Izvestia to carefully present official lines of policy and that instances of Soviet deception on foreign policy matters in these newspapers are exceedingly rare.[3]

Returning to the HOC scheme and its application, provided below in Table 8 are the eleven years the HOC scheme was applied to*, and their rank orderings as to how harsh or mild relations were during each year -- "I" connoting the most mild state of relations, "XI" the most harsh.

An analysis of these two rank orderings juxtaposed one against the other, as well as their relation to the results of the Detente Index will be drawn out in the next section of this chapter. As for the performance of the scheme itself, it basically produced expected and wholly interpretable results. For years usually associated with unadulterated cold war, such as 1949 and 1953, the volume of criticisms is heavy, and they cluster conspicuously at the top end of the hierarchy, hitting on life-or-death issues and reflecting a palpable absence of trust in the other. For years characterized by mixed tendencies of both cooperation and conflict, such as 1958, the volume of criticisms falls off markedly from the cold-war years, and the types of criticisms range up and down the scheme from the most serious to the less urgent and even hortatory types of criticisms, thus forming a crazy-quilt pattern (as might be expected). In years which we have conventionally characterized by the word detente, such as 1973, the proportion of criticisms to total statements is very small, and the proportion of criticisms in the lower -- increasing levels of trust-- portion of the scheme is higher. For the "HOC Scheme: Soviet Criticisms of the U.S.," which uses two designations which the "HOC

----

*Preliminary inter-coder reliability testing showed a duplicate coder to be able to reproduce the relative concentrations of criticisms ranging across the HOC scheme, but duplication of the volume of criticisms identified by the author was difficult. This is due to the nebulous nature of the "thematic analysis" technique (e.g., how explicit -- or diffuse -- must a theme be?). Strict reproduction of coding results will depend on sharpening the definition of thematic analysis, as well as integrating previously overlooked criticisms (e.g., quest for world domination; and, direct support for an insurgency) into the HOC lists. To the extent, however, that HOC scale scores are rank-ordered, and assuming that the more implicit criticisms are not consistently harsh or mild, then the volume of criticisms a coder chooses to identify need not significantly affect the type of image (based on scale scores) attributed to the subject at hand.

Table 8

Application of the HOC Scheme

	Soviet Criticisms	U.S. Criticisms
1949	X	X
1953	XI	XI
1956	II	IX
1958	V	VII
1963	IV	VI
1964	VI	II
1969	VII	III
1971	VIII	IV
1973	I	I
1976	III	V
1981	IX	VIII

Scheme: U.S. Criticisms of the USSR" does not -- namely, the "some circles" categories and the article/reference distinction (both designations discussed in Appendix C) -- we also get expected patterns. As the periodization moves from cold war, through mixed or ambivalent times, to detente, the use of qualified or oblique remarks (e.g., as a reference rather than an article, and attributed to some circles rather than to those responsible for the making of official foreign policy) increases.

C. Do the Two Scales Corroborate?

The purpose of this section is to investigate whether or not the two measurement techniques -- the Detente Index and the Hierarchy of Criticisms (HOC) scheme -- each utilizing quite different perspectives and methodologies, can produce similar evaluations of the state of the Soviet-American relationship at various points of time. If they do, then this heightens our sense of confidence in the validity of these measurement techniques, the concept(s) upon which they are based, the results they produce, and by extension the inferences drawn from these results. The raw scale scores of eleven random years, using both measuring devices (the Detente Index and HOC scheme) were rank-ordered and compared for degree of correlation using Spearman's rho. The HOC scheme was represented in three forms: according to Soviet criticisms of the U.S., U.S. criticisms of the USSR, and the averaged ranks of both side's results. All three were used since theoretical explanations as to why any one of the three would most closely mirror the occurrences taking place in the Soviet-American relationship may be adduced. Three versions of the Detente Index were also used, drawing on the suspicion that there is no reason to expect changes in imagery to occur simultaneously with changes in level or tenor of interaction; therefore, Detente Index scores were used for years corresponding exactly to those measured by the HOC scheme (time "T"), for years immediately following those measured by the HOC scheme (time "T + 1"), and for years immediately preceding those measured by the HOC scheme (time "T - 1"). Again, theoretical explanations to support the relationship of any of these three temporal configurations to imagery or perceptions may be easily conceived of.

Before presenting the results of the correlational analysis, I would like to mention that a Spearman correlation coefficient of .5, significant at the .05 level is obtained by comparing the "HOC Scheme: Soviet Criticisms" and "HOC Scheme: U.S. Criticisms" with each other. This fairly close association is important for two reasons: first, we can expect the three versions of the HOC scheme to behave similarly when compared to the Detente Index; and secondly, this association indicates a degree of interactiveness between the two sides and their images of each other -- this interactiveness being a key prerequisite for the logic of a detente process as I have presented it, as well as for a state's leadership to perceive a detente policy as promising to yield results.

The results of correlating the measurements produced by the HOC scheme with the Detente Index are found in Table 9; please consult the table at this time.

The results of Table 9 are quite suggestive. The fact that the strongest correlations (approximately or notably significant at most levels which the reader may choose for himself as appropriate) occur for all versions of the image-based measures when matched with events data from the previous year (Detente Index at time "T - 1"). The interpretation of this finding is that changes in concrete acts of policy (e.g., behavior) tend to precede subsequent changes in each side's perception of their relationship with the other. However, the correlation of the U.S. image of Soviet foreign policy (HOC Scheme: U.S. Criticisms) with the Detente Index is not appreciably lower at either time "T" or "T + 1". Perhaps a break-out of the Detente Index data from its current aggregate form (aggregate in the sense that it includes both U.S.- and Soviet-initiated policy acts) would reveal more distinct patterns.

Two theoretically appealing hypotheses could be tested out with the disaggregated data: first, that the "HOC Scheme: U.S. Criticisms" correlates well with Soviet (i.e., Soviet initiation or participation) policy acts at time "T - 1"; and second, that the "HOC Scheme: U.S. Criticisms" would correlate well with American (i.e., U.S. initiation or participation) policy acts at time "T + 1." The rank-order correlation

Table 9

Spearman Correlation Coefficients Between the Detente Index and
HOC Scheme's Per Annum Measurements

	Detente Index at Time "T"		Detente Index at Time "T + 1"		Detente Index at Time "T – 1"	
	Correlation	Level of Significance	Correlation	Level of Significance	Correlation	Level of Significance
HOC Scheme: Soviet Criticisms	.28	.19	.18	.30	.74	.007
HOC Scheme: U.S. Criticisms	.44	.08	.43	.10	.50	.06
HOC Scheme: Average Ranks	.23	.24	.16	.32	.64	.02
	n = 11		n = 10		n = 10	

produced by testing out the first hypothesis is .58, significant at .05. Similarly, the correlation of the two terms in the second hypothesis yields a coefficient of .82, significant at .01. In both cases, the coefficients associated with the two more refined hypotheses are stronger than those found in Table 9 which made use of aggregated data. The strengthened associations relating behavior to image (and vice versa) warrant the application of these same two questions or hypotheses to the Soviet image of American foreign policy. First, the correlation of the "HOC Scheme: Soviet Criticisms" with U.S. policy acts at time "T - 1" yields a coefficient of .61, significant at .04. Second, the correlation of the "HOC Scheme: Soviet Criticisms" with Soviet policy acts at time "T + 1" is insignificant. The strength of this second hypothesis (.82) using the U.S. case, however, should make us cautious about dismissing the relationship. A reconfiguration of the Soviet data may allow us to yet uncover an intelligible pattern. Given the truncated interest articulation process in the less open, oligarchical Soviet political system prior to a policy decision being made, perhaps the one-year lead time for expressed Soviet imagery (and related policy preferences) is too far removed from subsequent behavior. The grouping of the image-based data on an annual basis, however, precludes testing a lead time of less than 12 months. As an alternative, we will simply look at the simultaneous (time "T") correlation of Soviet foreign policy acts with their criticism of the U.S..* Although this configuration also results in an insignificant correlation coefficient, a graphic representation of the structure of the data yields a suggestive insight into why this level of association would be weaker than the implicit relationship warrants (please see Table 10).

Each year in the highlighted pairs (1949/1953, 1969/1971, and 1973/1976) of ranks per policy acts is separated from the other by a wide interval (greater than 4), which indicates a period of fairly rapid and extensive foreign policy change. During such periods of time, we might expect fast-moving events to outstrip rather stable existing perceptions of other actors and their interrelationships. Referring to Table 10, we would expect Soviet policy acts in 1953, 1971 and 1976 to be much more reactive to events, than to be mediated by existing images. Watershed influences on each of these three years readily come to mind: e.g., 1953 - Stalin dies; 1971 - Big-4 agreement on Berlin; and, 1976 - U.S.-Soviet clash over Angola. If indeed events during these years are outstripping images, then we might expect the Soviet image of U.S. foreign policy to be much more congruent with the thrust of Soviet behavior in the initial rather than concurrent year of each pair. An examination of Table 10 reveals this to largely be the

---

*The near-simultaneous correspondence of Soviet verbal behavior (as policy support or justification) with policy action may account for the slippage in the strength of the correlation (.74 to .61) between the Soviet image of U.S. foreign policy and events data at time "T - 1" when selecting out the USSR's own policy acts.

Table 10

Match of the Soviet Image of U.S. Foreign Policy with Soviet Policy Acts
(1 = most favorable)

Year	Policy Acts	Soviet Image	Interval Between Policy Ranks
⌈1949	9	10	(6)
⌊1953	3	11	
1956	5	2	
1958	7	5	
1963	4	4	
1964	8	6	
⌈1969	6	7	(4)
⌊1971	2	8	
⌈1973	1	1	(9)
⌊1976	10	3	
1981	11	9	

case. Only the pair 1963/64 (with a rank interval of 4) yielded an image of American foreign policy in 1964 that was not appreciably more consonant with the tone of Soviet behavior in 1963. With this caveat in mind, and given the strong correlation produced by the U.S. data, we will tentatively accept the proposition that State B's image of A works to condition State B's behavior toward A.

By imputing causality to the relationships suggested in the correlational analysis above, we can lay out a very simple (and tentative) model as to how superpowers formulate policy vis-a-vis the other; please see Figure 3.

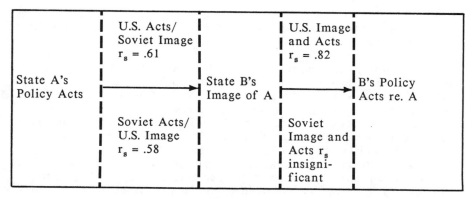

Figure 3

Partial Determinants of Inter-Superpower
Foreign Policy Behavior

This very simple model will be given added detail shortly. The
correlations from which this model is derived -- although significant at
.05 or better -- are certainly less than overpowering, and invite further
research into the questions underlying them.

At this point, the Detente Index and Hierarchy of Criticisms
measuring instruments -- both based on the concept of trust -- have
provided intuitively pleasing and mutually supportive evaluations of the
changing state of the Soviet-American relationship. Yet quite
plausibly, it might be argued that "trust" is epiphenomenal, and that
what really determines the ups and downs in superpower relations is
simply each state's disinterested calculation of its own self-interests.

Trust vs. Self-Interest

The challenge to trust as the key concept in this study can be
tested out using portions of our already collected data. Unfortunately,
the notion of "self-interest" (like national interest) can mean both
everything and nothing, and is very untidy to work with. If, however,
we treat "utility" or usefulness as the observable manifestation of self-
interest (meaning another state is useful only to the extent that it is
capable of satisfying one's own interests), then we now have a
measurable and analytically useful concept. Before outlining how we
might test the hypothesis that it is the calculation and recalculation of
self-interest, rather than transitioning levels of trust which dictate the
movements in the U.S.-Soviet relationship, let us first spell out
operationalizations of utility and trust. Trust in this context must be
conceived of narrowly, so that considerations of anticipated or desired
benefit (utility) do not overlap or intrude into it. This is the only way
to avoid the tautology of evaluating utility against trust when trust is

37

itself at least partially conditioned by the receipt and future prospects of benefit or reward.

Turning first to a measure of utility, assume that State A has a self-interest in garnering all needed (or possible) benefits -- at an acceptable price -- from any particular state capable of providing them. Assume also that every other state has a relatively unique endowment for providing State A with such benefits (some states being more endowed than others). Certain states, therefore, have a higher utility or usefulness than others to State A, so that State A acting in its self-interest should cultivate constructive relations with these high utility states. Constructive relations would be reflected by both volume of interactions as well as the degree of cooperativeness of relations. Since volume of interactions may stay at a relatively high level for two states which potentially threaten each other's security (e.g., due to hostile deterrent acts). we should therefore concentrate on the cooperativeness dimension. I propose measuring utility as "the ratio of State A's positive policy acts (where policy acts clearly have a certain State B as their intended target) to the total number of its policy acts which affect State B per annum."* Since the most fundamental aspect of utility may be reflected in the act of simply "making overture," the above percentage method may be the most appropriate.

To operationalize trust for use in testing the hypothesis presently under consideration, one may use the HOC scheme's method of calculation per annum for only criticism-types I - VI, thereby yielding a narrowly conceived measure of trust (threat/no threat) which is not significantly influenced by benefit provision. The logic of only using the top six criticism-types is graphically represented in Figure 4 (also refer back to Table 5, as needed).

----

*Positive policy acts involving third states (even if consonant with and supportive of State B's policies), as well as undirected or not explicitly directed acts (e.g., State A cuts its military budget) may be undertaken for various and extraneous reasons, and are therefore not counted in either State A's positive acts toward B, nor in the total (as this would diminish the overall percentage of the utility score, which may not be wholly appropriate). Negative acts involving third states are however counted in the total, since in theory such acts could have perhaps been avoided through superpower consultation and collaboration.

HOC Scheme: Soviet Criticisms of U.S.

Criticism Thrust	Relationship to Trust/Benefit	Region of Scale Measuring Only Trust
-I blanket indictments; predispositional basis -VI	no trust; no expectation of benefit	↑
-VII situational indictments; harsher versions of these same types of misdeeds possible -X	trust is possible; there is the prospect of benefit	
-XI indictments because preferable behavior is known to be possible -XXI	some trust exists; expectations of benefit are not being fully realized	

Figure 4

Region of HOC Scheme
Measuring Trust (Narrowly Conceived)

Now that the necessary operational definitions are in order, I would add the following assumption: namely, that a state's interests, and any other state's capacity for aggrandizing those interests are relatively stable. They may occasionally change due to new/alternate trading partners or suppliers of raw materials, an irresistable geopolitical opportunity, shifting international allegiances (e.g., Sino-Soviet rapprochement), etc. Interest in, or utility for another particular state will therefore be quite constant.

The fact that there have been wide swings or oscillations in the U.S.-Soviet post-war relationship -- as depicted by the Detente Index -- leads us to immediately suspect that a different or additional factor(s) other than the more constant influence of self-interest may be conditioning the relationship. The thesis of this study is, of course, that "trust" plays this conditioning role. If the concepts of trust and utility themselves are correlated, then we could hypothesize three possible relationships.

1. Utility with trust at Time "T + 1": because one needs State B, one must try to trust them.

2. Utility with Trust: levels of trust and utility simultaneously reinforce each other.

3. Utility with Trust at time "T - 1": trust determines the feasible range of bilateral interactions with State B, and thus the amount of utility it embodies.

If analysis shows the first relationship to be the strongest, then the assertion that self-interest (reflected by utility) is the most fundamental of considerations in determining one superpower's approach to the other will have been strengthened. If, however, the third relationship is predominant, then the treatment of trust as the more fundamental determinant of state relations will have been supported. Confirmation of the second relationship will render interpretation somewhat ambiguous. The results of the above correlational analysis using rank-ordered data are found in Table 11.

Table 11

Correlation of Utility with Trust

Utility with Trust at Time "T-1"		Utility with Trust at Time "T"		Utility with Trust at Time "T+1"	
Correlation	Significance	Correlation	Significance	Correlation	Significance
.83	.01	.63	.03	.36	not sig.
n=10		n=11		n=10	

The fact that the utility scores could vary so widely (with a range of 8% to 66%), and "follow" the trust scores so closely, lends added credence to the dominant influence of trust on shaping the U.S.-Soviet relationship. I would not, however, discard the concept of self-interest, but rather equate it with my treatment of background factors; an evaluation of which at a preliminary stage of foreign policy decisionmaking suggests the desirability of one or another broad course of action.

Although the evidence strongly suggests that utility is a derivative of trust, it is a conceptually useful notion in understanding the chain of factors influencing foreign policy behavior. Let us take the concept of "utility," as well as "background factors" (the evaluation of which was said earlier to be an important initial stimulus for defining foreign policy direction), and integrate them into the simple foreign policy model found originally in Figure 3. Please see Figure 5.

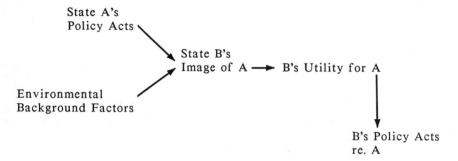

Figure 5

Determinants of Inter-Superpower Foreign Policy Behavior

A model such as the one above could have great usefulness in predicting or forecasting another superpower's (State B) near-term foreign policy behavior. We remember that the correlations between State A's policy acts and State B's image of A were approximately .6 (.61 when the U.S. was State A; .58 when the USSR was State A); therefore, let us weight the importance of State A's policy acts as a predictor of State B's image of A at .6. Next, taking both domestic and international background factors, let us hypothesize that in a tense interstate environment, international background factors come to the fore with a weight of .3*, while domestic factors are subordinate with a weight of .1; conversely, in a relaxed interstate environment, domestic background factors will predominate with a weight of .3, while international factors are considered with a .1 salience in policy determination vis-a-vis the other superpower (notice the effectiveness with which domestic groups in America voiced concerns affecting the USSR -- especially regarding trade and human rights -- in the relatively peaceful international environment circa 1974). This sort of a crude and simplistic formula provides us with three policy-relevant factors and the relative attention which should be directed to each. Such a formula can be expressed graphically in the following form:

---

*There will be substantial congruence between Superpower B's behavior and how international factors are assessed in a tense interstate environment.

Interstate Environment

	Relaxed	Tense
Factors		
A's Behavior	.6	.6
B's Domestic Factors	.3	.1
International Factors	.1	.3

Table 12

Forecasting State B's Inter-Superpower Policy
at Time "T+1"

In concluding this chapter, we have seen that at different levels of aggregation and with various time lags, the HOC scheme and the Detente Index do indeed substantiate each other, so that we can turn with confidence to the scale scores of the Detente Index, selecting years of marked amity or accommodation, and then combing these years for patterns or commonalities which might suggest useful prescriptive insights for the initiation and management of a process of superpower detente. This is the purpose of the next chapter.

Notes

[1] Byron Matthews, William Kordonski, and Eliot Shimoff, "Temptation and the Maintenance of Trust," Journal of Conflict Resolution, 27 (June 1983), pp. 255-277.

[2] Richard Cottam and Gerard Gallucci, The Rehabilitation of Power in International Relations: A Working Paper (Pittsburgh: University of Pittsburgh, University Center for International Studies, 1978).

[3] Robert Axelrod and William Zimmerman, "The Soviet Press on Soviet Foreign Policy: A Usually Reliable Source," British Journal of Political Science, 11 (1981), pp. 183-200.

CHAPTER 3

THE PATTERNS OF DETENTE

A. Commonalities Among Periods of Incipient Detente

This chapter will move away from the previous emphasis on data at aggregate levels, and revert instead to an examination of the building blocks -- in this case, policy acts -- which comprise such aggregations. Chapter 3 also makes a transition from the largely descriptive efforts of the first two chapters to more overtly prescriptive attempts, with prescription reaching its culmination in Chapter 5 -- "Detente: A Descriptive Essay." Using the Detente Index -- which strongly demonstrated its validity in the last chapter -- those years which produced positive scale scores, connoting relatively warm Soviet-American relations, will be selected, and the specific policy acts of each of these years will be combed to see if recurring types of actions can be identified. The years to be used in this analysis are 1955 through the first half of 1956, 1963, 1967 and 1969-1974. I refer to these years as periods of "incipient" detente, since obviously some sort of a process of reconciliation was launched during these times, yet just as obviously, these efforts at reconciliation failed to take root or persist; thus falling well short of transforming the bilateral relationship on a stable basis. Although 1956 had a negative overall scale score, the first half of the year, yielding a substantial positive score, seemed quite clearly to be a continuation of the "thawing" 1955 period, and it was only the tumultuous clashes between East and West over the upheavals in Eastern Europe and the Anglo-French invasion of Suez at the end of the year which lent the overall negative cast to the per annum evaluation. Also, my decision to use 1970 as part of the population of detente-relevant periods is a choice that could have been otherwise. I did use 1970, however, because it had a Detente Index scale score of zero, which meant that it ranked ninth out of thirty-three years in terms of relative Soviet-American accommodation, and by using 1970 a continuous period of time running from 1969 to 1974 was formed; thus allowing the examination of different segments of time within this period, which might prove illuminating regarding the sequence or progression of events as they occur in a detente process.

The policy acts of the years of incipient detente did indeed produce striking commonalities. The identification of types of initiatives which historically have been tightly associated with periods of incipient detente makes a useful starting point in collecting elements and ideas for a prescriptive theory of detente. The common features of an incipient detente have been labeled in the following way:

1. The big shift or spectacular event.

2. Put a new, more favorable face on, or solve a long-standing problem.

3. Do something (cooperative) that has not been done in a long time.

4. Do something (cooperative) that has never been done (post-war).

5. Cooperate to help the other with a problem.

6. Play-up and exploit common interests.

7. Do something unexpectedly lenient.

8. Encourage both public and private exchange activity.

9. Proclaim a (favorable) doctrinal shift.

10. Do something which transcends traditional concerns for secrecy and/or sovereignty.

11. Act to dampen third-area crises or problems.

12. In interacting with the other side, observe stylistic canons which they request or demand.

Casting these twelve features in functional terms, rather than in specific or nominal terms (e.g., a diplomatic summit, an arms control agreement, a cultural exchange agreement, etc.) is most useful. The reason is that actions which enhance detente are somewhat "contextual"; a diplomatic summit, for example, will produce a different impact at different points in time. Therefore, the functional emphasis aims at contextual relevance, so that prescription need not be time-bound. I do not wish to give the mistaken impression that the twelve labels I have chosen for these common features in any way entail some sort of rigorous typological work; they are meant only to be loosely descriptive of bundles of events which I have drawn together. I also do not wish to imply that detente is little more than the sum of a checklist of actions; it is an attitude or orientation as much as it is a repertory of policy acts. However, the kinds of attitudes represented in my original definition of detente -- namely, commitment, attentiveness, cooperativeness, etc. -- clearly pervade the spirit of these twelve common features or functions.

For each of the twelve common features of a detente in progress, each of the nine and one-half years of incipient detente will be listed and followed by an exemplary policy act. Some years may produce many more than one example per common feature, and some years may produce no examples. Only one example per feature for each year will be provided (except for no. 1 - spectacular events, which will list all examples by virtue of their spectacular nature). It might have been interesting to provide all examples, to see which types of features clustered in which years. The main problem, however, with doing this is that the descriptive labels I use for the twelve features are loosely formulated and there is some degree of overlap between them; for example, the distinction between "The big shift or spectacular event" and "Doing something (cooperative) that has never been done (post-war)," or between "Do something unexpectedly lenient" and "Act to dampen third-area crises or problems" is quite impressionistic, so that frequency counts of these items would be subject to much reinterpretation. The examples will, however, be helpful in demonstrating the tightness of these features as recurring, if not endemic patterns. The matching of policy acts to common features will be presented in straightforward catalogue fashion.

1. The Big Shift or Spectacular Event

    a. 1955 -   5/15: Austrian State Treaty signed.
        1955 -   June: Geneva Summit.
        1955 -   9/13: USSR recognizes West Germany, establishing diplomatic relations.

    b. 1962*- November: The Cuban Missile Crisis.
        1963 -   7/25: An East-West A-test ban treaty is initialed; prohibits space, atmospheric and underwater tests.

    c. 1967 -   June: Kosygin and Johnson meet in Glassboro, N.J.
        1967 -   8/24: U.S. and USSR submit a draft nonproliferation treaty to the Geneva 18-nation Disarmament Committee.

    d. 1969 -   11/17: Preliminary SALT talks open in Helsinki.
        1969 -   11/24: At simultaneous ceremonies in Washington and Moscow, Nixon and Podgorny authorize final ratification of the nonproliferation treaty.

    e. 1970 -   4/23: U.S. and USSR submit a joint draft treaty at the Geneva disarmament talks.

    f. 1971 -   8/5: U.S. and USSR present a joint draft treaty in Geneva banning germ weapons.

---

*The aftermath of this unprecedented confrontation was felt well into 1963.

g. <u>1972</u>   May: The Moscow summit, and attendant agreements, including SALT I.

h. <u>1973</u> - June: Brezhnev is in the U.S. for summit talks.
<u>1973</u> - 7/3: The 35-nation Conference on Security and Cooperation in Europe opens in Helsinki.

i. <u>1974</u> - 6/28: Nixon begins a summit meeting in the USSR.
<u>1974</u> - November: Ford and Brezhnev meet in Vladivostok.
<u>1974</u> - 11/24: Vladivostok arms pact sets a ceiling on all nuclear weapons, including MIRVs.

2. Put a New, More Favorable Face On, or Solve a Long-Standing Problem.

a. <u>1955</u> - 5/17: U.S. formally invites Soviet farm experts as "official guests" (after previous hassles over the fingerprinting of Soviet non-official guests).

b. <u>1956</u> - 3/1: U.S. proposes cooperative meteorological research with the USSR and other countries (after repeated Soviet protests that the U.S. uses meteorological research as a disguise for espionage).

c. <u>1963</u> - 7/23: The U.S. and Britain agree to negotiate a nonaggression pact with the Soviets after a test ban has been dealt with.

d. <u>1967</u> - 4/12: USSR says it would make a voluntary contribution to the U.N. to relieve the organization's deficit (the deficit being largely caused by the USSR's suspension of payments due to the U.N.'s invasion of the Congo).

e. <u>1970</u> - 3/26: Big-4 talks on easing tension in Berlin begin.

f. <u>1971</u> - November: Preliminary East-West MBFR talks begin.

g. <u>1972</u> - 6/3: Big-4 representatives sign the Berlin accords.

h. <u>1973</u> - 10/4: Nixon asks Congress for authority to grant MFN status to the USSR.

i. <u>1974</u> - 7/3: U.S. and USSR sign an agreement to keep "all" underground nuclear weapons tests to below 150 kilotons.

3. Do Something (Cooperative) That Has Not Been Done in a Long Time.

   a. 1955 - 10/31: U.S. lifts 1952 (year) restrictions on American passports' validity for Soviet-block countries.

   b. 1963 - 9/26: U.S.-Soviet negotiations are begun to reopen consulates closed since 1948.

   c. 1970 - 10/12: A new Soviet consulate opens in California.

   d. 1972 - 12/4: After ten years of negotiations, a U.S.-Soviet accord allows each to construct a new embassy in the other's country.

   e. 1973 - 9/10: The USSR stops jamming VOA and other Western broadcasts for the first time in five years.

4. Do Something (Cooperative) That Has Never Been Done (Post-War).

   a. 1955 - August: The Soviet Foreign Ministry plans for greatly increased tourism from the U.S.

   b. 1956 - 3/26: USSR offers to close-out its World War II lend-lease account.

   c. 1963 - 10/9: Kennedy authorizes a $250 million wheat sale to the USSR.

   d. 1967 - January: U.S. seeks a Soviet-American ABM treaty.

   e. 1969 - 12/5: NATO Council communique expresses receptiveness to a European security conference.

   f. 1970 - 11/6: Doubleday and Co. and the Novosti Press Agency sign the first U.S.-Soviet inter-publisher copyright agreement.

   g. 1971 - 6/3: The U.S. approves the export of truck-manufacturing equipment to the Soviet bloc.

   h. 1972 - 10/4: A U.S.-Soviet maritime accord is signed which sets shipping rates and port access rights.

49

i. <u>1973</u> - 3/9: USSR says that regarding international copyright obligations, U.S. authors would receive part of their royalties in dollars.

j. <u>1974</u> - 4/2: U.S. approves an Aeroflot route from Moscow to Washington, DC.

5. Cooperate to Help the Other with a Problem.

a. <u>1963</u> - 11/30: USSR gives the U.S. Justice Dept. its file on Oswald.

b. <u>1967</u> - 2/14: While in Britain meeting with Prime Minister Wilson, Kosygin and Wilson intercede with Hanoi and Washington, respectively, in seeking a formula for peace in Vietnam.

c. <u>1970</u> - 4/13: USSR offers aid to a malfunctioning U.S. Apollo 13 spacecraft.

d. <u>1971</u> - 1/17: Nixon dispatches sixty federal guards to protect the Soviet U.N. mission (after repeated Jewish Defense League attacks).

e. <u>1972</u> - 6/15: Podgorny goes to Hanoi ostensibly to push a solution to the Vietnam war.

6. Play-up and Exploit Common Interests.

a. <u>1956</u> - 5/5: The U.S.-Soviet joint production of five major films is agreed to.

b. <u>1963</u> - 9/20: Kennedy proposes that the U.S. and USSR work together for the first trip to the moon.

c. <u>1967</u> - 2/7: Kosygin cites opportunities for U.S.-European-Soviet industrial and technical cooperation.

d. <u>1970</u> - 10/29: A U.S.-Soviet agreement to cooperate on space rescues is signed.

e. <u>1971</u> - 10/22: U.S.-Soviet talks on preventing accidents at sea produce a communique claiming a preliminary understanding has been reached.

f. <u>1972</u> - General emphasis on arms control and trade; also a spate of exchange agreements signed.

g. <u>1973</u> - 6/27: U.S. firms sign a preliminary agreement to assist the USSR in the exploitation of Siberian natural gas.

h. <u>1974</u> - 9/24: U.S. and USSR, among others, agree to more stringent controls over the export of nuclear materials.

7. Do Something Unexpectedly Lenient.

a. <u>1955</u> - 9/17: USSR gives up to Finland its naval base on Porkhala Peninsula.

b. <u>1956</u> - 5/14: USSR announces a 1.2 million man reduction in its armed foces by 5/1/57.

c. <u>1963</u> - 6/10: Kennedy's American University speech includes a unilateral suspension of atomic testing.

d. <u>1967</u> - 4/17: The USSR agrees to reimburse the U.S. AAU for losses incurred due to the Soviet cancellation of a 1966 track meet.

e. <u>1969</u> - 11/25: Nixon renounces the use of biological weapons and orders the destruction of the U.S.' germ warfare stockpiles.

f. <u>1970</u> - 8/9: A Soviet government statement critizes radical Arab opposition to the Middle East cease fire.

g. <u>1971</u> - 6/10: Nixon revokes the requirement that 50% of the grain sold to the USSR must be shipped in American vessels.

h. <u>1972</u> - 3/16: After a 3/15 attack on a Soviet U.N. envoy, U.S. Ambassador-to-U.N. asks Congress to make it a crime to harass foreign diplomats.

8. Encourage Both Public and Private Exchange Activity.

This has been a clear feature of all years referred to as incipient detente. Public (governmental) exchange activity includes the exchange of legislators, technical experts, as well as the establishment of government-to-government research programs, and the framing of overall cultural exchange agreements to set and guide the exchange programme. Private exchanges include sports, church, mass media, academic, professional, artistic, touristic and other types of short- and long-range travel and work/study arrangements.

9. Proclaim a (Favorable) Doctrinal Shift.

   a. <u>1955</u> - The Soviet theme of "peaceful coexistence" is trumpeted and hailed as official policy.

   b. <u>1956</u> - The American policy of "liberation" for Eastern Europe is softened to "peaceful liberation."

   c. <u>1963</u> - 6/10: Kennedy's American University speech asks for a fresh start with the Russians.

   d. <u>1969</u> - 1/27: Nixon discards his stated preference for strategic superiority, and embraces the doctrine of "sufficiency."

   e. <u>1970</u> - 1/22: Nixon's State-of-the-Union message stresses moving from "an era of confrontation to an era of negotiation" with the USSR and P.R.C.

   f. <u>1972</u> - The word "detente" comes to characterize official U.S. policy toward the USSR.

10. Do Something Which Transcends Traditional Concerns for Secrecy and/or Sovereignty.

   a. <u>1955</u> - 1/14: USSR offers atom data for a prospective U.N. atomic-pool conference.

   b. <u>1956</u> - 3/26: The Eisenhower Administration proposes that the U.S. and USSR alert each other prior to major military movements.

   c. <u>1963</u> - June: A "hot line" teletype pact is signed.

   d. <u>1967</u> - 12/10: The U.S. and USSR cooperate with the IAEA to computerize atomic data for international use by researchers.

   e. <u>1970</u> - 10/17: A U.S.-Soviet agreement that the USSR will not build a submarine base in Cuba is announced.

   f. <u>1971</u> - 12/31: U.S. and USSR negotiate a program to exchange data on space exploration.

   g. <u>1973</u> - 9/26: USSR announces it has ratified two 1966 U.N. human rights covenants.

11. Act to Dampen Third-Area Crises or Problems.

   a. <u>1956</u> - 4/17: A Soviet U.N. appeal asks Arabs and Israelis to avoid warfare, and supports any U.N. action to prevent it.

   b. <u>1963</u> - 4/26: A joint U.S.-Soviet declaration supports a peaceful Laos.

   c. <u>1970</u> - 6/26: USSR urges that Indo-Pakistani differences be settled through negotiations.

   d. <u>1971</u> - 3/7: Nixon says the U.S. and USSR are exerting a restraining influence on Israel and Egypt.

   e. <u>1972</u> - 10/5: Sadat says the USSR has refused to grant MiG-23 fighter bombers to Egypt, and required that they accept a peaceful settlement with Israel.

   f. <u>1973</u> - 6/22: U.S.-Soviet agreement on the prevention of nuclear war is signed.

   g. <u>1974</u> - 1/30: USSR prods Syria to agree to a troop pullback with Israel.

12. In Interacting with the Other Side, Observe Stylistic Canons Which They Request or Demand.

Here we should note the persistent Soviet demands that U.S.-Soviet relations be conducted according to the principles of equality, mutual benefit and noninterference. Perhaps the Soviets should likewise accommodate themselves to the concept of "linkage" as a fact of American political life, as well as to the more mercurial and polyphonous style of American diplomacy.

These twelve patterns seem to be intuitively apprehensible as to their detente-enhancing roles, and the identified years of incipient detente present little trouble in providing examples which plug into these patterns. It strikes the author that the policy acts found in the previous exercise tend to be one of two kinds -- namely, "symbolic" (e.g. simultaneous treaty signing ceremonies in Washington and Moscow, reclassifying some Soviet visitors to the U.S. from non-official to official status, etc.) or "salutary" (e.g., the purchase/sale of grain, joint ventures to develop natural resources, etc.), and, of course, some endeavors seem to contain elements of both (e.g., arms control). This symbolic/salutary classification closely follows, and indeed gives some empirical validation to the original theoretical insight that actions which enhance a detente process do one of two things, or both; namely, "engender trust" and/or "provide benefit."

Although it is fairly clear that the twelve patterns are exemplified in each year of incipient detente, it is not obvious to the reader that these patterns are unique to only those particular 9 and one-half years. It is conceivable that each year in the post-war period contains at least one exemplary policy act per pattern, although in an aggregate sense they may be greatly outnumbered and overshadowed by conflictual acts. The reader, however, would not know this without processing reams of events data. Therefore, in order to establish the relative uniqueness of these patterns to the years of greatest Soviet-American accommodation, I will look at the first (1949), middle (1963)* and last (1981) years of my data set, and exhaustively catalogue all relevant acts under their most appropriate pattern for each of the three years. It is expected that 1949 and 1981 will have less success that 1963 in providing the variety and volume of such patterned acts. If this proves to be the case, we would have greater confidence in the association of these types of actions with periods of improving Soviet-American relations.

<u>1949</u>

1. The Big Shift or Spectacular Event.

    a. -   4/26: USSR offers to lift the Berlin blockade.

2. Put a New, More Favorable Face On, or Solve a Long-Standing Problem.

    a. -   5/28: The West offers a plan on unifying Germany.

    b. -   6/10: Soviets offer a draft peace treaty with Germany to the Western allies.

3. Do Something (Cooperative) That Has Not Been Done in a Long Time.

    a. -   9/22: U.S. removes oil-drilling machinery from export ban, and sells $5 million worth to the USSR.

4. . . .

---

*Although 1963 is not exactly the median year of my data set, its status is a period of incipient detente makes for a more interesting contrast with the chillier years 1949 and 1981.

5. . . .

6. Play-up Common Interests.

   a. - 7/5: Soviet President Shvernik says the USSR wants more trade with the U.S.

7. . . .

8. . . .

9. . . .

10. . . .

11. . . .

1963

1. The Big Shift or Spectacular Event.

   a. - 1/7: U.S. and USSR declare the Cuban missile crisis as closed.

   b. - 7/25: An East-West A-test ban treaty is initialed; prohibits space, atmospheric and underwater tests.

2. Put A New, More Favorable Face On, or Solve a Long-Standing Problem.

   a. - 5/31: Kennedy proposes fresh A-ban negotiations.

   b. - 7/23: The U.S. and Britain agree to negotiate a nonaggression pact with the Soviets after a test ban has been dealt with.

   c. - 8/14: U.S. in Geneva proposes controls on fissionable material.

3. Do Something (Cooperative) That Has Not Been Done in a Long Time.

   a. - 2/20: USSR presents a draft NATO-WTO nonaggression treaty to the 17-nation disarmament talks.

   b. - 3/27: USSR presents a plan in Geneva for missile ceilings, and eventual reductions.

   c. - 7/15: Moscow test ban talks open.

d. - 9/26: U.S.-Soviet negotiations are begun to reopen consulates closed since 1948.

4. Do Something (Cooperative) That Has Never Been Done (post-war).

a. - 10/9: Kennedy authorizes a $250 million wheat sale to the USSR.

b. - 10/9: Kennedy announces the joint U.S.-Soviet renunciation of putting nuclear weapons in space.

c. - 10/10: Test ban treaty enters into force with U.S.-British-Soviet ratification.

d. - 10/16: U.S. and USSR back a U.N. resolution banning orbiting nuclear weapon systems.

e. - 12/2: U.S. and USSR author a joint U.N. declaration of legal principles governing activities in space.

f. - 12/14: Khrushchev asks for mutual East-West troop cuts in Central Europe.

g. - 12/30: Congress drops a ban on credit sales to the Soviet bloc.

5. Cooperate to Help the Other with a Problem.

a. - 1/1: U.S. refuses to aid a Soviet religious sect which forced its way into the U.S. Moscow Embassy, asking help in fleeing religious persecution in the USSR.

b. - 1/24: Kennedy refutes the charge that there has been a Soviet military build-up in Cuba since the missile crisis.

c. - 2/18: Kennedy says the U.S. domestic furor over the Soviets in Cuba made it difficult for Khrushchev to withdraw them.

d. - 3/13: West offers three major concessions in Geneva regarding the policing of a test ban treaty.

e. - March: U.S. pledges every effort to halt Cuban exile attacks originating in the U.S.

f. - 4/30: U.S. gov't stops financial aid to Miami-based anti-Castro Cuban exiles.

g. - 5/20: State Dept. denies a Senate subcommittee report that the Soviets maintain a naval base in Cuba.

h. - 5/22: Kennedy denies a Soviet build-up in Cuba.

i. - 11/6: Dobrynin says the American military convoy (near Berlin) is being released, and says the detention did not signify an altered attitude toward the U.S.

j. - 11/30: USSR gives the U.S. Justice Dept. its file on Oswald.

6. Play-up and Exploit Common Interests.

a. - 1/1: Kennedy's New Year's message to Khrushchev says the U.S. will miss no opportunity to advance the cause of peace with the USSR.

b. - 1/1: Khrushchev's New Year's message to Kennedy urges energetic U.S.-Soviet efforts to solve urgent problems.

c. - 3/20: A detailed program is reached on U.S.-Soviet weather and communications satellite cooperative projects.

d. - 7/19: Khrushchev says the USSR is prepared to enter into negotiations on a broad range of issues aimed at lessening East-West tension.

e. - 9/10: Kennedy proposes that the U.S. and USSR work together for the first trip to the moon.

f. - 9/17-18: White House Conference on Export Expansion overwhelmingly supports easing trade restrictions with the Soviet bloc.

g. - 10/7: Kennedy letter to Congress supports U.S.-Soviet space cooperation.

h. - 10/9: U.S. Senate Foreign Relations Committee undertakes a study to expand East-West trade.

i. - 10/10: Khrushchev hails the test ban treaty, and pledges to capitalize on improving the international situation with further efforts at relaxing tensions.

j. - 10/19: Kennedy speech defends his administration's move to enhance a thaw in U.S.-Soviet relations.

k. - 11/1: Khrushchev supports the idea of a U.S.-Soviet moon project.

l. - 11/6: Khrushchev sees a group of American businessmen.

m. - 12/3: Khrushchev pledges to work with new President Johnson in the lessening of East-West tensions.

n. - 12/15: Rusk in Europe tells allies that the time is right for new East-West negotiations.

o. - 12/26: Commerce Dept. authorizes the export of 500,000 tons of wheat to the USSR.

7. Do Something Unexpectedly Lenient.

a. - 2/18: USSR informs Kennedy that it will further withdraw troops from Cuba.

b. - 6/10: Kennedy's American University speech includes a unilateral suspension of atomic testing.

c. - 12/14: USSR announces it will cut military expenditures by 4.3%.

8. Encourage Both Public and Private Exchange Activity.

a. - March: The second in a series of U.S.-USSR church delegation exchanges takes place.

b. - 9/20: 11th Pugwash Conference opens.

c. - 11/17: U.S. agrees to proceed with negotiating a cultural exchange pact.

9. Proclaim a (Favorable) Doctrinal Shift.

a. - 6/10: Kennedy's American University speech asks for a fresh start with the Russians.

10. Do Something Which Transcends Traditional Concerns for Secrecy and/or Sovereignty.

a. - 1/7: Khrushchev agrees to New York talks on nuclear-test inspection.

b. - 1/20: Khrushchev reveals a nuclear inspection offer.

c. June: A "hot line" teletype pact is signed.

11. Act to Dampen Third-Area Crises or Problems.

a. - 4/24: Kennedy sends Harriman to Moscow to discuss Laos with Krushchev.

b. - 4/26: A joint U.S.-Soviet declaration supports a peaceful Laos.

c. - 5/1: Kennedy and Khrushchev messages to each other hail the peaceful addition of West Irian to Indonesia.

d. - 5/29: USSR and U.K. appeal for a Laos truce.

e. - 9/17: Kennedy rules out an invasion of Cuba.

f. - 10/29: Western Big-3 military authorities inform the Soviets of the conditions under which they would submit to dismounted inspections on the route to Berlin.

g. - 12/14: Rusk supports an international conference on Cambodian neutrality.

h. - 12/17: USSR supports an international conference on Cambodian neutrality.

1981

1. The Big Shift or Spectacular Event.

   a. - 9/24: U.S. and USSR announce that the two countries will begin negotiations on 11/30 to limit medium-range nuclear weapons in Europe.

2. Put a New, More Favorable Face On, or Solve a Long-Standing Problem.

   a. - 2/23: Brezhnev proposes a moratorium on the deployment of new medium-range missiles.

   b. - November: Brezhnev proposes a freeze on the deployment of medium-range missiles in Europe.

3. Do Something (Cooperative) That Has Not Been Done in a Long Time.

   a. - 4/24: Reagan lifts the 15-month old embargo on grain sales to the USSR.

   b. - 9/23: Haig and Gromyko meet in New York; the first high-level encounter between the two countries since the Reagan Administration came to office.

   c. - 10/26: Arthur Hartman presents his credentials in Moscow as U.S. Ambassador-to-USSR after a 9 month period in which the U.S. had no ambassador there.

59

4. Do Something (Cooperative) That Has Never Been Done (post-war).

    a. - 3/25: (It is reported that) the U.S. and USSR have exchanged history textbooks to allow each side to point out possible misrepresentations.

5. Cooperate to Help the Other with a Problem.

    a. - 4/1: After being shot in an assassination attempt, Reagan receives a get-well message from Brezhnev.

    b. - 7/29: U.S. approves the Caterpillar Tractor Co.'s sale of $40 million worth of pipe-laying equipment to the USSR.

    c. - 9/2: U.S.-Soviet technical talks on how to verify a SALT agreement open.

6. Play-up and Exploit Common Interests.

    a. - 2/23: Brezhnev suggests a U.S.-Soviet summit as a way to help restore normal relations between the two countries.

    b. - 5/4: Haig says the U.S. is ready to enter talks with the USSR on reducing missiles in Europe.

    c. - 6/9: U.S. authorizes Soviet grain purchases for the remainder of the trading year.

    d. - 7/24: U.S. and USSR agree on talks to negotiate a new grain agreement.

    e. - 8/13: Reagan says he thinks a meeting with Brezhnev sometime is a good idea.

    f. - 10/1: U.S. doubles the amount of grain stipulated in the current 5-year agreement which the USSR may purchase during the current trading year.

7. Do Something Unexpectedly Lenient.

    a. - 4/10: USSR signs U.N. treaty which aims to protect civilians from napalm, land mines, and booby traps during war.

    b. - 10/20: The U.S. National Security Council dismisses its chief military advisor for having made an uncleared speech which predicted an imminent Soviet attack on the U.S.

8. Encourage Both Public and Private Exchange Activity.

a. - March: USSR undertakes a massive public relations drive in the U.S. for an improvement of bilateral relations, with Soviet representatives appearing on American television, lecturing to American audiences, etc.

b. - 7/4: U.S. prepares a carefully worded July 4th message for broadcast over Soviet television.

c. - 8/31-9/5: Two U.S. Senators visit the USSR, and confer with high-level Soviet officials.

d. - 9/3: Pugwash Conference convenes.

9. . . .

10. Do Something Which Transcends Traditional Concerns for Secrecy and/or Sovereignty.

a. - February: Brezhnev offers to extend the amount of territory upon which the movement of troops requires prior notification of the other.

b. - July: U.S. follows up on Brezhnev's proposal of extending the amount of territory which requires prior notification of troop movements, by offering to include trans-Atlantic troop movements.

c. - 11/2: Brezhnev interview, among other things, provides Soviet missile data.

d. - 12/2: WTO renews an offer to disband simultaneously with NATO.

e. - 12/8: Moscow allows the wife of Sakharov's stepson to emigrate to the U.S., after Sakharov had undertaken a hunger strike on her behalf.

11. Act to Dampen Third-Area Crises or Problems.

a. - 4/7: Brezhnev speech says that Polish communists would be able to solve Poland's problems without Soviet and allied help.

b. - 4/23: Brezhnev asks for an end to the Iran-Iraq fighting.

c. - 4/29: U.S. expresses concern and dismay over Israeli air strikes into Lebanon which resulted in the downing of 2 Syrian helicopters, and asks all governments in the area to help ensure calm.

d. - 5/5: U.S. sends Philip Habib to the Middle East to try to avert a Syria-Israeli confrontation.

e. - 5/6: A Soviet official arrives in Damascus to try to ease the budding crisis between Syria and Israel.

f. - 5/22: Brezhnev urges an international conference on stabilizing the Middle East.

g. - August: U.S. offers secret talks on a settlement in Afghanistan.

h. - 8/13: U.S. ACDA Director says preliminary U.S.-Soviet talks were underway to arrange negotiations on banning nuclear weapons from the Middle East.

The unexpected conclusion reached after a first glance at the patterned acts for these three years is that 1981 (ranked 33rd, or last, for its approximation of a detente-style U.S.-Soviet relationship) performs reasonably well as compared to 1963 (ranked 8th) in containing acts of detente enhancement. A closer look, however, reveals important divergencies. First of all, 1981 did not encompass the proclamation of a "favorable doctrinal shift" (pattern #9), which is probably quite important in framing the desired direction one side (or both) seeks for the bilateral relationship. Secondly, the ratio or positive policy acts to total acts (55-to-228) for 1981 translates into a rather unassuming 24%, whereas for 1963 (82-to-159) the proportion is a much more substantial 52%. Thirdly, I had anticipated that the average value (risk times magnitude) of positive policy acts in 1963 would be greater than that of 1981 (given the somewhat more trusting U.S.-Soviet relationship of 1963). This was borne out to an insignificant degree; .052 and .050 for 1963 and 1981, respectively. It occurred to me, however, that a number of the positive acts in 1981 could not objectively be considered as contributory to detente enhancement. Some acts merely tended to make amends for one's own prior instigative behavior in a specific situation, and, at best, returned the bilateral relationship to the status quo ante. For example, in 1981 when the Soviets were heavy-handedly pressuring the Polish government to quash the Solidarity movement, we find the following policy act: "WTO military maneuvers in and around Poland end." Contrast this type of act with those which could be characterized as new or additional departures in supportive behavior or suggested cooperation: e.g. "Brezhnev offers to extend the amount of territory upon which the movement of troops requires the prior notification of the other." Those proposals or actions which seek to build are certainly interpreted more favorably in most cases by the other side than those which merely seek to amend or ameliorate. 1981 had 14 amendatory acts (25% of all positive policy acts), whereas 1963 had 10 such acts (only 13% of all positive acts). Although amendatory acts can often be highly significant for avoiding confrontation, if we were to devalue them for their role in detente enhancement (as they probably should be), then we would see a slightly greater difference between the average value (risk times magnitude) of 1963's and 1981's positive policy acts. In summation, having compared in a variety of ways the year of incipient detente (1963) with the other two, our confidence has been strengthened in the relative uniqueness of the association between years of incipient detente and the quality and quantity of policy acts fitting the patterns of detente enhancement.

As for the relationship of the twelve detente-enhancing patterns with all periods of incipient detente, due to the more-or-less uniform presence of these patterns throughout each period, as well as the non-mutually exclusive nature of how these patterns are labeled, we are able to derive little in the way of prescriptive insight as to a natural sequence in which types of policy acts should most effectively unfold or come on-line. This notion of sequence is a crucial one, and one to which I will return in the fourth section of this chapter. In baking a cake, even the best ingredients if added in wrong combinations or at the wrong times will yield a product which is a failure (i.e., inedible); likewise, a detente strategy, even one backed by effective instrumentalities, which launches its initiatives in inharmonious combinations or at inappropriate times will most likely fail. Another problem with theorizing based exclusively on historical patterns is that no historical period has yet yielded a successful detente, meaning a reasonably stable transformation of the U.S.-Soviet relationship. Barring the explanation that the necessary ingredients of a successful detente were completely present in the past, yet detente's nonoccurrence was a function of one or both sides simply mismanaging the process, it would appear that there has been a (at least one) phase or conceptual gap that has been missing from previous detente efforts. Before hypothesizing about the nature of this additional phase(s), I will now look at periods of detente reversal (those years immediately following the years of incipient detente), replicating the exercise of combing the specific policy acts of these years for patterns and commonalities. An example from each year of detente reversal will be adduced for each of these discovered patterns in order to document their pervasiveness and persuasiveness. By knowing what types of recurring problems and impediments have tended to interrupt attempts at detente in the past, we can more informedly speculate about what an additional phase(s) of a detente process must accomplish.

B. Commonalities Among Periods of Detente Reversal

The years I have chosen for scrutiny in this section are the second half of 1956, 1957, 1964, 1968, 1975 and 1976. They are, of course, the years which follow immediately after a year or sequence of years identified as a period of incipient detente. This is not to imply that many important seeds of a detente's destruction were not sown during periods of detente itself, only that the years subsequent to a period of detente are the most logical points in time to look for systematic symptoms of an unraveling detente. I chose to look at both 1975 and 1976 because they had been preceded by six continuous years of incipient detente, and a post-mortem covering a mere twelve months would certainly have been too brief. As an aside, I would point out that four of the six years of detente reversal I have chosen to work with were U.S. Presidential election years.* I leave it to students of American foreign policy decisionmaking to decide whether or not the quadrennial rite of American Presidential candidates posturing so as to not appear soft on communism somehow translates into lines of policy which also reflect an uncompromising if not confrontational tenor. This observation is supported by George Breslauer, who asserts that a strong correlation exists between the U.S. electoral cycle and assertive U.S. behavior at Soviet expense.[1] The patterns I have divined from the policy act-combing exercise described above are:

1. Perpetration of a Watershed Event of a Highly Emotional (Negative) Nature.

2. Unexpected Events of a Watershed (Negative) Nature.

3. Commitment of an Unpremeditated Offensive Act at a Local Level.

4. Embrace a Hostile Doctrine.

5. Make a Claim (About the Other) Clearly Divorced From Reality, or at Best, Only Tenuously Supported by Evidence.

6. Refuse Third-Area Cooperation with the Other, or Engage in Local Competitions and Rivalries.

7. Encourage Developments Which Will Make the Retention of Order in the Other's Sphere of Interest More Difficult.

8. Threaten the Use of Military Force.

9. Cut Cultural Exchange Activity.

10. Support a Plan Clearly at Variance with the Other Side's Interests.

---

*If you treat the years as comprising four periods -- 1955-56, 1964, 1968 and 1975-76 -- then "all four" of these periods involved a Presidential campaign and election.

11. Publicize East-West Controversies Widely.

12. Threaten to Augment Military Strength in a Major Way.

The format for presenting the patterns common to a reversing detente is the same as that used for the prodetente patterns of the last section.

1. Perpetration of a Watershed Event of a Highly Emotional (Negative) Nature.

   a. <u>1956</u> - 11/4: Soviet forces pour into Hungary.

   b. <u>1964</u> - The U.S. commitment to the military defense of South Vietnam becomes unequivocal.

   c. <u>1968</u> - 8/20-21: Soviet and WTO forces invade and occupy Czechoslovakia.

   d. <u>1975</u> - 1/10: USSR cancels the U.S.-Soviet comprehensive trade pact, due to links with Soviet emigration policy.

   e. <u>1975</u> - September: U.S. and USSR begin sending large sums of money (and arms) to the FNLA and MPLA in Angola, respectively.

   f. <u>1976</u> - (Western intelligence sources report) an accelerated Soviet and Cuban military build-up in Somalia and South Yemen, as well as Cuban encouragement of Dhofari rebels in Oman.

   g. <u>1976</u> - The Soviet and Cuban role in Angola escalates.

2. Unexpected Events of a Watershed (Negative) Nature.

   a. <u>1956</u> - June: Anti-regime riots erupt in Poznan, Poland.
   <u>1956</u> - Anti-communist counterrevolution flourishes in Hungary.
   <u>1956</u> - 10/31: British and French troops seize the Suez Canal.

   b. <u>1957</u> - Turkish-Syrian hostilities erupt.

   c. <u>1964</u> - Greek-Turkish hostilities break out on Cyprus.

   d. <u>1968</u> - Liberalization in Czechoslovakia.
   <u>1968</u> - January: North Korea seizes the U.S. naval vessel Pueblo.

   e. <u>1975</u> - Leftist coup in Portugal.
   <u>1975</u> - May: Cambodia seizes the U.S. naval vessel Mayaguez.
   <u>1975</u> - Angolan Civil War heats up.

f.   <u>1976</u> - Civil war breaks out in Lebanon.

3.   Commitment of an Unpremeditated Offensive Act at a Local Level.

   a.   <u>1956</u> - 7/10:   (The USSR protests) U.S. planes occasionally violating Soviet airspace.

   b.   <u>1957</u> - 4/8:   (Soviet note protests) the U.S.'s harassment of Soviet ships in the Panama Canal.

   c.   <u>1964</u> - The USSR downs an American plane over East Germany.

   d.   <u>1968</u> - 1/22:   A U.S. nuclear-loaded strategic bomber in Europe crashes while performing a drill.

   e.   <u>1975</u> - 1/21:   Rifle bullets are shot through the windows of the Soviet mission to the U.N.

   f.   <u>1976</u> - April: A shooting incident occurs at the New York residence of the Soviet Ambassador-to-U.N.

4.   Embrace a Hostile Doctrine.

   a.   <u>1956</u> - 10/27:   Eisenhower asks Congress to support an Eisenhower Doctrine; aimed at economic aid to the Middle East, and resistance to Soviet Middle Eastern penetration, with armed might if necessary.

   b.   <u>1957</u> - 4/22:   Dulles reaffirms the policy of peaceful liberation -- dynamic peace -- for East European states.

   c.   <u>1975</u> - 7/1:   The Schlesinger doctrine for firing nuclear weapons refuses to forswear first use.

   d.   <u>1976</u> - 3/1:   Ford drops the word "detente," and opts instead for "peace through strength."

5.   Make a Claim (About the Other) Clearly Divorced from Reality, or at Best, Only Tenuously Supported by Evidence.

   a.   <u>1956</u> - 7/2:   Soviet Central Committee resolution says the Poznan riots were financed by the U.S.

   b.   <u>1957</u> - 8/21:   Eisenhower says the USSR seeks to gain control of the Syrian government.

   c.   <u>1964</u> - 8/16:   Khrushchev charges a U.S.-British-Turkish plot to invade Cyprus.

d. <u>1968</u> - July: The USSR charges the U.S. with having planted arms caches in Czechoslovakia.

e. <u>1976</u> - 10/25: Brezhnev calls the Lebanese Civil War "a Western plot."

6. Refuse Third-Area Cooperation with the Other, or Engage in Local Competitions and Rivalries.

a. <u>1956</u> - 7/19: U.S. withdraws a $56 million grant to Egypt for the Aswan dam; U.S. State Department says due to Soviet bloc penetration of the Egyptian economy.

b. <u>1957</u> - 9/9: U.S. military aid arrives in Jordan to counteract Soviet arms shipments to Syria.

c. <u>1964</u> - May: U.S. and USSR reject and support, respectively, A French proposal for a Geneva conference on Laos.

d. <u>1968</u> - January: U.S. and USSR support and oppose, respectively, International Control Commission activities in Cambodia.

e. <u>1975</u> - February: Eritrean rebels use Soviet arms against Ethiopia.

f. <u>1976</u> - 10/29: U.S. warns the USSR against interfering in the progress of negotiations in southern Africa.

7. Encourage Developments Which Will Make Retention of Order in the Other's Sphere of Interest More Difficult.

a. <u>1956</u> - 10/27: Dulles promises economic aid to East European nations in the process of wrenching themselves away from the USSR.

b. <u>1957</u> - 5/20: USSR asks for bilateral disarmament talks with France.

c. <u>1964</u> - 12/16: USSR aids in the airlifting of arms and supplies to Congolese insurgents.

d. <u>1968</u> - 10/17-18: State Department officials visit Yugoslavia to express concern over Soviet pressure.

e. <u>1975</u> - 7/24: USSR starts a week-long solidarity campaign in favor of Korean reunification.

f. 1976 - 3/3: State Department reacts favorably to Sadat's repeated requests for U.S. assistance to help wean Egypt off Soviet arms.

8. Threaten the Use of Military Force.

   a. 1956 - 11/10: USSR threatens the use of volunteers unless Britain, France and Israel withdraw from Egypt.

   b. 1957 - 10/16: Dulles pledges that the USSR would face American retaliation if it attacked Turkey.

   c. 1964 - 8/15: USSR promises to defend Cyprus from foreign invasion.

   d. 1968 - 7/5: USSR tells Bonn that the U.N. Charter authorizes it to intervene unilaterally in West Germany if necessary.

   e. 1975 - 1/13: Kissinger hints at possible U.S. military action in the Middle East to prevent the strangulation of the industrial world.

9. Cut Cultural Exchange Activity.

   a. 1956 - 12/3: U.S. State Department suspends all cultural exchanges with the USSR in protest over Hungary.

   b. 1964 - 5/4: The USSR closes Time magazine's Moscow bureau.

   c. 1968 - 8/30: State Department cancels N.Y.-Moscow flights and a U.S. band tour of the USSR, as well as places the entire bilateral cultural exchange program under review in protest over Czechoslovakia.

10. Support a Plan Clearly at Variance with the Other Side's Interests.

   a. 1957 - 5/14: Dulles supports Adenauer's plan for German reunification, and the permissibility of NATO forces in former Western zones.

   b. 1968 - 4/5: USSR says the U.S. should end all bombing of North Vietnam and respond favorably to Hanoi's peace program if it really wants to end the war.

   c. 1975 - February: (The USSR accuses) the U.S. of seeking to exclude it from diplomatic efforts to help solve the Arab-Israeli conflict.

d. <u>1976</u> - 7/22: Kissinger proposes U.S.-China-North Korea-South Korea talks on reducing tensions in Korea.

11. Publicize East-West Controversies Widely.

    a. <u>1956</u> - 7/3: U.S. House resolution instructs Eisenhower to take the Poznan case before the U.N.

    b. <u>1957</u> - 9/10: U.S. U.N. representative urges the General Assembly to keep the Hungarian issue in the forefront of its discussions.

    c. <u>1964</u> - October: U.S. asks that the USSR be stripped of its U.N. vote for not paying its share of the Congo peace-keeping operation.

    d. <u>1968</u> - 8/23: U.S. co-sponsors a U.N. resolution asking U. Thant to intervene in the Czechoslovak crisis.

12. Threaten to Augment Military Strength in a Major Way.

    a. <u>1957</u> - 8/26: Soviets claim to have successfully tested an ICBM.

    b. <u>1964</u> - The U.S. pushes for the creation of a NATO Multi-lateral Force (MLF).

    c. <u>1968</u> - 6/25: The NATO Council vows to counterbalance the growing Soviet naval presence in the Mediterranean.

    d. <u>1975</u> - 6/10: (The U.S. charges that) the USSR has a considerable naval base at Berbera, Somalia.

    e. <u>1976</u> - 8/31: (U.S. announces that) the USSR is deploying an intermediate-range MIRVed missile (SS-20) in Eastern Europe.

    The labels or titles used for these twelve detente-reversing patterns were chosen for their descriptiveness and apprehensibility. It seems, however, that using the converse versions of the labels for the previously discussed detente-enhancing patterns (e.g., refuse cooperation in helping the other with a problem, deny common interests, do something unexpectedly harsh, etc.) would have accommodated the above policy acts almost as well. It also seems that if we take the converse of the logic that actions which enhance detente either "engender trust" and/or "provide benefit," then this would summarily characterize detente-reversing actions -- i.e., actions which tend to interrupt a detente process either "instill suspicion" and/or "threaten loss of benefit." I think a third characteristic is also clearly suggested by the detente-reversing patterns, but before divulging this characteristic, I would like to set the stage for it.

It should be noted that the twelve patterns of detente-reversing actions are indeed comprised of "acts" of policy, which imply an intentional or volitional element. A state, however, focusing all its attention on refraining from initiating any detente-reversing actions may enjoy a fairly placid situation on the East-West front, and yet still not induce a genuine detente. In addition to the problem of a refrain from initiating detente-reversing actions still being insufficient in and of itself for detente, there are two other genre of impediments to the successful prosecution of detente which must be surmounted or avoided -- they are: (1) judgmental errors and incorrect choices; and (2) organizational foibles. Examples of judgmental errors and incorrect choices include a state's leadership tackling complex problems too precipitately, and tolerating excessive ambiguity in documents. Regarding the tackling of complex problems too soon, if the fate of a mutually desired detente rested on the initial achievement of total disarmament, this detente process would be stillborn. An analogous situation would involve a promising young heavyweight boxer; if his first fight were against the reigning champion, both his ego and body would stand to receive a serious bruising. What needs to happen is for the fighter to be brought along slowly, allowing time for the development of both his confidence and repertory of skills. Regarding a tolerance for excessive ambiguity in documents, this has been a problem underlying the historical controversies over the Atlantic Charter, the Yalta Agreement, the Basic Principles of Relations Between the U.S. and USSR, the Helsinki Final Act, etc. This type of ambiguity obscures communication, as well as creates false and excessive hopes; both developments being detrimental to the cultivation of mutual trust. Turning to the second genre of detente impediments, examples of organizational foibles include malleability (in the face of domestic and international third-party counter-pressures), and capricousness or inconsistency (which affects one side's reliability, predictability and general suitability as a responsible partner for various types of interactions). These features -- malleability, capriciousness and inconsistency -- speak to the general problem of official control and institutionalization; which introduces the third characteristic (in addition to "instill suspicion" and/or "threaten loss of benefit") common to and pervasive among many detente-reversing patterns. This third characteristic is "subject policy to loss of control or central direction."

Note how absolutely serendipitous some of the detente-reversing patterns are (e.g., "unexpected events of a watershed (negative) nature," and "commitment of an unpremeditated offensive act at a local level"); and beyond this, many of the most momentous policy acts were undertaken as a response to a serendipitous, unplanned or undesired situation or development. Given the topsy-turvy nature of the international environment, a state's leadership must have the resources and commitment to control and sustain implementation of a detente

70

policy; therefore the primacy of detente must be institutionalized via appropriate personnel, routines and rewards so that when detente is buffeted by unruly events and unpersuaded third parties, the proclivity will be for a state to absorb such shocks and process their implications, rather than for elements of its leadership to jump ship at the first justification for abandoning an unsure and shallowly rooted policy. I see the relatively long-lived attempt at improving U.S.-Soviet relations of 1969-74 as having succumbed largely due to this problem of exposure to loss of control or central direction; therefore, whatever phases of a detente process which we may come to identify later in this chapter (inferred largely from attempts at improving relations to date), the phase necessary for a genuine detente to prosper, and which has never been realized to date, can be called the "institutionalization of detente."

C. The Institutionalization of Detente

The task of institutionalizing detente can be thought of as a problem of organizational learning. Although this concern with the institutionalization of detente is as important, or nearly so, for the Soviet political system as it is for the American, it will not be denied that my thinking on this matter draws more heavily on the U.S. case, upon which most of the available experimentation and research dealing with organization theory is based. Three elements can be identified as crucial in attempting to switch a governmental bureau's or agency's perception of, and interest in blunting, the other superpower's inherent bad faith, to a perception of, and interest in identifying and pursuing cooperative possibilities with the other side. These elements are: (1) elite values; (2) range of functions; and (3) incentives. Concerning the first element, the research of Hage and Dewer has found that elite values, rather than leader or member values, or structural (organizational) variables (e.g., complexity, centralization and formalization) best predict the acceptability and success of organizational innovation (i.e., learning).[2] It is crucial, therefore, that a newly elected U.S. President, his personal entourage, administration officials, and (through the prerogative of political appointments) high-ranking bureaucrats, all perceive significant potential latitude for improving U.S.-Soviet relations, as well as value the desirability and efficacy of a detente policy. It would then be up to these political and bureaucratic elites to inculcate their respective organizations with the belief that the East-West environment had changed, and that cooperatively engaging the other side was feasible and even advantageous. I assume that this perception of a changed environment is genuine, and has been arrived at after a detached analysis of domestic and international background factors. Yet the seeming reality of environmental trends is easier to ignore than the physical presence of a perceived enemy. Leaders receptive to a detente policy are not likely to spring full blown as a result of environmental changes (of

71

which there have been plenty in the post-war period). A careful and empathetic examination by these leaders of, for example, Soviet foreign policy behavior will have to cast doubt upon the assured futility of cooperatively approaching the other side. (Chapter 4 seeks a deliberate procedure for encouraging such an examination of the other superpower's behavior.) Certainly the patterns of detente enhancement culled from the post-war years and presented at the beginning of this chapter suggest giving immediate pause to the futility assumption. Also, since institutionalization is a case of organizational (and probably instrumental) learning, cues for such learning will come from the unfolding actions of the other side, as well as from the exhortation of one's own state leadership; this means that the full-scale replacement of political elites either through election, ouster or generational change is not necessary for a state to embark on a detente course. Widespread adoption of the belief in a changed environment would lead to the perception of organizational performance gaps[3] or performance failures[4] ; as standard operating procedures which are predicated on an assumed acutely adversarial Soviet-American relationship would no longer appear relevant or capable of furthering organizational goals. With the appearance of such a performance gap, substantial change becomes probable.

If policy elites are to effect substantial change without stepping on bureaucratic toes -- which would create latent hostilities and an orientation toward sabotage and revanche -- then a new detente policy line must stress reconceptualized, rather than lost or gained responsibilities. This notion speaks to the second crucial element for a state's leadership in seeking to change bureaucratic self-identities and activities; namely "range of functions." The tenacity with which organizations protect, if not covet to expand the scope of their actions is well documented. To use an illustration from the realm of reindustrialization policy, a state's leadership wishing to infuse the bureaucracy with a self-interest in East-West detente must focus on "re-tooling," rather than on "shut downs" or a "reliance on extant loci of comparative advantage."

A general policy line of detente which is largely supported by a state's leadership, which can more-or-less be accommodated by existing bureaucratic structures and arrangements, but which threatens a potentially drastic reallocation of resources will be resisted. This raises the issue of "incentives," which is the third element of a strategy for recasting bureaucratic values so that they support detente. If one were to take the components or issue-areas of my Detente Index (e.g., arms control, trade, cultural exchanges, etc.) and parcel out responsibility for these areas to relevant bureaus and agencies, then one could actually make resource allocation or bonus funding contingent on the extent to which the level and quality of the activities in each area were advanced by their responsible agency(s). One could even use an instrument such as the Detente Index to monitor such relative yearly advances. To make sure that advancement in these areas does not take on a parochial life of its own, something akin to heavy industrial production in socialist economies, with sole emphasis on surpassing norms or quotas rather than on utility, then we must assume that there will be oversight provisions, either from a certain branch or department of government or from apprised sub-unit directors, so that the efforts of governmental sub-units are harmonious with and contributory toward the overall national detente policy. Even instances of zealotry are not likely to be catastrophic, since genuine detente is only possible when both sides are committed to its pursuit, and occasional excesses in pushing for new or expanded provisions within a particular issue-area will not be betrayed with worst-case abuses by the other side. Even the branches of the military are amenable to this type of funding which is contingent on detente enhancement; for example, Department of Defense procurement planning reports could identify military acquisition moves which would be the least threatening, the most stable, and the most contributory to resolving associated political problems, and then grant financial incentives to the extent that each branch of the military pursued these guidelines. The idea is probably similar to what Morton Deutsch had in mind when he said, "the basic military axiom for both East and West should be that only those military actions that increase the military security of both sides should be taken."[5] Examples of low-threat, stable and politically conscious moves might include replacing plans for the MX missile with the new generation single-warhead Midgetman, replacing battlefield nukes in Europe with PGMs (precision-guided munitions), focusing spending efforts on spare parts and ammunition rather than on hardware, superhardening ICBM silos, etc.

In summary, it appears that if policymaking elites can appeal in a nonthreatening way to the bureaucratic organizations which constitute their political system, can generate enthusiasm for the pro-detente theme or policy, and can hold out the prospects of remuneration for successfully putting this policy into practice, then it is reasonable to expect that the dynamics of instrumental learning will act to imbue these organizations with a vested interest in the furtherance of detente. As time passes, the detente-enhancing procedures become routinized and internalized, at which point detente becomes institutionalized; or in other words, it becomes a structured and regularized way of doing things. It is possible that bureaucratic resistance to a detente policy might be somewhat less than I have posited. Much of the opposition to the Nixon-Kissinger foreign policy line (to the extent it was mistaken for an attempt at genuine detente) stemmed from unique circumstances in which Nixon was under fire for presiding over an "imperial presidency," and Kissinger had seemingly assumed the right to the sole, secretive and detailed manipulation of America's Soviet policy. Bureaucratic resentments would of course be amplified in such a setting. Yet it could be argued that bureaucratic organizations are only obdurate with regard to their standard operating procedures (SOPs), and that in the face of detailed directives and clearly delineated responsibilities, actual policy content is of secondary concern. Policy and process are, however, not so easily separable. For example, a U.S. AID program abroad which procures, disseminates and instructs in the use of contraceptives, will not be ambivalent about a directive from on high mandating the exclusive advocacy of natural birth control methods. The point is that SOPs themselves often need to be altered to conform with policy shifts. To the extent that a less centralized style of leadership may mute bureaucratic opposition, then the need to secure the backing of the governmental apparatus may be soft-pedaled; however, given counterpoised branches of government, agencies and departments acting like fiefdoms with their own interests, perspectives and sensitivities, and highly placed civil servants belonging to a political party other than the president's, bureaucratic acquiescence to a new foreign policy direction cannot be assumed. Also, perhaps the emphasis on overcoming bureaucratic resistance would have been less pronounced if a broader focus and some different terminology had been chosen. Looking instead at "institutional" opposition, one might have examined the bureaucracy, Congress, and societal interest groups. Congress, and its susceptibility to single-interest pressure groups was certainly a major obstacle to our having explored detente more closely during the 1970s. If the public at large is indeed more receptive to tranquil rather than bellicose themes, then perhaps popular referenda might play a useful role in offsetting the influence of such pressure groups. Although no state can afford to have its foreign policy completely dictated by an often whimsical populace, to the extent that single-interest groups tout themselves as representing the public, then occasional referenda would offer a popular means for expressing a preferred U.S. orientation toward the USSR.

To call institutionalization "the phase of detente which has never been" is to imply sequencing or stages in a detente process. The next section draws on empirical and theoretical research to answer the question of what is the most logical, if not optimal, sequence of policy acts and initiatives for the implementation of a detente policy.

D. The Phases of Detente

Just as with the steps or phases of a fishing trip, where one can focus on either the physical acts of rigging one's tackle, maneuvering to an appropriate location, baiting the hook and casting it into the water, or on the ultimate result of what one is able to display on his stringer at the end of the trip, so it is with detente, where one can focus on the policy acts and initiatives as they are sequentially launched, or on the effects of these acts as they manifest themselves over time. In this section I will only examine how different types of policy acts should be arrayed in time so as to most logically contribute to a policy of detente; it will be left to Chapter 5 to weave or integrate both acts and effects together. The genesis of my concern with sequence came about when I was considering the prevalence of arms control agreements as they occurred relatively early during various periods of incipient detente. Following the strict logic of "risk," as derived from level of threat to national capability, we would expect arms control agreements to occur relatively later in a period of incipient detente. This not being the case, it stood to reason that other factors also impacted on determining when a type of policy act should most naturally occur. I will now present a preliminary framework for establishing a simple order of precedence among detente-relevant acts of policy. I will then augment this framework according to the theoretical work of others, and finally, by moving into the empirical world, to use the framework to organize and temper the patterns of incipient detente which were distilled in the first section of this chapter. Please see Table 13* for the above-mentioned framework. This framework already makes the previously discussed puzzle of arms control agreements frequently occurring in the early stages of a period of incipient detente more understandable, as characteristics 3-5 of the Early Detente section of the above framework clearly apply to arms control. I am going to assume that the characteristics presented in Table 13 are self-explanatory (although most likely debatable), and their underlying logic apprehensible.

We know that two states wishing to improve relations with one another will not immediately erect a full blown range of interactions, but are more likely to collaborate on a few "test cases"; these test cases probably reflecting the characteristics of the Early Detente section of Table 13. The test cases establish a modicum of mutual trust, provide practice at cooperation, and create points of reference or argumentation for persuading domestic opponents of the feasibility of a

---

*This framework draws substantially from the work of Dan Caldwell.[6]

Table 13

Types of Agreements or Arrangements Entered Into:
"Pre- or Early Detente" vs. "Detente"

Pre- or Early Detente

1. Implicit regimes (e.g., deterrence)

2. Low risk/vulnerability

3. Results in a clear, major accretion to (both side's) national security*

4. Implementation = avowal (such as arms control -- e.g., promise not to surpass quantitative or qualitative limits, not to proliferate, not to test or deploy, etc.)

5. Central actors have control over the situational environment (e.g., in Europe)

Detente

1. Explicit regimes

2. Higher risk/vulnerability

3. Results in either a marginal or major accretion to national security (as long as benefit is approximately mutual)

4. Implementation takes place over an extended time frame (e.g., trade agreements)

5. Central actors have diminished or asymmetric control over the situational environment (e.g., in the 3rd World)

---

*Although this characteristic seems to somewhat contradict the "low risk/vulnerability" point, the logic here is that at this early stage of a detente process where the other side's trustworthiness is not an established fact, going out on a limb by dealing with the other side on any sort of a moderate-risk venture must prove unequivocally beneficial (or else inconsequential) to a state, as lesser rewards would not serve as sufficient enticement. Also, since both sides see themselves as superior to the other in terms of benevolence and legitimacy, there may also be a tendency for each side to expect differential levels of reward in agreements based on this differential legitimacy.[7] Assuming that the level of benefit entailed in an agreement is approximately equivalent for both sides, agreements which represent benefit of a large magnitude will result in inclinations to squabble over who is entitled to the greater share to be overshadowed.

detente policy. Yet eventually, the detente effort must broaden to form a kind of package or complex of interactions. Erich Weede, looking at various states at different points in history, has painstakingly shown how the separate manifestations of detente (e.g., economic cooperation, smooth diplomatic intercourse, lowered defense spending, etc.) do not individually correlate with enhanced peace.[8] * This broadening of the interactional range should be fairly natural; Rudolph Rummel, for example, has written of a "general cooperative structure of expectations," which integrates diverse genre of cooperative activities.[9] This cooperative structure of expectations makes the fastidious pursuit of progress within each genre of activities very important. Conflict or break-down within any one genre in the early stages of detente may produce the type of expectational nonrealization that tends to call into question the validity of the overall approach itself. Like the very first test-case initiatives, this broadening set of interactions should evince the characteristics of the Early Detente period as well.

As there is a difference between an act and its subsequent effect, so is there a difference between an act which is preliminary (e.g., negotiations) and one which is culminant (e.g., a bilateral agreement). Negotiations which are especially crucial to get underway early center on arms control and trade. Arms control has been called by a leading Western analyst the linchpin of the Soviet conception of easing international tensions.[10] A survey of the speeches on international affairs by Soviet leaders certainly reinforces this point. In general, with the threat of nuclear exchange looming as the most hideous spectre of the modern age, any endeavor which purports to even partially or incrementally rid us of the fear of nuclear war is going to be received with enthusiasm and hopefulness. As for trade, even putting self-aggrandizement aside, the Soviets have consistently viewed the development of U.S.-Soviet trade as making for the creation of a "material base" for a steady improvement of bilateral relations.[11] ** Certainly the trust engendering and benefit providing functions of arms control and trade cannot be overlooked.

Leaving the more theoretical discussion behind for a moment, after arriving at a few low-power strictures as to what types and volume of initiatives should be prevalent in detente's early stages, I would like to return to the historical record and to seek insights into the question of sequencing by performing various manipulations of my empirical data. It is hoped that these insights will dovetail, or combine easily with those from the theoretical discussion. For the first such

---

*So he mistakenly rejects all of them as inconsequential, rather than considering their (potential) effects as components of a coherent package or strategy.

**As we would expect from good Marxist-Leninists concerned with substructural features.

manipulation I will take the nine and one-half years identified as periods of incipient detente according to the Detente Index, and try to categorize them according to a low-power distinction between early or later stages of incipient detente. I suspect that there exists something which I will call "unconsummated" detente -- meaning the positive annual Detente Index score derives from the accumulation of low-magnitude acts (e.g., 05-.1) such as verbalized statements of opinions or orientation, diplomatic notes, proposed collaborative meetings or fora, etc. There also exists something I would call "consummated" detente, derived from the incidence of medium- to high-magnitude policy acts (e.g., .15-.25), including substantive proposals, and acts and agreements of various saliencies. What I will do will be to recalculate the Detente Indexes for the years of incipient detente, but to exclude policy acts with magnitude values of .05 or .1 from the recalculation. Annual scores which then approach zero or become negative are identified as periods of unconsummated detente, those that remain significantly positive are consummated. Prior to this procedure, I suspected that at least 1969 and 1970 would be relegated to the unconsummated category. It is hoped that the detente-enhancing patterns and commonalities identified in the first section of this chapter will adhere even more tightly in light of this new, more refined distinction. The results of the recalculations are presented in Table 14.

Table 14

Detente Index Recalculations:
The Unconsummated/Consummated Distinction

Year	Original Score		Recalculated Score	
	Raw	Rank	Raw	Rank
1955-56 (first half)	1.60	III	1.50	III
1963	.29	VIII	.74	IV
1967	.32	VII	.05	VIII
1969	1.50	IV	.47	V
1970	0.00	IX	.39	VI
1971	.82	VI	-1.90	IX
1972	2.76	II	2.26	II
1973	4.86	I	3.70	I
1974	1.35	V	.38	VII

The recalculations make for a very interesting interpretation. Although only one year (1971) dipped into the negative, the scores for 1967, 1969 and 1970 became the next three lowest, except for 1974 (which I will explain in a moment). Given these years' contiguity (broken only by the watershed Soviet invasion of Czechoslovakia in 1968), and their position just prior to the commonly accepted highpoint

78

of detente (1972-73), I will treat 1967 and 1969-71 as periods of unconsummated detente, 1955-56 (first half), 1963 and 1972-73 as consummated, and 1974 as an artifact of a hold-over or halo effect. When looking at the specific policy acts of 1974 it was noticed how many of them were private (on the U.S. side) economic ventures. Private ventures are crucial to a detente process, but not in the absence of official sanction. The removal of private acts of policy from the unconsummated/consummated recalculation would plunge 1974's score well below zero. This holdover effect can occur because even after a government's official foreign policy is backing off from a detente policy, it takes time to enact legislation which will stanch private initiatives. The policy inertia in the private sector from warmer times will persist a bit beyond the warmer times themselves. The level of private activity in 1974 may be no greater than that in any other year characterized as incipient detente; however, with the government's detente momentum in remission, the relative, if not all-determining, influence of private actors increases. Therefore, I will exclude 1974 from my analysis altogether, since it obviously functions as neither pre- (unconsummated) detente nor (consummated) detente proper.

Since each of the twelve detente-enhancing patterns presented in the first section of this chapter provides only one exemplary policy act per year (of incipient detente), rather than a comprehensive listing, the examples are rather disparate, and it is difficult to find specific acts which are common to the years of either unconsummated or consummated detente. Sequencing must therefore be approached in terms of the twelve functionally cast patterns rather than in terms of specific acts themselves. Since the twelve patterns are analytical constructs, they must be parceled out or sequenced according to a theoretical framework, such as the one provided in Table 13. On the level of the specific policy act, however, there did appear what seems to be a fairly strong cleavage between two specific acts and the unconsummated/consummated periods, respectively. Regarding the big shift or spectacular event (pattern no. 1), which by its nature contains a limited number of policy acts, each year of unconsummated detente produced an arms control agreement, and each year of consummated detente (except 1963*) included a summit. I will observe this arms control - then - summit sequence in my later prescriptive efforts (this sequence is also supported by the following manipulation of my empirical data).

This manipulation, or rather usage of my empirical data, is almost exclusively pertinent to the U.S. alone. The point to be made is itself problematic (i.e., based on inferences from small samples), yet interesting and perhaps important. I reason that due to the watchdog

---

*1963 is a rather anomolous case, as the U.S.-Soviet accommodation of that year was very much a reaction against the frightful prospects posed by the Cuban missile crisis of 1962.

function of the press in the West, it usually tends to act as a devil's advocate for policymakers, and most often skeptically distances itself from official policy stances -- e.g., is relatively pessimistic when the administration is enthusiastic about detente, and relatively optimistic when the administration is unenthusiastic about detente. To test this out I took the sample of years coded according to the "HOC Scheme: U.S. Criticisms" and called the five years above (I-V) the middle rank "warm," and the five below (VII-XI) "cool." My recorded criticisms for these years discriminated between "official" (elected and administration officials) and "nonofficial" (all others) criticisms. If the contrary orientation of the press toward current foreign policy is true, then we would hypothesize that the average criticism value for nonofficial sources would be lower, or reflect a milder image of the USSR than the average criticism value for official sources during each of the cool years; likewise, the average criticism value from nonofficial sources would be higher, or reflect a more severe image of the USSR than the average criticism value from official sources during each of the warm years. These predictions were correct in 4 of the 5 warm years, and 3 of the 5 cool ones. Although not a perfect association, the relationship suggested here certainly seems more likely than an assumed pattern of press and governmental concord.*

The recent tenth anniversary of the fall of South Vietnam, and all of the reexamination of this period which it generated (especially regarding the influence of Tet on the disaffection of the press with the war effort) illustrates well the adversarial press-government dynamics. Prior to Tet, facts on the military effort (body counts, pacified villages, etc.) had been encouraging; therefore official goals in Vietnam appeared "circumspect," and the press was largely "supportive." After Tet, North Vietnam's having had committed a large, well armed and highly aggressive force of army regulars to an assault on the South resulted in a factual picture that was perceived as most discouraging; the same official goals now seemed overly "ambitious," and in response the press became "critical."[12]

The benefit to an administration in understanding the above relationship is that if early detente-relevant forays are understated, the press is likely to seize upon them and inflate their potential significance; then as a government pursues its detente policy, it will appear to be responding to the popular mandate of the opinion shapers

---

*Unofficial sources -- in addition to editorial columnists-- included spokesmen such as reporters conveying digested statements from non-press sources, as well as readers' letters to the editor. Perhaps the contrary orientation of the press to government could have been more clearly demonstrated by content analyzing only press columnists as unofficial sources. The interrelationships of press, governmental and societal foreign policy imagery are certainly a topic worthy of further research.

and their readers/listeners, thus helping to garner popular support for such a course. Even if the press and official pendulums then swing somewhat in opposite directions, the Soviet-American bilateral relationship would have made some headway by that time, thus creating an evidential base that would tend to offset or counteract reservations starting to surface in the press. The above point argues against premature summitry (which in reaction would tend to elicit skepticism from the press), but perhaps indicates an early role for "Proclaim a (Favorable) Doctrinal Shift" (pattern no. 9). The years of unconsummated detente in the early 1970s produced such radical departures from previously verbalized policies as "strategic sufficiency," "the Guam Doctrine," the purported move from "an era of confrontation to an era of negotiation" with the USSR and PRC, etc. This notion of departure or a new beginning is an important one, for much as we common-sensically know the importance of first impressions in interpersonal relations, and the resistance of these first impressions to change, social scientists have shown how the primacy effect which occurs at the beginning of a relationship will actually condition inattention to subsequent evidence which contradicts the initial perception of the relationship.[13] The added advantage of the proclaimed doctrinal shift, unlike the summit, is that it is most likely to be too arcane for the average person to brood over, and therefore unpopular or short-lived as material for most publicists to dwell on.

We will now try to blend the insights from the analytical framework presented in Table 13 with those suggested by the empirical data. This will be done as part of a general exercise to parcel out different patterns of policy acts (and specific examples) into a temporally sequenced set of categories. The simple categories I will use are "pre-detente," "unconsummated detente," and "consummated detente." All acts having the other side as target are more-or-less equally relevant for initiation by either the U.S. or USSR; detente-enhancing acts focused on a target in a state's own domestic setting will most likely reflect my bias of simply knowing the U.S. case more intimately than the Soviet. In Chapter 5, as I weave policy acts and their effects together into a descriptive essay on detente, the three sequenced categories of policy acts will be somewhat expanded to form five phases. Let us begin with an examination of the "pre-detente" period.

Pre-Detente

This is the period of the detente test cases, where low-key, albeit demonstrable successes are sought. The salient characteristics of acts in this stage, drawn from the Early Detente section of Table 13, are that they be "low risk/vulnerability" and that "central actors have control over the situational environment(s)" in which they occur. These characteristics should be interpreted as enduring through subsequent detente periods unless explicitly superceded (e.g., "central actors have control ..." is replaced in the period of consummated detente with "central actors have diminished or asymmetric control ...").* The key types of activities fitting the above characteristics are "encourage both public and private exchange activity" and "play-up common interests."

Examples:

1. cultural exchange.

2. scientific and technical exchange.

3. cooperation, if not joint initiatives in international organizations (e.g., the U.N., U.N. specialized agencies, CSCE-related fora, etc.).

Exchange activity is especially important in this period; in theory, it fosters mutual understanding which aids communication, helps to avoid interpretational differences (which are often charged to bad faith or deception, rather than misunderstanding), and helps each side to understand the cultural cues of the other which allows for policy initiatives to be custom tailored for maximum receptivity by the other. Also of relevance here, as in all subsequent periods is pattern no. 12-- "In interacting with the other side, observe stylistic canons which they request or demand." This is not a matter of mere atmospherics, but a major precondition for the further improvement of bilateral relations. The USSR, for example, with its persisting demand for mutual equality (and on occasion mutual respect) considers a lowering of the pitch in the other side's vitriol to be a significant achievement in the betterment of relations.

Unconsummated Detente

In practice this period may span many years; therefore, the types of activities grouped in this section may seem overly compressed. With the finer break-out of phases provided in the next chapter, any problems of compression should disappear. Because a period which touches the boundaries of both pre- and consummated detente encompasses such a great transition, the characteristics of patterns of

---

*I will not deal with the implicit/explicit regime distinction concerning relatively early and later periods of detente, respectively, due to the unusual behavior of this regime-development process. For although many implicit regimes are replaced by explicit ones as detente develops, after a certain amount of time or certain amount of progress the tendency is to again revert toward implicit regimes. A real-life example of this logic can be illustrated by an individual consenting to a contractual agreement; from a mere acquaintance a contractor wants to see the client's signature on the dotted line, whereas from a trusted friend, a handshake or verbal commitment may suffice.

policy acts found in this period will draw from both the early and regular detente sections of Table 13. Such defining characteristics include "increased risk/vulnerability," "results in a clear, major accretion to (both sides') national security," and "implementation = avowal" (although the implementational time frame lengthens as you move through the period). In addition to embodying these characteristics, it must be kept in mind that the policy acts of this period seek to accomplish, at least, two main goals; namely, to markedly broaden the range of detente-relevant interactions inherited from the pre-detente period (and produce results when feasible), and to condition maximum public and private support for an accelerating detente imperative. To this end, we will find types of policy acts which are consciously initiated in order to reach into previously untouched or long ignored areas, and which strive for strong symbolic impact or significance. The key patterns of activities fitting these strictures are "put a new, more favorable face on, or solve a long-standing problem," "do something (cooperative) that has not been done in a long time," "do something (cooperative) that has never been done (post-war)," "do something unexpectedly lenient," and "the big shift or spectacular event (non-summit)."

Examples: (one example per pattern, same order)

1. collapse together, or disaggregate long stalemated negotiation topics or fora, for fresh new opportunities and perspectives.

2. upgrade diplomatic access for the other side, and the intensity of diplomatic act: ity toward the other side: e.g., preferential treatment for the other to ensure comfort or ease of access to diplomatic installations, diplomatic attendance at ceremonial occasions of importance to the other side, etc.

3. discuss limitation of a previously excluded weapon system(s), or trade a previously barred item or commodity.

4. eschew a foreign military base-leasing opportunity.

5. sign an arms control agreement (this serves as a bridge into the period of consummated detente).

Again I stress that the patterns of detente are cast in functional terms, and the identification of specific acts which fulfill these functions is contextual; therefore, the above examples are chosen from among many other equally valid ones. Examples no. 1 and 3 should make it clear that these acts need not be end-results in and of themselves, but may also simply initiate negotiations or discussions. Some issues are too thorny, or insufficient levels of trust exist at this stage to bring all negotiations to a settlement (and hence must await solution in the period of consummated detente). Domestically we assume that at least a cadre, if not majority of government officials are in place on both sides to support the initiation and acceleration of a detente policy. The promotion or recruitment of such like-minded officials should continue throughout the period of unconsummated detente. As detente's areas of concern expand, and an increasing number of bureaus, departments and agencies are drawn into the administration of detente, detente must be promoted as bureaucratically non-threatening, and the application of pro-detente moral suasion and new types of budgetary incentives must be stressed and be favorably received.

Consummated Detente

The third category of policy acts, and one lattermost in time, represents the period of consummated detente. In practice, this period is the one most likely to span the greatest number of years, and a successful end-result would be a transformation in popular perceptions of the relational-type which obtains between the U.S. and USSR; e.g., from enemy to collaborative peer. With the institutionalization of this new relationship the process of detente is technically complete, and what then becomes necessary is the institution of a strategy for relationship insurance or maintenance (which may, although, bear a striking resemblance to the last phase or two of detente). Characterizing the patterns of policy acts found in this period are such descriptors as "uppermost levels of prudent risk/vulnerability," "results in either a marginal or major accretion to national security (as long as benefit is approximately equal)," "implementation may take place over an extended time frame" and "central actors have diminished or asymmetric control over the situational environment." As with an infant and adult human being, the difference between a fledgling and full blown detente is that gratification need not be immediate and overt. Carefully cultivated and expanded levels of mutual trust allow for previously unimaginable vistas of cooperation, as well as the maturity and security to grapple with disconcerting global developments without childishly and reflexively attributing them to an omnipresent bugaboo (i.e., the other side).

The key patterns of policy acts which are implicated by the characteristics discussed above are "the big shift or spectacular event (summit)," "cooperate to help the other with a problem," "do something which transcends traditional concerns for secrecy and/or sovereignty" and "act to dampen third-area crises or problems."

Examples: (one example per pattern, same order)

1. a diplomatic summit: although certain to raise popular expectations, an infrastructure should have been laid during the period of unconsummated detente sufficient to realize these expectations. Also, since a spate of agreements will

84

most likely be available for signing at the summit, this is a fitting symbolic reinforcement of the U.S.-Soviet movement into the period of consummated detente.

2. act as an advocate for the other side in lobbying one's allies to embark on East-West initiatives which will extend detente on a multilateral basis.

3. allow on-site inspections to supervise and verify arms control arrangements.

4. apprise the other side if one becomes alerted to impending third-area turmoil or hostilities, and be prepared to reign-in errant clients seeking to change the international status quo in a fashion which is categorically unacceptable to the other side.

Political cooperation on international issues is a crucial development in this period. Speaking impressionistically, it seems that whereas years of tense bilateral relations exude conspicuous political conflict while trade and cultural exchange activity shrinks, years of relatively warm or improving relations achieve this status due to a diminution in political conflict, and the reappearance of trade and cultural exchange ventures, although not due to a palpable increase in political cooperation on traditional issues of high politics. Given the high risk nature of bilateral political cooperation, our striving to achieve it, and its elusiveness to date, internalized habits of political cooperation are truly the culmination of consummated detente. Political cooperation means that state interests have come to be somewhat co-determined, rather than unilaterally determined; thus reflecting the spirit of our original definition of detente, which concerns such attributes as attentiveness, empathy and cooperativeness. This is not to say that both sides will adopt policies of complete passivity in the Third World, or find no satisfaction in validating the vigor of their own system by third-area advances; only that both will refrain from actively seeking advantages which are "strategically decisive," and that both will have the capacity to discern the difference between actions by the other which are merely "unilateral," and those which are decisive.[14]

Political cooperation must take place in a topsy-turvy world, and what is more, the detente process which ultimately makes political cooperation feasible must unfold in this same topsy-turvy environment. Yet the dilemma of national security is such that policymakers must always assume the worst about the other superpower in order to prepare for any potential challenge to the national security which they earnestly seek to protect, often to the point of straining to find the hand of the other behind all points of turmoil on the globe. With points of turmoil almost certain to erupt with discouraging frequency, the worst case assumptions -- especially if publicized or used to confront the other side -- are sure to slow, if not terminate a detente process still in its early phases. The Catch-22 aspect is that detente is never given a chance -- often due to accidental and even unrelated events -- to develop long enough so that rising levels of mutual trust make it possible to discount the threat posed by all indigenous points of turmoil. Given this endemic problem, the institutionalization of detente (discussed as the third section of this chapter) is vital. Without personal and organizational commitments to, and routines in support of detente, this line of policy would never survive the habitual recriminations generated by various types of national security watchdogs. Therefore, it is crucial that domestic detente institutionalizing actions undertaken and supposedly having taken root in the period of unconsummated detente be in place and firm for the period of consummated detente (when efforts at international political cooperation become so important). If political leaders and entities can resist the temptation to retreat from detente when the first disparaging tocsins are sounded, subsequent evidence may disconfirm the alarums voiced by the security watchdogs. In this way, the watchdogs' credibility to cry wolf diminishes, official susceptibility to reacting to these dire prognoses wanes, detente persists, and new and broader types of U.S.-Soviet collaboration and cooperation become tenable as mutual trust builds, so that the probability of power-grab scenarios (involving the other side) originally painted by the security watchdogs becomes less and less likely.

I might make explicit the point that along with various mutual undertakings of the unconsummated and consummated detente periods (e.g., trade and arms control arrangements), conscientious efforts at "bilateral" institutionalization also takes place (in addition to domestic institutionalizing efforts on each side). Standing consultative fora both facilitate frequent contact which fosters an air of normalcy, and make provisions for issue-specific conflict resolution at low levels before it has a chance to become politicized and possibly take on an additionally acrimonious air.

An issue which has not been addressed, and which is perhaps the most troubling to persons considering the propriety of a detente policy concerns the motivations behind the steady Soviet conventional and nuclear military build-up of the last two or more decades. As for the strategic nuclear build-up, and especially its attributed role in helping to dash detente during the mid-to-late 1970s, I agree with Raymond Garthoff's position that the American political acceptance and public impression of nuclear parity (early 1970s) was not in synchronization with the Soviet attempt to consolidate parity during the latter 1970s.[15] In fact, I suspect that Kissinger -- the consummate political strategist-- intentionally declared strategic parity prematurely. This put the Soviet Union in the awkward position of either having to recant on its claims of parity and admit inferiority, of pursuing military programs that would appear as a drive for superiority, or of accepting an unattractive status quo. If this U.S. move was a conscious diplomatic tactic, it was brilliant; it if were meant as a detente enhancement, it was at best ineffective.

There are a number of political, bureaucratic and economic reasons for the powerful influence of the military within the Soviet policymaking system; an adequate treatment of this topic would warrant at a minimum another book. At bottom line, however, the USSR seems to expand the instrumentalities of its military force because it has the technological/productive capacity to do so.[16] This process receives two types of periodic stimuli: first, the challenge of a foreign military program (an action-reaction dynamic); and second, the opportunity to achieve preeminence within a category of military hardware. This second stimulus, no matter how regrettable, should not be surprising. It must be remembered that the USSR is a superpower primarily if not only by virtue of its potent conventional and nuclear arsenals. To complete the model (technological/productive capacity spurred by occasional threat or opportunity), military missions (actual and potential) give priority to certain military technologies, and bureaucratic politics/organizational processes give shape to the end-products that these technologies render. The above model portrays what appears to be an incessant Soviet military build-up; one not particularly responsive to acts of restraint on our own side. The U.S. therefore has limited leverage against such a process, and without a Soviet political commitment to detente, this leverage will be insignificant. Erosion of the action-reaction threat can be started, however, by undertaking joint cooperative efforts at the lower reaches of the risk ladder. We have also seen in the third section of Chapter 3 that some U.S. arms acquisition programs may be selected due to features which promote stability and somewhat reduce Soviet insecurity. Additionally, conferred status via the collaborative peer relationship may mitigate the USSR's compulsion to express its superpower status through military outlets. Military-industrial advocates in the USSR may come to be shown by burgeoning Soviet-American cooperation to have prognosticated incorrectly, may lose influence, and therefore warrant less resource aggrandizement in return for their political support. If these developments can come to rein in or dampen Soviet military programs, then the positive impact this would have in the U.S. should foster momentum for addressing the upper rungs (expanded trade, disarmament, and international political cooperation) of the risk ladder.

This chapter has covered quite a broad stretch of intellectual terrain -- distilling a repertory of detente-enhancing acts of policy, and discussing their sequential application. Is there a concept which can tidily pull these various strands of analysis together into a coherent package? The concept of "political strategy" seems to be a promising candidate, and in a brief and concluding section of this chapter, I will examine the definition and utility of political strategy.

87

E. Political Strategy: A Unifying Concept?

The main elements presented in this study which should be relevant to a conceptualization of political strategy are:

1. A repertory of (twelve) functionally couched patterns of policy acts.

2. A disciplined discussion of how these policy acts should be sequenced.

3. A policy goal or desired end-state (e.g., relational change).

4. A formula which accounts for the movement toward or away from the desired goal (i.e., engender trust/provide benefit).

My definition of political strategy accommodates these elements as if it had been constructed specifically for the purpose of encompassing them. I define political strategy as "the formulation of a sequence of discrete yet interrelated policy acts for the purpose of manipulating a perceived environmental trend(s) in a desired direction and in support of a desired goal."* The fit of my four main elements into this definition is relatively self-evident. It should perhaps be pointed out that fluctuations in the levels of mutual trust and benefit provision over time are the "trends" referred to abstractly in the definition, and it is these trends which form the actable bridge between instrumentalities and goals. I submit that the concept of political strategy should receive more explicit and rigorous treatment in assisting the formulation of prescriptive theory.

Delving a bit deeper, we might say that a trend manipulative formulation (or strategy) for the purpose of planned foreign policy change must ask two basic questions; 1) how will it be done (approach); and, 2) to whom will it be done (target). In addition, we could add a third, yet more policy-specific question; namely, what will be done (action). This third question has been addressed in the case of detente by the trust/benefit formulation. All three questions or considerations may be arrayed together, as is done in Figure 6.

---

*The notion of "trend alteration" as the central analytical focus for a treatment of political strategy was borrowed from Dr. Richard Cottam.

88

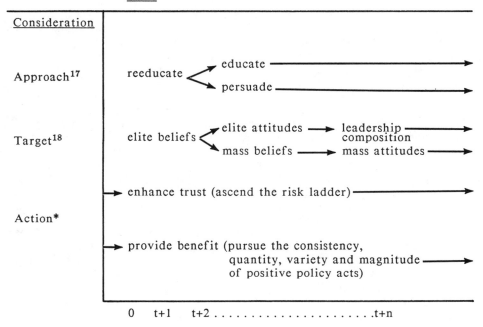

Figure 6

Interstate Considerations in Formulating
Foreign Policy Change

The initial "approach" shown in Figure 6 is one of "reeducation." The implication here is that foreign policy change involves the abandonment and reorientation of existing psychological and physical patterns. This approach is based on an unambiguous demonstration of behavior or presentation of fact. At a later time, the approach bifurcates to either (or both) an "educational" (with less emphasis on contrast with the past) or "persuasive" (assertions or entreaties are backed up by an evidential base) one. As for the second consideration -- "target"-- the initial target or aim of a foreign policy change strategy is the beliefs of the other side's elites. In general, over time both elite attitudes and a mass audience come to be targeted (as shown in Figure 6). Beliefs, which are based upon factual proof are much more amenable to change than are attitudes (which are grounded in values), and are therefore the most logical to be confronted first. I might point out that whereas the elite and mass target tracks diverge in

---

*Note - planned actions should be closely cued to the content of target beliefs and attitudes.

89

Figure 6, they are in fact interactive (certainly more so in Western-style democratic political systems). The "action" consideration has been discussed at length in this manuscript. An expanded deductive framework such as the one presented in Table 13 will help to order or discipline the implementation of a particular action program. The stages at which the three above considerations would be (in terms of extensiveness of change) during any one particular slice in time would be compatible and mutually supportive.

The three previously discussed considerations are identified as applying to the interstate aspects of one country attempting to influence another; yet we know that there is a necessary and significant intrastate component to, for example, a detente policy, as well. I might point out that the logic underlying the "approach" and "target" tracks of Figure 6 are to a great extent applicable to the domestic (intrastate) enlistment of supporters for a foreign policy change; and that the policy responses of the other member of an interstate dyad to one's own "action" track feed back directly on the entire domestic aspect of a change strategy. This feedback would be bolstered by domestic policy actions aimed at bureaucratic alteration and institutionalization. Strategic concerns such as the ones presented in Figure 6 have been consciously observed in composing the descriptive essay on detente in Chapter 5.

The very notion of strategy formulation, however, presumes a highly placed group of decisionmakers committed to a particular policy direction. Yet in the case of a detente policy, this would be an excessively optimistic expectation. The necessary precondition to a major foreign policy shift must be that certain decisionmakers come to see the feasibility of such a shift. If the contemplated shift involves a desirable policy characterized by expanding commitment or risk, then its precondition need not involve a fundamental change in values or assumptions, but simply a challenging of assumptions.[19] As a precipitant of this necessary precondition, Chapter 4 lays out a procedure for prompting the challenging of policy-relevant values or assumptions.

Notes

[1] George Breslauer, "Do Soviet Leaders Test New Presidents?" _International Security_, 8 (Winter 1983/84), pp. 83-107.

[2] Jerald Hage and Robert Dewar, "Elite Values Versus Organizational Structure in Predicting Innovation," _Administrative Science Quarterly_ (September 1973), pp. 277-290.

[3] Anthony Downs, _Inside Bureaucracy_ (Santa Monica, CA: The RAND Corporation, 1967), p. 191.

[4] John D. Steinbruner, _The Cybernetic Theory of Decision_ (Princeton, NJ: Princeton University Press, 1974), p. 74.

[5] Morton Deutsch, "The Prevention of WW III: A Psychological Perspective," _Political Psychology_, 4 (March 1983), pp. 3-31.

[6] Dan Caldwell, _American-Soviet Relations From 1947 to the Nixon-Kissinger Grand Design_ (Westport: Greenwood Press, 1981).

[7] Morton Deutsch, op. cit.

[8] Erich Weede, "Threats to Detente: Intuitive Hopes and Counterintuitive Realities," _European Journal of Political Research_, No. 5 (1977), pp. 407-32.

[9] Rudolph Rummel, _Peace Endangered_ (Beverly Hills: Sage Publications, Inc., 1976), p. 43.

[10] William Husband, "Soviet Perceptions of U.S. Positions-of-Strength Diplomacy in the 1970s," _World Politics_, 31 (July 1979), pp. 495-517.

[11] Leonid Brezhnev, _Peace, Detente and Soviet-American Relations_ (New York, NY: Harcourt, Brace and Jovanovich, 1979), p. 86.

[12] Thanks to my friend John Hoffman for pointing out this example to me.

[13] J. K. Chadwick-Jones, _Social Exchange Theory_ (London: Academic Press, 1976), p. 54.

[14] See, E. Raymond Platig, "Crisis, Pretentious Ideologies, and Superpower Behavior," _Orbis_, 25 (Fall 1981), pp. 511-24.

[15] Raymond L. Garthoff, "American-Soviet Relations in Perspective," _Political Science Quarterly_, 100 (Winter 1985-86), p. 556.

[16] For an excellent discussion of this point and others in this paragraph, see Stephen M. Meyer, "The Study of Soviet Decisionmaking for National Security: What is to be Done," in _Soviet Decisionmaking for National Security_, eds. Jiri Valenta and William Potter (London: George Allen and Unwin, 1984).

[17] See, Gerald Zaltman and Robert Duncan, _Strategies for Planned Change_ (New York: Wiley, 1977).

[18] A superb exposition of this type of strategic thinking can be found in George Kennan's famous "X" article: X, "The Sources of Soviet Conduct," Foreign Affairs, 25 (July 1947), pp. 566-82.

[19] See, Richard Mason and Ian Mitroff, _Challenging Strategic Planning Assumptions_ (New York: John Wiley and Sons, 1981).

CHAPTER 4

PROBING THE FEASIBILITY AND ADVISABILITY
OF DETENTE

Although we have surveyed environmental background factors to establish the "desirability" of detente, given the true and perhaps unrecognized basic foreign policy thrust of, for example, the USSR, a detente policy (such as one incorporating the features discussed in Chapter 3) may be both infeasible and unwise. If the USSR's foreign policy drives are in fact similar to those of Hitler's Germany, a demonstrated American interest in moving toward detente would be interpreted by the Soviets as an attempt at appeasement, and therefore most likely deserving of exploitation. If, however, Soviet foreign policy is primarily defensive, an American move toward detente would be an appropriate approach to shaping bilateral relations. At present, it must be realized that the image of the USSR held by most of the governing elite and public opinion shapers in America is closer to that of Hitler's Germany than to that of a state driven by defensive or non-aggressive motivations. To these persons, therefore, a U.S. push for detente makes no sense. Although there are certainly American policymakers such as George McGovern and Jesse Jackson who as President would from the start see wide latitude for the improvement -- perhaps even at an imprudent pace -- of Soviet-American relations, an erosion of the enemy image seems to be a necessary precondition before any specific detente policy would be feasible. To this end, it is possible for the analyst to construct tests using historical data, which aid in determining an answer to the question concerning the prevalence of either defensive or offensive motives primarily animating Soviet foreign behavior. But before it becomes profitable to engage in this type of motivational assessment, there is a preliminary issue which must first be dealt with.

If a person believes that the U.S. has pursued at least one episode of detente vis-a-vis the USSR in the past, and that detente has always come unraveled and ultimately failed, then it makes little sense (in order to render detente as an appropriate policy response) to produce evidence for this person which indicates a non-imperialistic Soviet Union has by and large been the case in the post-war period. Why demonstrate the feasibility or applicability of detente, when one already knows that the policy itself is faulty? If one views the past failures of detente as caused by an aggressive USSR, then historical tests which suggest the post-war existence of a largely status-quo USSR should shake that person's confidence in detente even further by removing the Soviets' imperialistic appetite and implacable hostility as an explanation for detente's flaws. The analyst needs to therefore be in a position to disarm the charge that a detente approach has already shown itself to be ineffective. In this instance, it must be demonstrated that whatever the failings of past U.S. or Soviet policies toward the other, and for whatever reasons, these shortfalls cannot be called failed "detentes." For this purpose, being able to accurately evaluate the extent to which past "incipient" detentes had developed or progressed is a crucial capability. The analyst must usefully define detente, and then show how far short of this standard past efforts have actually fallen. By demonstrating detente's non-occurrence to date, one can preserve the credibility and potential utility of a detente strategy as a policy option.

If the detente process can be thought of as a ladder requiring slow yet persistent ascent, then extant analytic frames have not produced evaluative results to demonstrate how far up the ladder past efforts have gone. Assessing the state or course of a nation's foreign relations vis-a-vis another nation or group of nations using the stock "year-in-review" format is much too impressionistic for persuasive evaluative accuracy. Monitoring shifting perceptions and interpretations of a particular key concept (e.g., positions-of-strength diplomacy, human rights, peaceful coexistence, etc.) over time is an interesting approach, and one which often proves insightful; yet this approach is also too limited or narrow for extrapolating confidently to an evaluation of larger and more complex political processes. Historical periodization is another evaluative tool, used by historians to characterize different slices in time -- usually periodized according to changes in one or more key dimensions; yet this approach, while impressive in its sweep, is simply too crude and undisciplined for more focused evaluative efforts. The most successful evaluative approach, namely, where a complex political process is broken down into key dimensions, empirical indicators are chosen per dimension, and then all indicators are combined into an aggregate measure, has an important drawback. This approach calculated over time will show fluctuations in a measure -- each measure being relative to the years of the sample-- but it does not show the degree to which the overall process (as measured) has moved, for example, two states toward either complete hostility or a completed detente. The high point on a graph of plotted measures does not necessarily represent detente. Even the high and low points in my Detente Index scores -- 4.86 and -6.5, respectively-- represent the best and the worst of the lot, and do not convey information as to what amount, proportion or percentage of a detente process (or its converse) had been traversed.

What can the analyst tell a person who disparages detente, citing the transient, inconsequential, if not dangerous effects of the Eisenhower/Khrushchev incipient detente of the mide-50s, and the Nixon-Kissinger/Brezhnev incipient detente of the early 70s? He must show that these attempts at detente really did not reach very far. A valid evaluative tool for showing this is not dependent on, for example, Eisenhower-Dulles, Nixon-Kissinger and the analyst all sharing common views and assumptions about detente; therefore, the categories of the Detente Index -- ranging from cultural exchanges to political cooperation on matters of high politics -- comprise a valid tool which

94

can be applied to all so-called detentes. If the two episodes mentioned above were indeed instances of a genuine detente, then we would expect to find cooperative policy behavior taking place at the upper end of the ladder, or in other words, on weighty matters of international security (high politics). The occurrence of a historical pattern of this type, however, has not developed. One may argue that there has been conspicuous success nonetheless at arms control, which shares the penultimate position on the detente ladder. Yet the term "arms control" was chosen in connection with the Detente Index, which is a device for measuring empirical reality. We could not have used the term "disarmament," for which there would have been no historical instances (barring the retirement of obsolete weapon systems). Disarmament, however, would be an important component of a true detente; therefore, if we substitute the term disarmament for arms control when evaluating past attempts at detente, the nonoccurrence of this significant type of activity becomes clear. Our historical episode of incipient detente therefore can be seen to have traversed the lower and middle ranges of the detente ladder (approximating Phase III, as I have layed it out in Chapter 5) -- well below the point where one might expect a stable transformation of the enemy image each superpower holds of the other.

Although one can evaluate the extent of past incipient detentes without taking their authors' assumptions into account, one can best explain the fate of these episodes in assumptional or perceptual terms. Nixon and Kissinger initiated their opening to the East for reasons of international political expediency, and although rarely recognized as such, it was nonetheless a product of the traditional enemy stereotypical view of the USSR. This view affords little leeway for evidence which would be perceived as contradicting a perception of the basically and immutably inimical position of the Soviets vis-a-vis American interests. No wonder then that genuine detente -- entailing relational change -- never really showed consistent signs of attainability during the Nixon-Kissinger era. This is not to say, however, that there was no potential in the system at this time for detente, as some elements actually responded to evidence which suggested such a potential (see discussion of the "halo" or "holdover" effect on page 79 of Chapter 3). Policymakers must be forced to examine their assumptions about superpower behavior, and should these assumptions prove wanting, to construct an alternate or revised picture. How would one go about testing the accuracy of his perceptions?

If one accepts the premise that detente is not an already demonstrated failure, then it becomes possible to explore the feasibility of moving in this policy direction. Feasibility can be established by producing evidence which suggests that the USSR may in fact be a state driven primarily by defensive motivations, and one whose actions are largely reactions to perceived (unfounded, or not) American threats. The method for testing whether such evidence exists will be called the "retrodictive strategic probe."[1] The retrodictive probe is based on the

95

fact that persons having different assumptions about the fundamental nature of another actor, e.g. the USSR, will also generally have differing expectations about how that actor will respond to any of one's own specific acts of policy. What the probe device seeks to accomplish is to reconstruct the historical setting "prior to" an identified act of policy, and at this point to explicate how persons adhering to different assumptional bases would predict another actor's response to this impending policy act. Predictions which come to be borne out lend credence to the assumptions from which they spring, and should a particular assumptional base repetitively predict correctly, confidence in the verisimilitude of that base is strongly enhanced. Approaches that use the historical record to test the veracity of different assumptional bases have already yielded encouraging results.[2]

The model I use to elicit and order predictions about Soviet behavior appears graphically as follows (please see Figure 7):

Issue Area

Not Valuable   Valuable

		Not Valuable	Valuable
	Active	I	II
USSR			
	Reactive	III	IV

Figure 7

On the left-hand border of the model, the terms "active" and "reactive describe a person's fundamental belief about the basic thrust of the USSR's foreign policy: active connotes an aggressive, imperialistic state, reactive connotes a primarily defensive state that is satisfied with protecting the status quo. Although the active/reactive dichotomy seems to be an oversimplification of how people view Soviet motivation, this is a fundamental dichotomy, and one that has been proffered by others. A recent newspaper editorial used the terms "power maximizing" and "mirror imaging" to approximate the meaning of the active/reactive terms.[3] The top border labelled "Issue Area" refers to the specific nature or identity of the policy question being examined; "not valuable" implies that a person sees the USSR as uninterested in a certain type of interaction or issue, "valuable" implies interest. The constituent categories of the Detente Index can satisfy the need for a range of issue-areas to accommodate the model, and I will use the "cultural exchange," "trade" and "arms control" areas to illustrate general predictions for each quadrant or assumptional base of the model. Assume that the situation is this: the U.S. is considering the

96

proposal of a significant cultural exchange (trade or arms control) agreement to the USSR; how will persons with differing views of the Soviets expect the proposal to be received and acted upon? If we were dealing with an actual proposal at a real point in time, predictions could be framed in much more detail. We must assume that all U.S. proposals are made in good faith, otherwise, there is little vindication for the person who predicts a Soviet rejection of a proposal which has been made in bad faith or is hopelessly self-serving and one-sided. Following the cultural exchange, trade and arms control examples, I will provide one additional example, namely, for the "international political cooperation" issue-area. This example is a bit more complex than the other three, and will require some elaboration. I will also use an actual historical case -- the Austrian State Treaty -- to be plugged into this model.

I would like to point out that that other configurations besides the one used in Figure 7 are possible for use in ordering predictions for retrodictive strategic probes. The main dimension we are interested in is, of course, the Active/Reactive one; especially if one reasons that a reactive USSR is likely to be amenable to most if not all types of bilateral cooperation. In fact, one might simply want to order predictions based upon each of the four hypothetical state profiles used in the HOC Scheme of Chapter 2 -- these profiles running on an adversarial scale from the dire enemy to the complex competitor poles. I personally feel, however, that this much nuance is not necessary for testing an intrinsically dichotomous view of the USSR. Dichotomies are crude as measuring devices, but not necessarily as testing devices. Four gradations in the adversarial dimension would also blur the distinction between predictions used in an actual case study. So why not simply predict along active/reactive lines? This would leave open an important ambiguous outcome whereby the nonoccurrence of an expected cooperative (or hostile) Soviet reaction to an American action could be explained away by saying that the issue simply wasn't important or germane enough to the current Soviet political agenda to warrant a response. This disclaimer practically destroys the possibility of devising relatively uncontestable probes. This is why I have added the "Valuable"/"Not Valuable" dimension to the model in Figure 7. For my purposes, it allows me to array policy predictions in the most non-overlapping and centrally relevant form.

At this time, for sample models per three specific issue-areas, please see Figures 8 through 10 (remember that distinct contextual detail can only be added when plugging an actual case into one of the models).

Situation: The U.S. is considering the proposal of a significant cultural exchange agreement to the USSR.

Cultural Exchange

	Not Valuable	Valuable
Active	1. Reject agreement I	1. Technology theft. 2. Use as a propaganda forum. II
USSR	III	IV
Reactive	1. Token participation; or 2. Alternative interaction suggested.	1. Enthusiastic (yet wary) participation. 2. Faithful adherence to agreement's provisions.

Figure 8

Situation: The U.S. is considering the proposal of a significant trade agreement to the USSR.

<u>Trade</u>

	Not Valuable	Valuable
Active	I 1. Reject agreement.	II 1. Technology transfer. 2. Disruption of Western markets. 3. Transhipment with resale at higher prices. 4. Trade tied to major concessions (e.g., loans, credits, low shipping rates, etc.)
Reactive	III 1. Marginal trade activity; or 2. Alternative interaction suggested.	IV 1. Enthusiastic and faithful participation. 2. Equal exchange.

<u>USSR</u>

Figure 9

99

Situation: The U.S. is considering the proposal of a significant arms control agreement to the USSR.

Arms Control

	Not Valuable	Valuable
Active	1. Reject agreement. I	1. Seek quantitative and qualitative advantage. 2. Seek only to limit areas the other side leads in. 3. Sign an agreement and then cheat on it. II
USSR **Re-active**	III 1. Meaningless (e.g., exceedingly high) limitations. 2. Interminable negotiations without movement toward agreement; or 3. Alternative interaction suggested. III	IV 1. Enthusiastic and faithful participation. 2. Equal sacrifice. 3. Equal security. IV

Figure 10

100

Before presenting the general model for the International Political Cooperation (Political Cooperation - High Politics) issue-area, it should be pointed out that there is a difference between this issue-area and the three previous ones, in that such international political cooperation may be bilateral in the sense that there is a proposal for joint action in some third area, and cooperation may also occur in response to a U.S. action made directly to a third party (third party overtures on less important issues are not likely to consistently draw significant Soviet reaction). If, for example, the U.S. was to prod Israel in an attempt to move toward settlement on the fate of the West Bank, the USSR would basically have the choice of either opposing, ignoring or supporting the American initiative. The point here is simply that the occurrence of policy questions which could involve both the USSR or other states as the direct target expands the range of predicted Soviet responses. It may be that the USSR has no interest in cooperating directly with the U.S. on international political questions; however, the terms "not valuable" and "valuable" regarding issue-area importance must take on slightly different meanings when assessing a possible Soviet response to an American move directed at a third party. Even if the Soviets do not value undertaking bilateral initiatives with the U.S., the U.S. may nonetheless move on its own in ways that very much affect Soviet interests. In this case, "not valuable" simply means low-priority or unimportant regarding the status of the third party being approached by the U.S., "valuable" means important or high-priority: the predictor makes these assessments for himself. Since the parameter (not valuable/valuable) may legitimately shift from case to case regarding American overtures to third parties, rather than from issue-area to issue-area, Quadrant III predictions which are borne out may be at least as welcome as those of Quadrant IV. This is an acceptable situation, as it is the active/reactive parameter in which we are the most interested.

Below, in the sample model for international political cooperation, each quadrant is bisected by a dotted line; predictions above the line pertain to direct U.S. approaches to the USSR regarding some type of joint cooperative activity*, predictions below the line pertain to significant U.S. initiatives to third parties which may or may not indirectly touch upon Soviet interests -- all predictions are made here in only the broadest terms (please see Figure 11).

---

*Remember the good-faith assumption about American initiatives, meaning that they aim at problem solving or security enhancement.

International Political Cooperation

	Not Valuable (Direct)	Valuable (Direct)
Active	1. Reject cooperation. 2. Unilateralism (Indirect) 1. Verbal opposition I	1. Use as entree for influence building. 2. Mislead re. willingness to lobby/pressure allies or clients. 3. Maneuver the U.S. into unpopular, no-win situations. (Indirect) 1. Oppose/Aggravate II
	III	IV
Reactive	(Direct) 1. Decline cooperation due to (e.g.): a) fear of condominium charge; b) belief in the autonomy of the national liberation movement; c) belief in the inevitable decline of capitalism; or 2. Token participation. (Indirect) 1. Verbal support.	(Direct) 1. Demonstrate restraint. 2. Push de-escalation and demilitarization. 3. Accept possible loss of role or influence in an area. (Indirect) 1. Support/facilitate.

USSR (row label spanning Active/Reactive)

Figure 11

To help sharpen the distinction between quadrants, one may wish to define or characterize the interface between cells (in addition to Figure 11's provision of exemplary behavior within cells). Please see Figure 12 for such an interface focus.

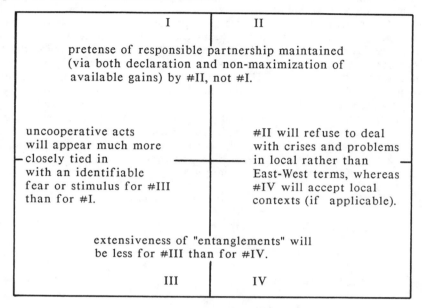

Figure 12

Interface Characterization Between Quadrants
of the Strategic Probe Device

The characterizations of the boundaries in the model above may after repeated use prove to not be the most useful or discriminating. A future direction for the analyst might therefore be to deduce operating principles for each quadrant (e.g., Quadrant I: a. actively cultivate new opportunities for influence expansion; b. maximize short-term gains; c. act unilaterally; etc.), and then characterize each interface or boundary according to these principles. Yet even with refinements such as these, explicit predictions of another state's anticipated behavior can only be achieved within the context of a specific case. To illustrate this purported explicitness, a case study -- the Austrian State Treaty- will now be employed.

Going to 1955, the first year identified as one of incipient detente, the Austrian treaty was selected for its momentousness as a test of East-West cooperative possibilities. The treaty, signed on May 15th, defined the character of Austria's post-war foreign and to some extent internal affairs. After little movement since the war toward the

103

signing of a peace treaty, in April of 1955 the Austrians and Soviets began bilateral talks on appropriate provisions for a peace treaty. At this point, Americans could hardly have known how punitive or mild the Soviet suggestions or demands might be. The outcome of the Austro-Soviet talks was a communique called the Moscow Memorandum, which spelled out provisions for a treaty that was more wildly lenient than most persons would have dared to imagine. The retrodictive strategic probe is constructed to occur before the Memorandum was produced. Therefore, in early April of 1955 with Austro-Soviet talks just getting underway, and given a U.S. and Western allied readiness to end occupation of Austria and conclude a four-power treaty, how would persons operating from different assumptional bases predict the provisions soon to be advanced by the Soviets? I will use the model for international political cooperation which was just discussed to lay out the predictions which should have flowed logically from each of the four assumptional bases. Each base will express a view on four key dimensions of the Austrian situation; namely,

1) the size/duration/type of Austrian payments;

2) possible oil and shipping concessions;

3) political obligations and restrictions; and

4) military restrictions.

Predictions per base are provided below:

Quadrant I: USSR Active - International Political Cooperation Not Valuable

1) removal to the USSR of former German-owned facilities; demand for dollar reparations (from Austria as a belligerant, rather than occupied nation);

2) full or partial Soviet control of Austrian oil production and Danubian shipping;

3) retention of Soviet sphere of occupation: demand for Austrian neutrality immaterial;

4) size and composition of Austrian armed forces dictated by Soviet preferences.

Quadrant II: USSR Active - International Political Cooperation Valuable

1) extraction of as large a payment in cash and kind as quickly as possible;

2) obtain reasonable, long-term interests in oil and shipping operations;

3) preference for a 4-power Council to administer Austrian affairs; at worst, constitutional provisions for significant communist participation in any coalition government: explicit linkage of negotiations over Austria to other political questions, such as the fate of Germany;

4) constraints to keep prospective Austrian armed forces at a marginal capacity; link their autonomy to a diminished role for an integrated West European defense community.

Quadrant III: USSR Reactive - International Political Cooperation Not Valuable

1) modest/sustainable payments in cash or kind for formerly owned German properties;

2) Austrian control of its oil and shipping activities;

3) political neutrality with a clause for intervention by the communist states if needed to help decide future problems (e.g., re. displaced persons);

4) demilitarization.

Quadrant IV: USSR Reactive - International Political Cooperation Valuable

1) modest short-term payments in cash or kind for formerly owned German properties;

2) short-term 4-power administration of, or Austrian autonomy for oil and shipping concerns;

3) political neutrality;

4) Austrian armed forces permissible; military nonalignment.

I feel that the logic behind each quadrant's predictions is readily discernable and can be extrapolated from the two dimensions which constitute the assumptional base of each quadrant. Although there is a temptation with hindsight for the analyst to gear the predictions of the particular assumptional base to which he subscribes toward the subsequent outcomes of which he is already aware, this is, however, a problem of human foibles, not necessarily of the approach itself. Given a reasonably objective analyst, or better yet a team of analysts, coupled with increasingly fleshed out predictions for the general model of international political cooperation itself, then the predictions associated with a specific case could be explicated with little bias deriving from political preferences. Comparing Quadrant IV -- USSR Reactive - International Political Cooperation Valuable -- with the actual eventualities connected with the Austrian treaty, it is fairly clear that the assumptional base associated with this quadrant yielded the best predictions, and therefore the most accurate view of reality. One case hardly makes for a definitive test; therefore, other instances of prospective political cooperation must also be examined, as well as policy questions from other issue-areas. It must also be acknowledged that some probes just will not produce neat, clear-cut results. In some cases the elements of the eventual outcome will be mixed across both an active and reactive quadrant. In other cases, predictions ther selves will be difficult to make; e.g.: should a predicted strong Soviet reaction/overreaction be placed in a reactive quadrant due to paranoic albeit legitimate factors (such as border insecurity, xenophobia, spy mania, etc.), or in an active quadrant due to malevolent assertiveness? An ambiguous outcome neither proves nor casts doubt on any of the assumptional bases, it only means that the interpretation of an outcome is contestable (i.e., we do know who is right). Since the retrodictive strategic probe is meant to be used serially anyway, when the occasional ambiguous outcome occurs, the analyst should simply select another policy episode from the same issue-area and approximately the same period.

It is the author's suspicion, however, that the USSR Reactive-International Political Cooperation Valuable view would prevail after continued testing in making the greatest number of correct predictions, and therefore afford the truest picture of reality. The fact that within months of the Austrian treaty, the USSR also engaged in summitry at Geneva, established diplomatic relations with West Germany, and gave up its naval base on Porkhala Island in Finland -- ostensibly in pursuit of their post-Stalin policy of peaceful coexistence -- certainly lends substantiating evidence to the credibility of the Quadrant IV view (at least during this time period). Each of these three policy episodes (as well as any other, given a certain level of significance or visibility) easily lends itself to scrutiny using the retrodictive strategic probe format. If U.S. government analysts had used a device such as the strategic probe back in 1955 which forced them to see the Quadrant IV motivations behind the above acts of Soviet foreign policy, they may have determined this point in time as a marvelous opportunity for truly pushing U.S.-Soviet reconciliation. Given the frequency with which historians characterize the Cold War as a series of missed opportunities, this is no mean achievement. Had the process of reconciliation flowered, it is even conceivable that the trust and understanding fostered during this period would have made the upheavals in 1956 over Hungary and the Middle East unnecessary. The analyst must also be sensitive to the possibility that the USSR's basic foreign policy objectives may shift over time in accordance with perceived environmental conditions.

Since motivations may shift with environmental changes, such a prospect has implications for the future, especially once a policy of detente has actually been embarked on. As the Soviet perception of threat continues to atrophy during the early stages of an evolving detente, it is conceivable that the discarded threat perception will be replaced with an energizing perception of emancipation and opportunity. Should this phenomenon occur, the continuance of a detente policy toward a confident and outwardly oriented USSR would be a mistake. Assumptional testing, as was done retrodictively in this chapter, should also be carried out continuously as policy unfolds; constant probing to reaffirm the primarily defensive motivation of the USSR's foreign policy is a good safeguard for ensuring the appropriateness of detente. The most accurate way to guarantee that future-oriented predictions of Soviet responses correspond to the logic of each assumptional base would be for actual adherents of each view to post their predictions.

Concluding that the USSR does not seem to act like a highly aggressive state bent on conquest is only one side of the coin used in establishing the feasibility of detente. The USSR if defensively motivated will see the U.S. as a threatening and aggressive state, which makes Soviet concurrence on the wisdom of detente unlikely. As the U.S. aggressor image of the USSR erodes, policies should be designed to give the Soviets cause to question this same image as it is applied to the U.S. What the U.S. must do is to adopt a policy of conciliation. This policy will be highly situational, where the U.S. seizes every opportunity to make an accommodating overture or response to the USSR. These gestures will not be giveaways or blatant concessions, but will merely be a running series of policy acts which exude empathy for the Soviet position. This period of conciliation is meant to shock Soviet leaders, and force them to try to square this reasonable American behavior with the enemy image they hold. At first, Soviet leaders will suspect they are being tricked or deceived, yet the persistence of a conciliatory American attitude will eventually suggest a notable U.S. policy shift toward increased pragmatism. If at this point the analysis of U.S. policymakers has cast doubt on the dire enemy status of the USSR, and the Soviets in turn accept that they are not being tricked by a state which appears to have shed its Russophobic delusions, then detente becomes feasible, and joint consultation on its initiation and management seems warranted. Should the Soviets, through an analytical process similar to the retrodictive strategic probe exercise which I have outlined, first come to suspect the distortion and exaggeration bound up with their image of the U.S., then it would also be effective for them to adopt the conciliatory policy which I have for exemplary reasons prescribed above for the U.S. In either case, threat perception on both sides will fade to the point where detente is admissible. To then embark on a coherent, mutually understood detente plan of action is to take steps which increasingly preclude the reappearance of the dire enemy image.   Chapter 5 presents a detente plan for accomplishing this very task.

Before turning to the next chapter, it seems necessary and important to ask: despite the obvious importance of assumptional testing, what are the chances that a practitioner in the foreign policy establishment -- harried by factual complexities and fast-paced change -- will heed the naive advice of the academic analyst and submit to an exercise as trifling as the retrodictive strategic probe?   The answer may not be an overly encouraging one.   Unfortunately, there is no one masterstroke that will render academic research and advice more relevant and attractive to the practitioner.   Instead, a variety of trends must be moved forward.   First, the standard format for the preparation of official policy analyses and position papers should be made to require a section which forces the explication of that paper's assumptional underpinnings.   Secondly, foreign policy analysts in academe must recognize their charge to critique these assumptions for their empirical justification.   Thirdly, and perhaps most importantly, effective channels or points of access into the bureaucracy must be cultivated.   Why, for example, do Rand and Brookings -- both quasi-academic/quasi-governmental organizations -- enjoy such credibility in government?   I might suggest that this is due to the prevalence of their recruitment and use of the "inner-and-outer" -- meaning that type of individual who migrates back and forth between stints of government service and intellectual rejuvenation in the academic community. If this were indeed the case, perhaps more value should be placed on this type of individual; not necessarily because he can master performing in both worlds, but because he can act as a conduit between them.   If one added into this multi-pronged approach, federal hiring and promotion practices which sought to identify and deflect from upper-grade positions persons with rigid personalities who would not be open to academic counsel, as well as added institutional arrangements for surfacing and scrutinizing unbiased (or at last "recognizably" biased) information, then official receptivity to all types of inputs, including academic ones, will be appreciably enhanced.

Notes

[1] Please see Richard W. Cottam, <u>Foreign Policy Motivation</u> (Pittsburgh: University of Pittsburgh Press, 1977), pp. 326-32; and, <u>Competitive Interference and 20th Century Diplomacy</u> (Pittsburgh: University of Pittsburgh Press, 1967), pp. 139-40.

[2] Please see George Breslauer, "Soviet Policy in the Middle East, 1967-72: Unalterable Antagonism or Collaborative Competition?", in <u>Managing U.S.-Soviet Rivalry</u>, by Alexander George (Boulder: Westview Press, 1983), Chapter 4; and William Gamson and Andre Modigliani, <u>Untangling the Cold War</u> (Boston: Little, Brown and Company, 1971).

[3] Charles Wolfe, Jr., "Why the Experts Disagree About the Soviets," <u>Washington Post</u>, 25 July 1984, p. A17.

CHAPTER 5

DETENTE: A DESCRIPTIVE ESSAY

This chapter sets out to move beyond the rather halting writing style often found in parts of the study thus far; a study laden with tables, schema and typologies. Chapter 3 was intended to be overtly prescriptive in terms of laying down a blueprint for the content and context of a coherent detente policy, and Chapter 4 sought to demonstrate the admissibility and appropriateness of employing this blueprint. Policy acts and their cumulative effects germane to specific phases of a detente process will now be lashed together and described in a narrative fashion. The phases I will use are:

Phase I	:	Test Cases
Phase II	:	Unconsummated Detente
Phase III	:	Consummated Detente - Early
Phase IV	:	Consummated Detente - Late
Phase V	:	Institutionalized Detente

There is nothing inexorable about these phases. There is no magic spell in the detente ritual that precludes either side's defection from such a course. Moving through the (at least, first three) phases depends on strict good faith -- meaning both sides have evaluated objective domestic and international conditions (background factors), have perceived their own resource finiteness as well as Soviet-American common interests, have found a detente policy to be in their states's best interest, and therefore resolved themselves to its pursuit. Superpowers are too autonomous, too wary, and too haughty to be manipulated into a detente they do not desire. Neither side is capable of playing Pied Piper, sounding the notes of a detente melody that the other finds irresistible. Nor are either side's unilateral good deeds so unambiguous that they will be received by, or have full effect on a rejectionist opponent. Both sides must seek detente, and their efforts must be both swift and effective, or these very efforts will be swamped or outstripped by events at large.

The phases themselves are arbitrary in terms of boundaries, and in reality would meld one into another. This is unlike Charles Osgood's conception of Graduated Reciprocation in Tension-reduction (GRIT),[1] where a future set of initiatives is clearly lined up ready to go upon the other side's reciprocating the last set of initiatives, in a sort of "you scratch my back, I'll scratch yours" fashion. Yet like the regular intervals at which the GRIT strategy is evaluated for progress, so must my five-phase detente strategy be closely monitored for the occurrence of anticipated effects. Should anticipated effects lag too slowly or not occur at all, we must realize that the underlying logic for subsequent phases has been contravened. A detente strategy is not an all or nothing approach toward the other superpower. Presumably U.S.

decisionmakers have a quiver or repertory of policy alternatives ready for employment should an approach presently in place prove inadequate. The alternative may take the form of a different strategy within the framework of a continuing detente policy, or more likely, it will be a substitute policy in toto (e.g., malign neglect).

Given favorable background factors, and effective U.S.-Soviet leaderships receptive to improving relations, I am nonetheless optimistic that the following strategy would stand a considerable chance of success; we will now describe hypothetically how such a strategy would unfold phase by phase.

A. Phase I: Test Cases

Extensive in-house analysis and evaluation shows the leaders of one or both superpowers that the other's behavior does not preclude the initiation of a desirable policy of detente. Diplomatic signalling then alerts the other side of one's own developing pro-detente inclination. After a period of mutual scrutiny, the dominant coalition of political forces in both the U.S. and USSR come to realize that the other side is sincere about engaging in a long-term process of improving relations -- perhaps to dramatic proportions -- and that their own side has successfully conveyed interest in participating in such a process. Envoys are exchanged to probe fruitful areas of initial contact. These areas are chosen for their low visibility, relatively uncontroversial nature, and high prospects for being successfully carried out. A new biennial U.S.-Soviet cultural exchange agreement is framed, signed and instituted. The provisions of the agreement create artistic, theatrical, student, journalistic, professional, athletic and clerical exchange programs. Government-to-government agreements for joint scientific research are signed on such problems as acid rain, desulfurization of coal, hydrological management, storage of nuclear waste, entomological methods of crop protection, etc.

On a multilateral basis, U.S. and Soviet delegates to the Conference on Security and Cooperation in Europe (CSCE) review meetings and spin-off conferences (e.g., The Conference on Confidence- and Security-Building Measures and Disarmament in Europe) make conciliatory speeches, and pledge their countries to the furtherance of the CSCE process. In a different forum, drawing on the acrimonious legacy of the downed Korean civilian airliner in 1983, U.S. and Soviet representatives to the International Civil Aviation Organization collaborate on authoring a slate of proposed remedial actions which would seek to help avoid similar airline disasters in the future.* As for the United Nations, U.S. and Soviet representatives to its specialized agencies lobby each other to support projects of particular interest to themselves, and a variety of mutually held concerns are identified. Joint ameliorative actions taken to confront these concerns include the enhancement of U.N. resources for administering disaster relief aid, and the submission of recommendations on removing or circumventing the more contentious aspects of law-of-the-sea negotiations so as to get these talks rolling again.

This phase need not last long, perhaps six months to one year. The absence of rancor in the East-West dialogue subtly nudges most persons on both sides into musing about the possibility of constructive Soviet-American intercourse. For those political leaders on both sides who had orchestrated the detente test cases, their hopes have been vindicated and their confidence emboldened. The detente process is now ready to have its range of activities deepened and broadened.

B. Phase II: Unconsummated Detente

In detente's second phase the number and variety of cooperative policy acts increases. This acceleration, as well as the recent examples of smooth running or fruitfully concluded test cases cause many persons to reflect seriously on the possibility of, at long last, a viable detente. The initiation of this phase should be accompanied by landmark speeches by the U.S. President and the CPSU's General Secretary; each pledging a determined effort to explore all opportunities for improving Soviet-American relations, and divulging the other side's similarly expressed interest, which heretofore had been knowable mainly through diplomatic channels only. The students of Soviet-American relations must be sure not to misinterpret detente as a bilateral covenant hashed out by political leaders and then followed by a mutually choreographed stylized dance that seeks only to legitimate the covenant in the eyes of skeptical domestic forces on each side. For a state's leaderhsip, detente is more akin to a balancing act; on one hand cultivating a reputation for trustworthiness and good faith with the other side, and on the other, leading and shaping opinions and potentialities at home so that broad social groupings and forces may align with and contribute to the official husbanding of cooperative interstate relations. Many Soviet-American undertakings bolster both international and domestic

---

*Note: Since the writing of this manuscript, in July of 1985 the U.S., USSR and Japan concluded a Pacific Air Safety Pact. As such an isolated instance of cooperation, however, it is likely to be observed at best to the letter of the agreement, rather than in any sort of cooperative spirit.

113

confidence in the wisdom of a detente course. Should official efforts get out of balance with regard to either the other side or one's own fellow countrymen, the result will be a non-starter.

Unilateral initiatives in this phase often aim for psychological impact to reinforce the perception of a break with superpower business-as-usual. A useful device for doing this would be to clear away the vestigial rubble from failed incipient detentes of the past. Specifically, one should examine previously negotiated but still unratified treaties. In the U.S. case, a treaty may be withheld from submission for ratification due to an attempt to discredit the previous administration, or to send a signal to the Soviets as to the desired direction for more viable future treaty arrangements. If in addition to these two considerations, the only other objection to a treaty is that its provisions are not far-reaching enough, then that treaty should be ratified; both the Threshold Test Ban Treaty and the Peaceful Nuclear Explosions Treaty would seem to fit in this category. If a treaty is indeed unacceptable due to a changed environment, then it should be quietly scrapped, or placed in some sort of a status which does not imply pending ratification (as perhaps we should do with SALT II, whose numerical ceilings play an apparently useful role). Drawbacks which led to a treaty's scuttling or removal from consideration for ratification should be addressed as soon as possible in on-going or prospective arms talks. The process of removing previously negotiated treaties from the curious limbo of nonratification would perceptually free policymakers from having to attend to old business, and create a type of clean slate for forward movement. A further example for demonstrating a break from business-as-usual might be each side's navy being granted ports of call in the other's country. Perhaps a variety of high visibility cases involving family reunification, the emigration of religious activists or even political dissidents to desired new locations, and the exchange or large-scale release of the other's nationals incarcerated on espionage charges could be arranged. Good will can also be demonstrated as much by opportunities foregone as by deeds performed; for example, pro forma denunciations of the other at various multilateral convocations (e.g., the annual economic summits of Western industrial democracies, sessions of the non-aligned movement, etc.) are passed up.

On a more strictly utilitarian level, arms control talks (medium-range and strategic) begin. On a multilateral basis, the U.S. and USSR emphasize the need for more attention to the issue of nuclear nonproliferation, and initiate within the U.N. the drafting of stricter more enforceable standards for preventing such proliferation. In addition to arms talks, state-to-state trade negotiations likewise begin. Also, a number of private U.S. firms sign contracts with Soviet enterprises, and economic joint ventures start to appear. Cultural and scientific exchanges initiated in Phase I continue to flourish, and broaden in scope. Exchanges also include legislators from each side, who visit the other regularly on fact finding or clarifying missions. A

114

number who visit the other regularly on fact-finding or clarifying missions. A number of facilitative acts which lay the groundwork for future progress also take place. Each side maximizes diplomatic access for the other, and the hardware and practices for interstate communication are updated and given prominence. In way of communication, the U.S. President and the Soviet General Secretary come to establish a lively personal correspondence. Also, as contacts proliferate, joint coordinating and adjudicating organs or bodies are created; these bodies give institutional reality and stability to detente, and embody a constructive problem-solving philosophy.

Domestically, the U.S. President undertakes an animated and prolonged campaign to rally bipartisan political support for detente; this is crucial, for it is Congress which must pass much of the legislation which alters agency funding criteria to detente enhancement (discussed in Chapter 3, Section 3), which in turn is crucial for deeply rooting detente into bureaucratic practices. Agency heads are outspokenly reassured by the President and Administration officials that a policy of U.S.-Soviet detente will not diminish the prestige and resources granted to their organizations, although missions may, and indeed probably will evolve or change. Supportive agency heads are, in turn, enlisted to lobby their colleagues. It is likely that agencies having an international dimension (as most do) will receive words of encouragement and commendation from their counterparts abroad (e.g., Europe, the developing world) regarding the emerging pro-detente tendency in the U.S. government. The leadership's courtship of the bureaucracy is just as important in the USSR as it is in the U.S. Appropriations criteria for agency funding remain unaltered in this phase; the notion of "unconsummated" detente connotes tentativeness, which is reflected by the heads of governmental units and subunits seeking to test the detente ground on the basis of its moral attractiveness while operating within conventional parameters.

As for negotiations, they can be thought of as being either one of two types -- those instituted mainly for the sake of talking as a benefit in and of itself (e.g., MBFR, START); and those undertaken with a tacit mutual timetable in mind, including a prospective date by which to have hammered out an agreement (e.g., SALT I). Given the purposeful nature of initiatives in a phased detente strategy, we would hope that most negotiations undertaken in Phase II would be of this second type. Given the mutual emphasis on arms control negotiations, and the assumed purposiveness of these talks, the phase of unconsummated detente should produce a major arms control agreement, which will then serve as a bridge into the next, and higher, phase of detente. The specific provisions of the agreement are not themselves all-important or all-determining; although given the hair-trigger situation involving medium-range missiles in Europe, perhaps provisions for reducing these missiles, folded into a larger START agreement (thus ensuring central relevance for Americans) would be the most dramatic and beneficial. This agreement would most likely take treaty form, and its forthright ratification by both sides should not be underestimated for symbolic import.

Phase II has progressed through the first fledgling attempts at building upon the test cases of Phase I, to the conclusion of a major arms control agreement. The cumulative effect of these various acts and initiatives may be taken stock of. Given the U.S. government's circumspect, if not reserved pursuit of detente, the press has tended to exhort the value of a detente policy and its continued implementation. Press treatment, as well as events themselves are shaping a mood (on both sides) of cautious excitement; and a subconscious feeling pervades that the elements of a detente policy are approaching critical mass, which would be followed by a perceptual take-off point whereby the fortunes of many public and private individuals and organizations become bound up with and committed to detente. Economic interchange is helping to disperse the benefits of detente, and scrupulous attention to economic self-interest and mutuality of benefit strives to offset potentially explosive popular tendencies to speak or vote in consultation with their pocketbook. The high ratio of successful to failed initiatives and joint endeavors -- originally selected according to characteristics which maximize their chances of viability -- has begun to raise long-frozen levels of mutual trust, and preliminary attempts to inculcate pro-detente bureaucratic processes within each side's government structure aim to create preconditions for the eventual institutionalization of this inchoate trusting relationship.

C. Phase III: Early Consummated Detente

The period of consummated detente (Phases III and IV) sees the realization of the promise contained in the detente ideal. Phase III, in the level of goodwill and mutual trust achieved, as well as the types of initiatives undertaken, somewhat resembles the historical era of 1972-73. These two years comprised the historical highpoint of Soviet-American (incipient) detente, and it is interesting to note that a hypothesized "successful" detente process requires two additional phases beyond the one (Phase III) mirroring 1972-73.

The notion of "consummation" connotes accomplishment or achievement. A summit meeting between the President of the U.S. and the CPSU's General Secretary is a perfect platform from which to trumpet cooperative achievements to date. The arms control agreement which concluded the phase of unconsummated detente, as well as other bilateral agreements husbanded together from the close of Phase II, would be signed at the summit. The summit seeks to initiate a spectacular momentum to detente, with skeptics risking being bowled over should they attempt to impede this momentum, much as a snowball collecting mass as it hurtles downhill has the capacity to scatter or absorb recusant objects in its path.

116

The acts and agreements of Phase III impinge on areas usually shielded by the prerogatives of national security. Economically, the U.S. allows itself (and its allies) to import, as well as cooperatively develop Soviet natural resources (e.g., fuel, raw materials). An extraordinary, but feasible development would be for the USSR to build into its 5-year economic plans a section premised on the U.S.' supplying of goods and services. Scientifically, the U.S. and USSR map out an ambitious program of joint research in such areas as atomic energy and space exploration. Encounters in these areas have occurred in the past, but usually only involving low-level, if not obsolete technology and data. This type of cooperation becomes even more intimate in Phase IV, as the mandate for military application of these technologies wanes. On a different side of this same coin, decreased military demand may lower the number of spin-off technologies, which would put even more pressure on U.S.-Soviet scientific cooperation to prove fruitful. Confidence-building measures find a central role in this phase, especially regarding surveillance and advance notification. Various modes of on-site observation and verification become standard practice; war games and maneuvers are attended by observers from the other side, troop exits or missile dismantlings are counted by the other side, the thwarting of national means of verification is eschewed, and should points of contention over these matters arise, settlement may be pursued through arrangements for limited access to the other's military installations. Each side permanently stations military monitors on the other's terrain, and the relationship betwen military attaches and their host-country counterparts becomes almost collegial. In highly charged settings such as around Berlin, the U.S. Potsdam liaison office and its Soviet counterpart in West Germany lay out explicit ground rules for regulating the types of surveillance functions each performs on the other's soil. Both sides notify the other prior to all major occurrences of a military nature; e.g. troop movements, missile tests, modernization and replacement programs, etc. Also, an agreement on numerical quotas for the testing of nuclear devices is reached, thus taking a step in the direction of slowing the heretofore unconstrained pace of qualitative improvements in the superpowers' nuclear arsenals.

Domestically, riding the crest of detente's momentum, institutionalization efforts are intensified. In both the U.S. and USSR, government officials still opposing detente are removed if possible, and made to feel anachronistic if not irrelevant should they resist. With new detente-regime officials added to original supporters, organizational practices and criteria which dictate fund allocation are ready to be revised. With resources becoming partially contingent on contribution to detente enhancement, and with pro-detente values prevalent, organizations and their sub-units have palpable incentive to abandon many, now counterproductive practices which had served them well during and after the Cold War. As with bilateral U.S.-Soviet acts of engagement, which gradually migrate upward in terms of risk and magnitude, so must the institution of a new organizational incentive system be gradual. The system must first condition pro-detente

117

responses to an organization's peripheral areas of concern. A gestalt switch in an organization's mission would produce only chaos; and bureaucratic breakdown is hardly conducive to bolstering detente's advocates. Regarding interstate institutionalization, Soviet-American disagreements which had to be suppressed in the interest of detente during the first two phases need no longer be treated in such a manner, but may be referred instead to an increasingly accommodating network of bilateral institutions, such as various standing consultative committees usually associated with an issue-specific agreement or field.

The cumulative impacts manifested during this phase continue the pro-detente trend lines of Phase II. The American press which led the way in exhorting the pursuit of detente during the period of unconsummated detente feels vindicated by the events of Phase II, and favorable press attention to detente-relevant activities continues. The benefits of detente become more abundant and widely dispersed. This is especially true if one considers the intangible benefits of civil peace of mind or psychological liberation from acute fears of nuclear holocaust. Since many of the acts and agreements of this phase touch on traditional concerns of secrecy and sovereignty, the trust fostering capacity of these actions, if managed faithfully is great. Institutionalization has progressed to the point where most units of government are autonomously experimenting with the initiation of pro-detente endeavors without strict central direction, and the motivation for such endeavors has been in response to entreaty rather than compulsion. Inaugurated with a spectacular summit, and strewn with confidence-building measures highly contributory to detente, Soviet-American mutual trust has been annealed by one's own exposure to risk, self-created vulnerability displayed by the other side, and good faith all around. Although political courage and determination are necessary from the leaders of both sides for detente to have prospered through three phases, a bit of luck is also desirable, in that one hopes that a searing international conflict does not raise its head early in the detente process, thus forcing Soviet and American decisionmakers to make difficult and often polarized policy choices. Yet with detente's fourth phase, even this dreaded type of occurrence may not be sufficient to shake popular and official confidence in the policy's correctness.

D. Phase IV: Late Consummated Detente

The entry into this fourth phase is marked by the appearance of a type of bilateral cooperation basically heretofore unseen in the history of superpower relations -- namely, political cooperation with respect to third-area conflicts. Two key events almost universally cited as leading to or sealing the demise of the incipient detente of the early 1970s are the reluctance of the superpowers to collaborate during the Arab-Israeli war of 1973, and unilateral orientation each side adopted

118

toward the Angolan civil war of the mid-70s. When we compare 1972-73 to the description of detente's Phase III, although similar, it is clear that Soviet-American relations at that time did not develop the degree of intimacy hypothesized to exist at the close of Phase III, and it is therefore not surprising that Arab-Israeli and Angolan conflicts had the effects they did. For political cooperation to be feasible, the benefits of a constructive relationship with the other superpower must outweigh any marginal gains which might accrue from the exploitation of local instabilities or hostilities, and one must trust the other superpower enough to feel confident that it also will not stoop to such exploitation. The non-zero-sum game of superpower cooperation means that few local settings genuinely engage a superpower's vital interests, and those which do (East and West Europe) are clearly and mutually understood. This means that the superpowers need not posture and haggle with one another trying to demonstrate a preponderance of interest in every local issue around the globe, which in the past has led each side to see imperialistic if not rapacious designs in the other. Within the framework of a relatively trusting relationship, the dictation of outcomes in fluid third-area situations will not be seen as compelling, and local conflicts will be allowed to burn themselves out -- although the superpowers may collaborate to geographically confine a conflict, or press for its termination on the grounds of averting human tragedy. The role of trust in interpreting conflicts can be seen in the 1982 Falkland Islands war. No American commentator at that time saw British participation in this war as heralding the beginning of a new era of British imperialism and aggressiveness; whereas had the Soviets played the exact role that Britain did, the prognostications about future Soviet behavior would have been most foreboding and ominous.

Political cooperation occurs both in each superpower's conduct of its own relations with third states, and in their mutual collaborative efforts focusing on third states or areas. Political cooperation can be seen as occurring in the absence of, prior to, during, and after third-area disruption (e.g., coup, initiation of hostilities, etc.). In the absence of an impending disruption or problem, each superpower refrains from a concerted strengthening of a friendly state (e.g., Somalia, Ethiopia) or political faction (e.g., FNLA, MPLA) which is pledged to the elimination of a state or faction supported by the other superpower. A general U.S.-Soviet (or multilateral) agreement regulating conventional arms transfers would be of great assistance here. Prior to a budding international problem, if both superpowers are cognizant of the problem, they confer extensively so as to co-define the nature of the threat, its potential for escalation, and each side's interests (if any) in the situation. Should only one superpower become aware of the impending problem, it notifies the other promptly that drastic eventualities might occur, and in this way preempts any subsequent suspicions on the part of the other side that the problem may have been originally engineered, or at least welcomed by oneself. Should hostilities appear imminent between states each friendly to one of the superpowers, and this hostility was not preceded by an egregious

119

provocation, then the superpowers in good faith counsel prudence or caution from their associated states. Superpower exertions at pleading for calm reason may, however, fail; in which case each superpower will withhold all personnel, arms and supplies from the combatants. Jointly they communicate throughout the crisis to avoid misinterpretations based on each side's slightly different store of information, and they author and forcefully promulgate cease-fire proposals. Assuming that the conflict is eventually arrested, the superpowers attempt to construct a plan for stabilizing the now quiet area of conflict, and when feasible, to contribute to the amelioration of those conditions which initially gave rise to the conflict.

Three joint bodies are formed to perform the functions and crisis avoidance and management discussed above. To facilitate their interaction, the three bodies are actually teams organized within a single U.S.-Soviet Center for International Political Cooperation.* The teams are:

I. Third-Area Crisis Diagnosis and Conferral

II. Nuclear Outbreak Prevention

III. Interchange on Strategic Doctrine

The first team deals mostly with predicting and assessing the political ramifications of budding crises anywhere in the world. If a crisis promises to be or becomes so acute that a superpower military response is possible, the second team is employed to deal with defusing the perceived need for a nuclear option. This team also handles technical problems such as disconfirming (or confirming) in-coming nuclear attack alerts generated by computer malfunctions. The first team would be staffed by analysts, whereas the second team should be made up of official U.S. and Soviet representatives with access to their respective leaderships. The third team operates under less time sensitive circumstances than the other two, handling issues that are not as urgent as crises, yet every bit as contentious (and explosive in the long run). Here such topics as strategic defense, launch on warning, and perhaps scientific questions concerning such things as nuclear winter could be discussed. Frank discussion on doctrinal matters would aim to make each side's strategic posture seem more comprehensible, less threatening, and perhaps even deserving of adoption or emulation.

The U.S. and USSR observe the above norm of international political cooperation not because it has been canonized by a written

---

*Creation of a joint center for risk control has been prominently discussed in specialized journals recently.[2]

agreement, but because both sides seek to preserve the radically improved state of their relationship. The discarding of the diabolical enemy image of the other, which occurs as levels of trust rise, allows each superpower to empathize with the other, and thus understand the type of behavior the other would find reassuring. Increased trust also allows each superpower to practice or demonstrate the type of behavior it desires, and has reason to expect will be reciprocated. It would be naive to expect the superpowers to become so harmonious in their perceptions that they come to similarly identify the guilty and the innocent in all local conflicts; third states are simply too adroit at appealing to a superpower in its own political idiom. This by no means implies that the value of a local sycophant outweighs inter-superpower considerations, only that different local parties are likely to be more-or-less exclusively attractive to one superpower or the other.

The word "empathy" used in the last paragraph raises another style of superpower behavior appropriate to Phase IV; namely, the willingness to help the other with a problem. Possible actions include refuting unfair criticisms of the other superpower made by third states, promoting the other's negotiating efforts with third states that contribute to a more peaceful world, as well as stepping into the breach to assist in times of emergency such as air or sea disasters, crop failures, etc. The willingness to help the other with a problem is an "orientation," much as the proclivity to browbeat the other or let them "stew in their own juices" was a cold war orientation. Helping the other does not mean signing one-sided agreements, which would be an abnegation of self-interest, and ultimately detrimental to detente; but simply means being attentive to the other's needs, which is a sign of magnanimity, and can only enhance mutual trust and goodwill. I might add that as opposed to the early phases of detente, which were more formulaic, and well recognized signposts (e.g., cultural exchanges, trade agreements, arms control, summitry, etc.) were necessary to reinforce the perception of cooperation and progress, the latter phases of detente and the acts of policy which characterize them are more free-form or instinctive, based increasingly on orientation (e.g., relational-type) rather than formulae, much as the Cold War was based on orientation or relational-type. This apparent transmigration from one orientation to another indeed signals a succeeding detente process.

The in-sight success of detente gives this policy an unassailable momentum. Decisionmakers in the U.S., USSR and other countries as well, must operate within a detente frame of reference if they wish to be relevant to contemporary policy debates. The perception of momentum predisposes decisionmakers to be enthusiastic about contributing to a policy which has so captured the world's imagination. Bureaucracies which had previously only experimented at the margins with detente enhancement, now do so vigorously, in part because of a bandwagon effect, but also because of the truly riveting impact of the transformation which has occurred in superpower relations. Yet momentum may slow or sputter to a halt, and fond images may blacken;

therefore, it is not until Phase V that detente can be considered ultimately successful.

E. Phase V: Institutionalized Detente

This phase is characterized by effect or outcome rather than by actions or initiatives -- for institutionalizing actions were begun and continued since detente's second phase. Most of the literature which diagnoses the death of detente during the 1970s discusses the problems of policy legitimation and consensus building for such a policy, both among the public at large and within government itself. These problems of legitimation and consensus building suggest two main considerations; the first is the existence of significant sectors of unpersuaded groups and individuals (public and private), and the second is official susceptibility to being swayed by these unpersuaded elements. The concept of institutionalization connotes both a minimization of unpersuaded elements, and a maximization of official imperviousness to disagreeable or undesired influences. Institutions -- meaning regularized ways of doing things -- must be both strong and flexible; strong in that no policy ever achieves unanimity in backing and will be assaulted by various elements (often for parochial if not greedy reasons), and flexible so that responsiveness to contextual factors (e.g., popular needs and environmental conditions) will be high.

This chapter's presentation of a sequenced approach to bureaucratic courtship and instrumental learning, as well as the grooming of an international environment facilitative of this learning is aimed at, and thought to be sufficient to produce the type of institutional development discussed above. Institutionalizing efforts are necessary in a detente process to build a capacity for fending off emotionally based, yet often politically potent interpretations of international events -- such interpretations usually being couched in rote or habitual (e.g., cold war) terms. Institutionalization at more developed stages lends stability and predictability to the overall relationship, only to be reversed as a result of a truly catastrophic disturbance, the stable relationship emerging in Phase V grants perspective and legitimacy to U.S.-Soviet competition, which itself has been significantly limited or circumscribed as compared with the period prior to detente. Relational change is complete; the deeply ingrained enemy image which the superpowers held of each other has been exorcised and gradually replaced with a new perceptual and physical reality associated with the collaborative peer relational-type.

F. Summary

As one thinks about the postulated five phases of a detente process, and the types of initiatives and accomplishments they contain, it is tempting to muse about how long such a process would take. Given the interactive and mutually contingent nature of this process there is obviously no firm timetable or schedule; however, I might casually offer an estimation of 7-10 years as being necessary to traverse the five phases. This lengthy time frame is quite daunting when one considers possible detente-enhancing moves that could be seized upon at the present moment, and finds himself advocating an arms control agreement on medium-range missiles in Europe, a political settlement in Afghanistan, normalized U.S. relations with Cuba, East-West cooperation in genuinely assisting strife-torn Central America, relaxation of repression in Poland, Soviet and U.S. cooperation to persuade associated states to withdraw from Lebanon, etc. Yet this type of an ambitious slate for action violates the very lessons pulled from the theoretical and empirical observations presented earlier in this text, and which are infused into the five-phase detente construction. There seems to be at least as much impatience in wishing to do good as there is in meting out punishment. Yet impatience and overexuberance are likely to produce a pattern of fits and starts, which has been so familiar to us in the past. Commitment need not be synonymous with haste. Detente is best served by official sensitivity to the evolutionary nature of this process, and by official demonstration of the political wisdom and courage to intelligently shape and manage this evolution.

If detente is a process of relational change, then its successful prosecution and completion must be followed by a policy of relationship preservation. Although trust/benefit maximization is still germane to a post-detente period, its focus may differ slightly from that of detente's due to two problems. The first problem is that as the tenure of Soviet-American peaceful engagement lengthens, an increasingly exhaustive attempt to identify and explore avenues of mutual cooperation is made; this tends to preclude future possibilities for embarking on precedent-setting ventures, with an attendant loss in symbolic power. Under such circumstances, the value of traditional utilitarian ventures such as trade and economic cooperation goes up, and the high-risk visibility of political cooperation remains crucial. The second problem is that as conditions on the East-West front become relatively quiescent, there may be a tendency for the superpowers to turn their attention to other areas such as the development of relations with their European allies; although such a development is likely to have a positive effect, there is the risk nonetheless that such a diversion of attention will be interpreted by the other superpower as complacency toward it or taking it for granted. It therefore seems vital that established bilateral institutions such as planning groups and consultative commissions have provisions

123

for frequent if not continuous employment. Stipulated contact such as this helps to avoid perceptions of estrangement from the other, and should such perceptions begin to develop, regularized contacts should help to diagnose and counteract them in their early stages. High-level annual political summits may also be a useful institutional device for demonstrating to the other its priority position, and since political leaders are sure to change occasionally on both sides, summits would serve to socialize these new leaders into the cooperative culture of U.S.-Soviet relations. In any case, given the history of failed U.S.-Soviet attempts at detente, and the prodigious requirements of orchestrating a prospective detente strategy, the task of preserving a bilateral relationship already altered to amicable propensities would certainly be a luxurious one.

Notes

[1] See, Charles E. Osgood, <u>An Alternative to War or Surrender</u> (Urbana: University of Illinois Press, 1962), Chapter 5.

[2] See, for example, Richard K. Betts, "A Joint Nuclear Risk Control Center," <u>Parameters,</u> 15 (Spring 1985), pp. 39-51.
and, John W. Lewis and Coit D. Blacker, "Next Steps in the Creation of an Accidental Nuclear War Prevention Center," <u>Arms Control,</u> 5 (May 1984), pp. 71-84.

CHAPTER 6

CONCLUSIONS: UNANSWERED QUESTIONS AND UNUTILIZED ANSWERS

A. How to Dismiss Detente

Despite this text's presentation of a reasoned analytical framework, effective methods of measurement, application of these measuring methods to the historical record which produced detente-relevant patterns of activity, and the utilization of these patterns in conjunction with related theorizing to yield a prescriptive strategy for the conduct of a detente policy, persons viscerally opposed to detente may seek to dismiss such efforts with one of several sweeping indictments. Three basic indictments as to why U.S.-Soviet detente is implausible, if not dangerous, involve the following reasons: (1) compelling geopolitical competition; (2) implacable and irreconcilable ideologies; and (3) domestic political systems which are incapable of participating in a genuine international detente. In reality, all three reasons are interrelated and touch on factors which are indeed important in determining a state's foreign-policy outputs; however, I will now examine each of the above three reasons and suggest that persons who cite them as having an invariably deleterious effect on detente are not looking at all the evidence.

Looking first at geopolitical competition, there are two aspects to this problem; first, that U.S. and Soviet interests overlap in a mutually exclusive manner, and second, that both states are predisposed to pursuing their interests in an aggressive and destabilizing fashion. I think that both of these conditions may be proven erroneous. It has been stated that the essence of geopolitical analysis is the relation of international political power to the geographical setting[1], and by virtue of each superpower's "super power," and interests defined expansively by this power, that U.S.-Soviet interests, of necessity, impinge upon one another (note: the overlapping and exclusive interests aspect of the geopolitical problem). This mode of reasoning is premised on two assumptions; first, that international politics must only be played as a zero-sum game, and second, that unitary actions are the best way to enhance a state's power and prestige. Both assumptions are falsifiable. Although both superpowers possess massive power, these quantities are not limitless, and when perceptions of finiteness impel superpower collaboration, even to the point of co-defining certain interests, the zero-sum assumption clearly does not hold. Should the superpowers' mutual threat perception be lowered, the zero-sum premise recedes even farther. As for the second assumption -- the advantages of unitary action -- without resorting to the cliches of interdependence theory, the fact that a state's advantage and reputation may be enhanced through cooperative or multilateral forms of behavior is almost incontrovertible.

The second aspect of the geopolitical problem is that the superpowers are destined to pursue their interests in an aggressive and destabilizing fashion. The fact that an excellent study by Gamson and Modigliani[2] using a deductive decision model found that a hypothesized "consolidationist" rather than "expansionist" motivation for both U.S. and Soviet foreign policy behavior best predicted their actions in the post-war period raises immediate doubts as to the veracity of the aggressive pursuit of national interests assertion. Most Americans are probably comfortable in assuming that American foreign policy has been rather benign as compared with the USSR's; therefore, if one were to become convinced that Soviet foreign policy has been largely imitative of the U.S.', this should be a comforting thought. To a large extent, the USSR's emulation of American foreign policy does in fact appear to have been the case.

> Just as in military hardware the Soviet Union has been 3-5 years behind the U.S. in developing major new weapons systems, so in acquiring the political accoutrements of superpower status-- "show the flag," naval power, proxy armies, military aid -- the Soviets have been imitators.[3]

This realization may not mean the Soviets have had an ideal role-model, but it does tend to put things into perspective. It has even been suggested that the Soviets embarked on a detente course in the early 70s out of aggressive impulses; but as Robert Horn has pointed out, Soviet apprehension over China, the need for economic help, and the desire to stabilize a hold on East Europe were all salient factors impelling a Soviet-American detente -- and each of these factors is clearly defensive in nature.[4] The U.S. generally escaped being charged by the USSR with aggressive and destabilizing pursuit of geopolitical advantage during the 1970s, and in fact Soviet commentators attributed the U.S.' acceptance of detente to contracting capabilities and diminished effectiveness abroad; however, there were plenty of other Soviet indictments of America's conduct of detente, and these will be discussed shortly. The specific charge made most frequently concerning the USSR's offensive motives in undertaking, or at least pretending to undertake a detente policy concerns a Soviet desire to immobilize the West with detente rhetoric, while then being free to press wars of national liberation in the Third World with lowered risk. If, however, one reads the detail of Soviet policy pronouncements carefully, rather than just looking for the first justification of what one already "knows" to be true, one will find that the Soviets' claim the era of detente presents the most favorable conditions for the national liberation movement, not because the USSR is now free to export revolution, but because the improving international environment has caused the more 'rabid imperialists in the U.S. government to lose their preeminent positions, and therefore their calls for imperialistic adventure are less likely to be heeded; thus, with Washington's heavy-handed interventionism having been rescinded, third-world peoples are given the freedom to effect the changes they themselves have long desired. This line of reasoning may be largely rhetorical or a case of Soviet wishful thinking, and there may even be a grain of truth to it, but in any case, it most likely does not support the aggressive pursuit of national interests charge.

If the superpowers are not destined to pursue their national interests in an aggressive or destabilizing manner, and if their interests are not in fact exclusive of one another, then there are certainly grounds for rejecting the argument that compelling geopolitical competition precludes Soviet-American detente. In fact, instances where both the U.S. and USSR passed up opportunities (e.g. both capabilities and some pretext for action were in place) for geopolitical advance during the 70s falsify, at least, the "inexorability" of geopolitical competition. Perhaps Khrushchev was being something less than disingenuous in 1962 when he said, "nowhere do (U.S. and Soviet) interests clash directly, either on territorial or economic questions.[5]

The second overarching indictment or reason often offered in ruling out the possibility of Soviet-American detente centers on one or both side's adherence to an implacable and irreconcilable ideology. Although ideology is important in contributing to a person's mind-set or attitudinal prism, there are good reasons for not overstating its potency. Two properties of ideology make it an unlikely and insufficient inhibitor of a desired detente process; these properties are, first, its vagueness, and second, its surrogate use or substitution for other factors and considerations.

Looking first at the vagueness property, Morton Deutsch writes

...the vagueness of ideologies permits a redefinition of who is "friend" or "foe." There is ample room in the myth systems of both the U.S. and Soviet Union (or China) to find a basis of amicable relations.[6]

It has been observed that the American perception of Marshal Tito in the post-war period as measured by his treatment in the press varied tremendously, at times being depicted as little more than a tyrannical despot, and at others almost as a liberal democrat; this treatment tending to vary over time according to whether or not Tito was reconciling with the Soviets, or tweaking their noses.[7] U.S. ideology did not prevent Sino-American rapprochement in the early 70s -- this occurrence taking place between two states which could hardly have been more ideologically antithetical -- nor does it prevent contemporary American support for authoritarian third-world political systems whose leaders merely mouth the catch-words of pluralism. Persons who argue that these political linkages are possible precisely because the U.S. is not ideologically oriented are probably in error.

129

The fact that American ideological beliefs have largely remained unrecognized may well be a tribute to the force of their general acceptance rather than an indication of their lesser importance.[8]

As for Soviet ideology, it did not prevent the USSR's rapprochement with the capitalist countries of the West in the 1960s and 1970s, nor does it prevent their close association with third-world despots who simply mouth the jargon of scientific socialism. Given the vagueness or malleability of ideology, a situation can easily be visualized where the focus or target of ideological admonitions would be conceptual or tendential, rather than a physical embodiment. Guarding against the communist or imperialist threat would then involve campaigning against the perceived attractiveness and widespread adoption of one of these tendencies or orientations, rather than containing either the USSR or U.S. as the incarnation of communism or imperialism, respectively. In fact, this is largely what happened during the incipient U.S.-Soviet detente of the 1970s when the USSR divorced the ideological struggle from state-to-state relations, thus reducing it to near inconsequentiality.

The second property of ideology which diminishes its potential for precluding detente involves the fact that it is often used as a surrogate for other considerations. This means that ideology may be used to justify or interpret actions which are actually unrelated to ideological considerations, or which have long-standing roots in a tradition other than the ideological one. Alexander Yanov throws light on the proposition that actions are often interpreted in terms of ideology which are actually unrelated to ideological concerns, by discussing the pulling and hauling of Soviet political decisionmaking. He writes that from this standpoint, "the endless debate about which motives dominate Soviet policy -- ideological or pragmatic -- loses its meaning. 'Interests' dominate ...."[9] America's often unfortunate experience with group or single-interest politics implies a very similar dynamic. Regarding ideological incantations which often cloak more traditional influences, the point is frequently made, and sometimes persuasively so, that the tenet of world revolution enshrined in Marxism-Leninism is just a repackaged version of traditional Russian slavophilism. None of this is to say that interests (institutional or national) or traditional yearnings -- all of which may be wrapped in ideological trappings -- are not important in determining the desirability of, or prospects of success for a state pursuing a detente policy; only that attribution of this importance to the specific nature of the ideology itself is likely to be fallacious. In conclusion, we might logically assume that due to the vague and surrogate qualities of ideology, a state's official ideology, no matter how vitriolic, need not preclude the detente option.

The third and final reason I have identified as being often given in arguing against the feasibility of Soviet-American detente is that one or both superpowers' domestic political systems are incapable of participating in a genuine international detente. Pertaining to the USSR, the most frequently cited characteristics which give rise to this critique are, 1) the closed, secretive and undemocratic nature of the Soviet political system; and 2) the ruthlessness ingrained in Soviet leaders by having to have prevailed in an environment of cut-throat (perhaps literally) political in-fighting: as for the United States, the Soviets excoriate the decentralized and volatile nature of American political decisionmaking. Although there is some "functional" logic to this critique -- e.g., the personal power drives of the top political leaders in a dictatorship are not tempered by the peaceful proclivities of its citizenry; merciless political instincts will manifest themselves regardless of a policy issue's domestic or foreign orientation; and the cacophonous and volatile nature of American-style democracy is incompatible with the predictability and dependability necessary for the development of mutual trust -- the critique is basically a "stylistic" one. It asks: "since we are the good guys, how can we trust those other guys who are so suspiciously different from ourselves." Yet a stylistic problem is infinitely remediable. To hold detente hostage to stylistic differences is as much a case of putting the cart before the horse as is Chapter One's discussion of eschewing detente until U.S. and Soviet aims and perceptions somehow converge to the point where the explication of an international code of conduct becomes possible, and subsequent observance of this code produces detente. A detente process facilitates mutual understanding, familiarity with the other side's cultural cues, and the consolidation of mutual trust -- all of which assist in making the other side's differing decisionmaking style appear peculiar or intriguing, rather than sinister.

As for the validity of the admittedly plausible functional aspect of the domestic political systems critique, I would argue that political leaders in states offering competitive elections are at least as prone to manipulating patriotic symbols and national sentiment, with chauvinism being the end-result, as are a state's political leaders who are members of an entrenched oligarchy. Two interpretations then become possible: first, that both electoral democracies and pseudo-electoral oligarchies are equally incapable of acting peacefully enough to cultivate a policy of detente; or second, that the method of leadership selection and degree of access to this leadership are not likely to be determining factors in the probability of a state leading a peaceful foreign policy. Since most Americans (or Soviets) are not prepared to accept the first interpretation, the second becomes the most plausible. Deserving of thoughtful attention, however, is the previously mentioned assertion that the rigors of political survival in the USSR have imprinted on the minds of Soviet leaders that the political traits of expediency and brutality are the most useful and important. Distinguished historian Richard Pipes writes:

(The Soviet governing elite) "rose to positions of power in the 1930s, in the turmoil of Stalin's purges and massacres - that is, under conditions of the most ruthless political infighting known in modern history. No ruling elite in the world has had to learn survival under more difficult and brutal circumstances. This elite is the product of a process of natural selection under which the fittest proved to be those who knew best how to suppress within themselves everything normally regarded as human... No one dealing with Brezhnev and his colleagues ought to forget this fact."[10]

Yet the Pipe's piece was written during 1973-74, and we are, of course, no longer dealing with Brezhnev and (by and large) his colleagues. The long touted generational change within the Soviet leadership, if it has not already arrived, it certainly has begun. With Gorbachev's emphasis on competent, self-sacrificing (at least in terms of past levels of privilege and self-aggrandizement) communist leaders, and with the succession mechanism for Party leader moving away from one of lethality towards one of legality, the jury must certainly be out on whether or not the relationship suggested in the Pipe's quotation (e.g., ruthless political instincts lead to exploitative foreign policy behavior) is perpetual.

With the functional aspect of the domestic political systems critique appearing somewhat dubious, this leaves only the stylistic aspect which has been diagnosed as remediable, thus casting serious doubt on the overall assertion that U.S. and/or Soviet domestic political systems are incapable of detente policies.

Despite the just-attempted summary dismissal of the domestic political systems critique, there is a version of this critique as it pertains to the U.S. which deserves examination by virtue of its widespread and frequent voicing; namely, that the anti-detente interest of the influential American military-industrial complex predisposes this confederation to veto any attempts at genuine detente. Should a military-industrial complex actually exist as a functional entity, then it would indeed be logical that this entity is best served by a tense international environment. Rather than dispute this logic, it seems more profitable to question the very existence of a unified and coherent military-industrial complex. Using an indirect first tack into disproving the coherence of a military-industrial complex, one might assume that given military and industrial collusion, a slack U.S. economy would prompt military chieftains to run-up military expenditures and in this way bail out their industrial co-conspirators. Yet Frei and Ruloff find strong support for the fact that "the U.S. does not try to mitigate economic problems by increasing her defense budget and thereby yield to pressures exerted by the military-industrial complex."[11] A second tack at the question of whether or not a monolithic military-industrial complex exists is drawn from a classroom exercise devised by Richard Cottam. Let us assume that the President of the United States has appointed a blue-ribbon commission to make a recommendation on the advisability of cementing a military alliance with the Peoples' Republic of China, and let us assume that four of the commission's members are top-ranking executives of a multinational corporation that is popularly perceived as benefiting from its close cooperation with the American defense establishment, for example, International Telephone and Telegraph (ITT). We would expect the ITT executives to invariably support the notion of a military alliance with the P.R.C.; but let us take a closer look at each of the four hypothetical executives. The first heads a task force of ITT subsidiaries which produce armaments for the U.S. military. The second heads a branch of subsidiaries seeking contracts with the USSR and the countries of Eastern Europe, after in-house research has shown these countries to be promising new markets. The third heads a group of subsidiaries seeking business opportunities in China, including the sale of arms there. Finally, the fourth represents ITT subsidiaries concerned with questions of urban renewal and education in America. Now with this additional information, do we still think that all four executives will be supportive of the military alliance with China? Most likely, two of them will, and two of them will not. If we cannot get concordant actions from members of a single firm on a single question of obvious importance to the supposed military-industrial complex, then how can we expect uniform behavior across firms, across public/private boundaries, across issues and geographical areas, etc.? Roles, which are highly determining in policymaking settings, are simply too diverse, and interests too variegated to produce the type of conspiratorial behavior postulated by adherents to the notion of a military-industrial complex. Given the uncoordinated behavior occurring among the constituent parts of a reputed military-industrial complex, as highlighted in the two lines of reasoning presented above, we can therefore assume that such an entity does not have the coherence or unity to decisively obstruct an official political move towards detente.

Even if U.S. and/or Soviet domestic political systems do not preclude either state from being able to pursue a policy of detente, some might still ask the related yet separate question -- if we find the other side's domestic political system distasteful, and would feel better about our participating in a detente if the other side would alter or at least begin the evolution of their system in ways that are appealing to us, then is this type of alteration not fair game as part of the search for a sustainable detente? There is a certain logic to a question phrased this way, yet due to practical considerations, such a sought-after alteration is not fair game. The proclivity to seek transformation of the other superpower's politico-economic system is actually an American trait; yet there are two practical reasons -- quite divorced from considerations as to whether or not such a transformation would be normatively desirable -- which argue strongly against such interference. The first reason involves the norm of reciprocity. Soviet attempts to influence, much less change the American political system are deemed intolerable; how in the interest of fairness could we expect to be accorded the privilege of tampering with Soviet internal affairs, while refusing to grant the reciprocal privilege to them? The second reason why attempts at interfering in the other side's internal affairs should not be conceptualized as a component of a detente strategy is that such attempts would be unsuccessful. Examining the incipient detente of the 1970s, Frei and Ruloff have shown that there appears to be no clear relationship between detente and internal Soviet liberalization measures.[12] Despite explicit American attempts at linkage during this period, the inducement of Soviet liberalization as part of detente's quid pro quo failed. Given Soviet sensitivity to the principle of noninterference in each other's domestic affairs, we could expect future attempts at inducing liberalization to fail as well. Only in the case of Jewish emigration from the USSR was there a clear relationship between detente and liberalization.[13] This is a very interesting case, and I would put forth the proposition that perhaps the Soviets were beguiled by their own propaganda concerning the exaggerated controlling influence of powerful "Zionist circles" in the U.S. Under these conditions the Soviet leadership probably saw increased Jewish emigration as an extremely poignant goodwill gesture that would earn them the appreciation of these Zionist leaders, thus facilitating the receipt of future benefits that would outweigh the temporary costs in terms of manpower and sovereign control. The case of Jewish emigration is therefore likely to be an anomalous development due to particularistic factors, rather than a half-proof of the principle that detente can be an effective springboard for changing the other side domestically. The types of restriction in the USSR which Americans find most objectionable (e.g., lack of transnational contacts between the two societies, and lack of contact or access between ordinary Soviet citizens and their own leaders) are primarily a result of the Soviet oligarchy's drive to protect their own privileged position. Changes in East-West relations will not affect this commitment to privilege protection, and if anything, a prospective detente which promised to open transnational channels and more widely disseminate the forbidden fruits of the West (e.g., travel, consumer goods, information) may even result in more vigorously applied restrictions. Overall, not only are attempts at changing the other's domestic system likely to fail, but they are also likely to make detente itself a victim of these attempts; therefore, despite the anguish of having to make moral trade-offs, sacrificing the greater good of international detente for the long-shot lesser good of, e.g., liberalizing Soviet society is a poor exchange. This moral dilemma is eloquently addressed by George Kennan in the following passage.

> "the task of the United States government will be to see how these feelings (human rights concerns) of the American people can be communicated to the Soviet government in a way that will help, rather than damage, the fortunes of those to whose strivings and sufferings they are addressed. But this government will also have to be concerned to see that these expressions of sympathy do not take forms that are misinterpreted in Moscow as direct efforts to shape the course of internal political developments in Russia, and that they do not, in this way, interfere with the completion of the main task of American

statesmanship with relation to Russia, which is, as noted above, to reduce the danger posed for both countries and for the world by the present military rivalry.[14]

In recapitulation, reasoned arguments have been offered to refute the three most commonly levied indictments against detente's feasibility -- namely, compelling geopolitical competition, irreconcilable ideologies, and preclusive domestic political systems. With such indictments anticipated and refuted, does this mean that my research now emerges unscathed as the first and last word on Soviet-American detente? Unfortunately, the answer is "no." No researcher can anticipate at the beginning of a research project all of the insights, questions and uncharted areas of intellectual concern. There is, however, an obligation to float these possibly underdeveloped question-areas, rather than to sweep them under the rug. One such underdeveloped area that suggested itself during the course of my research concerned the manifold functions of psychology in determining and helping to understand the dynamics of a detente process. The following section highlights some of the more important psychological aspects that should be reckoned with in the study of detente.

B. Psychology: The Missing (and Certainly Complex) Dimension

I do not wish to imply that this study has been completely oblivious to psychological factors; the discussions of trust, criticism, relational-type, policy momentum, etc. are inherently psychological in nature to the extent that they are perceptually determined. This is not to suggest that there has not been a "value-conflict" dimension to U.S.-Soviet post-war relations, only that perceptual factors, especially those associated with mistrust, have greatly inflated the scope of potential value conflicts. What I would like to say here is that perhaps some of the psychological underpinnings necessary for an understanding of detente have not been systematically explicated by myself, or by others for that matter.

I first sensed a psychological component to interpreting detente's relative presence or absence when calculations of the events-based Detente Index (Chapter 2) for 1958 and 1959 showed them to not be years of incipient detente (by my standard), even though I had suspicioned they would be. There was something striking among the occurrences of these years that had made me feel as if they were years of incipient detente, even though cumulative calculations (including half-year break-outs) proved this to not be the case. Writing on the topic of psychological influences on the interpretation of events, Charles Osgood says the psychological impact of an action does not necessarily depend on its military significance, although it may. Certain announcements and subsequent actions have the property of being dramatic, of catching the eyes and hearts of people all over the world; others do not.[15]

In a very preliminary manner, I will suggest two concepts that seem promising in helping to understand and predict which acts might, as Osgood puts it, catch the eyes and hearts of people; thse concepts are, (1) precedence, and (2) the collective evoked set. Although the concept of "precedence" is fairly self-explanatory, let me explain the meaning of "collective evoked set." Evoked set is a psychological term for that group or set of things on someone's mind at the moment when an incoming piece of information is received, and which acts to color the interpretation of this piece of information. If one were able to infer the collective evoked set of a target group, one would have a powerful analytic tool that would suggest what type of an act has the greatest potential for popular impact. Since so many detente-relevant initiatives have an attention-grabbing function, especially in detente's early-to-mid phases, this would be a most useful capability. I will now turn to some examples of psychological dynamics at work in detente-relevant situations, as well as tersely examine the possible roles of precedence and collective evoked set in understanding these dynamics.

To illuminate the role of precedence, consider the following question; because the Detente Index score for 1981 was the largest (connoting a hostile U.S.-Soviet relationship) of the post-war period, does this mean that popular, e.g. American, perceptions in 1981 reflected a view of a more acutely dangerous and threatening situation than that which was perceived in the late 1940s and early 50s? The answer, I feel, is "no." In the early 50s, for example, there had been no serious attempts at post-war incipient detente, and people were understandably fearful. For all people knew at that time, detente was impossible, East-West conflict was inescapable, and the boundaries to which this conflict might extend were horrifyingly wide. Although 1981 was characterized by a complete absence of constructive U.S.-Soviet intercourse, there had been several previous episodes of incipient detente to reflect on, including the especially promising attempt of the early 1970s, and persons knew that to back away from the precipice, and indeed to strive to avoid such precarious situation in the future was possible. Much as it is easier to relearn or brush up on a foreign language than it is to learn it from scratch, so do people feel that it is more easy to reactivate once attempted cooperative habits than to forge them for the first time. The above example illustrates how precedence colors the interpretation of facts whose objective meaning should be otherwise.

Another feature of my research that suggested unprovided-for psychological dynamics involved the magnitude scale used in coding the momentousness of individual policy acts. Let us take a hypothetical

U.S. proposal to the USSR about undertaking some sort of a cooperative joint venture; this policy act would receive a magnitude score of .15. Let us also assume that the USSR rejects this proposal, which as an act of policy would draw a magnitude score of -.15. So on balance, .15 plus -.15 equals zero, and in terms of a Detente Index figures cumulatively, it is as if the proposal and subsequent rejection had never existed (e.g., produced no effect). Yet even a rejected proposal may produce a very real effect, either negatively or positively. If State A makes a low-risk proposal to state B, and is sure State B will accept the proposal, then if State B unexpectedly rejects the proposal, this is likely to leave a bad taste in State A's mouth and thus affect how forthcoming it is likely to be in near-term diplomatic intercourse. However, if State A makes a high-risk and far-reaching propsal that State B rejects largely out of surprise or lack of psychic preparedness, then State B may revise its image of State A as being more forthright and generous than previously thought, thus conditioning State B to be much more receptive to near-term diplomatic overtures from State A as well as more forthcoming in proposed overtures of its own. The simple proposal-rejection sequence can therefore be seen to produce markedly different residual effects. In the above example we can see the influence of precedence (i.e., the expected vs. far-reaching proposal) and the collective evoked set (i.e., whether or not a state is prepared to accept a proposal, and if not, whether or not the rejected proposal might be interpreted favorably enough to produce a positive residual effect). There may be good prospects for typologizing policy proposals according to such characteristics as precedence and degree of expected receptivity based on the current make-up of the target's evoked set; one can then hypothesize expected policy outcomes per proposal type (e.g., accepted/rejected, accepted with deflation/accepted with elation, rejected with rancor/rejected with enticement). I do not want to leave the reader with the impression that my Detente Index completely fails to handle the differential and residual effects of single policy acts, because residual effects manifest themselves in the number and type of policy acts which follow any one particular act, and my chronological method would pick this up. If, however, one were to zoom in on a particular sequence of policy acts (e.g., proposal then rejection), one might be hard pressed to infer the specific influence of this sequence on the immediate bilateral climate (in which instance one should use a more appropriate approach such as the case study).

Chapter 4 (Probing the Feasibility and Advisability of Detente) also implicates, but does not fully develop a psychological underpinning. The principle implicit here is that only persons of a flexible personality-type would be capable of profitably engaging in an assumption challenging exercise. Perhaps key American and Soviet leaders -- at the very least the U.S. President and the CPSU's General Secretary -- having a flexible, open (as opposed to rigid and dogmatic) type of personality should be incorporated into the earlier discussion of domestic background factors as a necessary condition for detente.

Although this study may evince a less than sophisticated utilization of psychological theory, I think this lacuna hardly detracts from its overall utility. I would like to cast this utility within a larger context, namely, the role of policy-relevant theory , and do so in the concluding section of this text.

C. The Role of Policy-Relevant Theory

This study began with the charge that American foreign policymaking vis-a-vis the USSR has most often been inconsistent, haphazard and anything but guided by empirical research or well tested theory. Not surprisingly, I feel that the scholarly production of theoretical research can indeed be a useful guide to action for receptive decisionmakers. What type of theory would be the most useful, or in other words, how would one define policy-relevant theory? Policy-relevant theory can be defined as the supporting arguments and conclusions of a piece of research which investigates an issue or problem likely to be encountered by decisionmakers, and which stands the chance of being more persuasive than, and likely to be incorporated in lieu of, the simple or intuitive models in use by decisionmakers.

In abstract form, it is difficult to discern whether the above definition is ambitious in scope or whether it is rather modest. Actually, the definition is quite flexible; it accommodates theoretical input for both one-time episodes as well as for recursive policy problems, and for bit parts (e.g., diagnosis and options assessment[16]) as well as for full-blown process-oriented prescription. I do not wish to denigrate the importance of the bit-part function, but only to emphasize the ambitious or audacious version of policy-relevant theory, simply because it has not been adequately treated. I would like to part company in two ways from what I understand Alexander George's conception of policy-relevant theory to be. As for Professor George's views, he seems to, (1) favor explanatory theory that is policy-relevant without being prescriptive,[17] and (2) emphasize the diagnostic and options-assessment functions. In the first place, I think that explanatory theory which is devoid of an "implementability" dimension is not truly policy-relevant. Theory may be "policy-appropriate," as in the case of much explanatory theory, but without strict prescriptive attention to usage or implementability, such theory is not likely to dislodge the simple or intuitive models currently being used by decisionmakers, which almost by definition precludes true policy relevancy (i.e., aptness to be applied to a policy problem). Secondly, George's diagnostic and options assessment functions are extremely limited in that they are inherently reactive. In light of this two-pronged critique, I advocate theory which consciously weaves considerations of implementation throughout (i.e., purposefully combines both "process" and "substantive" theory, to use Professor George's terminology[18]), and which is proactive (in a forward-looking sense), rather than reactive. Despite the explicit attention to implementability, some might argue that the audacious version of policy-relevant theory is simply too complicated to be realized through a large, lurching governmental bureaucracy. Attention to phasing or periodization, however, is one method of combatting this problem. Policy-relevant theory which makes provisions for policy phases allows bureaucracies to only have to deal with a small number of critical variables per phase, and to monitor only a discrete temporally specified range of variable values per phase.

What is the relation of policy-relevant theory (audacious version) to the political strategy concept introduced at the conclusion of the third chapter? A political strategy can be thought of as an applied policy-relevant theory. Applied in the sense that: 1) the relationship between two or more variables, 2) is seen to correspond to a real-world trend, and 3) this trend in turn partially or fully accounts for an actual policy problem. For example: 1) a tripolar or triangular diplomacy among three great powers is thought to compel a short-term moderation in the behavior of each, 2) and this theory is seen to be relevant in light of a militarily ascendant Peoples' Republic of China, 3) which could be used in tackling the foreign policy problem of hamstringing an adversarial USSR. A political strategy is likely to be more intricate than a policy-relevant theory, seeking at times to manipulate a variety of trends in pursuit of a single goal; therefore, a political strategy may be considered as an applied complex of compatible policy-relevant theories. It is the business of the political strategist to ensure this presumed compatibility, and to rely on theories which have been empirically tested to the maximum extent possible. Whereas the term political strategy connotes the preserve of the high-level practitioner or government official (where an action potential exists), and policy-relevant theory implies that of the academic analyst, despite the differences in flavor both seek the same prescriptive function and utility. I would define policy-relevant theory which does not aim at bringing about a policy end-state or point of closure as non-audacious or circumscribed; for example, shaping the orientation of the mass media to produce a situation which will eventually be facilitative of a goal or end-state. As I mentioned previously, I would treat explanatory theory, or theory devoid of implementational concerns as merely policy appropriate. In summation, audacious policy-relevant theory can be seen as a blueprint; a set of directions for transforming one's policy environment.

Any foreign ministry or department of state which aims for preparedness and flexibility in its operations must maintain in its policy quiver a variety of basic policy designs (e.g., containment, modus vivendi, detente, etc.). Departments of defense seem to understand this, given their reliance on contingency planning. Once the detente option is in place, the key then becomes having the wisdom to know when to launch (or interrupt) such a policy.

Notes

[1] Saul B. Cohen, <u>Geography and Politics in a World Divided</u>, 2nd ed. (New York: Oxford University Press, 1973), p. 29.

[2] See, William Gamson and Andre Modigliani, <u>Untangling the Cold War</u> (Boston: Little, Brown and Co., 1971).

[3] Richard Barnet, "U.S.-Soviet Relations: The Need for a Comprehensive Approach," <u>Foreign Affairs</u>, 57 (Spring 1979), p. 783.

[4] Robert Horn, "Detente and Soviet Foreign Policy," in <u>From Cold War to Detente</u>, eds. Peter Potichnyi and Jane Shapiro (New York: Praeger Publishers, 1976), p. 108.

[5] Quoted in, Dan Caldwell, <u>American-Soviet Relations from 1947 to the Nixon-Kissinger Grand Design</u> (Westport: Greenwood Press, 1981), p. 198.

[6] Morton Deutsch, "The Prevention of WW III: A Psychological Perspective," <u>Political Psychology</u>, 4 (March 1983), p. 9.

[7] Richard Cottam, <u>Foreign Policy Motivation</u> (Pittsburgh: University of Pittsburgh Press, 1977), p. 87.

[8] Christer Jonsson, "The Ideology of Foreign Policy," in <u>Foreign Policy USA/USSR</u>, eds. Charles Kegley, Jr., and Pat McGowan (Beverly Hills: Sage Publications, 1982), pp. 93-94.

[9] Alexander Yanov, <u>Detente After Brezhnev: Roots of Soviet Foreign Policy</u> (Berkeley: University of California Institute of International Studies, 1977), p. 77.

[10] Richard Pipes, <u>U.S.-Soviet Relations in the Era of Detente</u> (Boulder: Westview Press, 1981), p. 71.

[11] Daniel Frei and Dieter Ruloff, <u>East-West Relations</u>, 2 Vols. (Cambridge: Oelgeschlager, Gunn and Hain Publishers, Inc., 1983), Vol. 1, pp. 248-49.

[12] Ibid., p. 253.

[13] Ibid.

[14] George Kennan, <u>The Nuclear Delusion - Soviet-American Relations in the Atomic Age</u> (New York: Pantheon Books, 1982), p. 118.

[15] Charles E. Osgood, <u>An Alternative to War or Surrender</u> (Urbana: University of Illinois Press, 1962), p. 115.

[16] See Chapter 14, Alexander George, <u>Presidential Decisionmaking in Foreign Policy: The Effective Use of Information and Advice</u> (Boulder: Westview Press, 1980).

[17] Alexander George and Richard Smoke, <u>Deterrence in American Foreign Policy: Theory and Practice</u> (New York: Columbia University Press, 1974), p. 512.

[18] Alexander George, "Bridging the Gap Between Theory and Practice," in <u>In Search of Global Patterns</u>, ed. James Rosenau (New York: The Free Press, 1976), p. 114.

A Select Bibliography

Adomeit, Hannes. Soviet Risk-Taking and Crisis Behavior. London: George Allen and Unwin, 1982.

Alexandroff, Alan. The Logic of Diplomacy. Beverly Hills: Sage Publications, Inc., 1981.

Andropov, Yuri. "U.S. is Undermining Detente." Pravda, 12 February 1980, p. 2.

Axelrod, Robert and Zimmerman, William. "The Soviet Press on Soviet Foreign Policy: A Usually Reliable Soruce." British Journal of Political Science, 11 (1981): 183-200.

Barber, Bernard. The Logic and Limits of Trust. New Brunswick: Rutgers University Press, 1983.

Barnet, Richard. "U.S.-Soviet Relations: The Need for a Comprehensive Approach." Foreign Affairs, 57 (Spring 1979): 779-95.

Bell, Coral. The Diplomacy of Detente. New York: St. Martin's Press, 1977.

Betts, Richard. "A Joint Nuclear Risk Control Center." Parameters, 15 (Spring 1985): 39-51.

Bilder, Richard. Managing the Risks of International Agreements. Madison: The University of Wisconsin Press, 1981.

Birnbaum, Karl. The Politics of East-West Communication in Europe. Stockholm: Swedish Institute of International Affairs, 1979.

Blau, Peter. Exchange and Power in Social Life. New York: John Wiley and Sons, Inc., 1967.

Bonoma, Thomas. Conflict: Escalation and Deescalation. International Studies Series, No. 02-033, Vol. 3. Beverly Hills: Sage Publications, 1975.

Brauer, Sanford and Barnett, Bruce. "Perception of Opponent's Motives in a Mixed-Motive Game." Journal of Conflict Resolution, 18 (December 1974): 686-99.

Breslauer, George. "Do Soviet Leaders Test New Presidents?" International Security, 8 (Winter 1983-84): 83-107.

142

_____. Why Detente Failed. Philadelphia: A paper presented to the 22nd annual meeting of the International Studies Association, 1981.

Brezhnev, Leonid. Peace, Detente and Soviet-American Relations. New York: Harcourt, Brace and Jovanovich, 1979.

Bueno De Mesquita, Bruce. The War Trap. New Haven: Yale University Press, 1981.

Burgess, Philip and Lawton, Raymond. Indicators of International Behavior: An Assessment of Events Data Research. Beverly Hills: Sage Publications, Inc., 1972.

Caldwell, Dan. American-Soviet Relations From 1947 to the Nixon-Kissinger Grand Design. Westport: Greenwood Press, 1981.

Callahan, Patrick, Brady, Linda and Hermann, Margaret, eds. Describing Foreign Policy Behavior. Beverly Hills: Sage Publications, 1982.

Chadwick-Jones, J.K. Social Exchange Theory. London: Academic Press, 1979.

Cohen, Saul B. Geography and Politics in a World Divided. 2nd ed. New York: Oxford University Press, 1973.

Cohen, Stephen, Rabinowitch, Alexander and Sharlet, Robert, eds. The Soviet Union Since Stalin. Bloomington: Indiana University Press, 1980.

Confino, Michael and Ahamir, Shimon. The USSR and the Middle East. New York: John Wiley and Sons, 1973.

Cottam, Richard. Competitive Interference and 20th Century Diplomacy. Pittsburgh: University of Pittsburgh Press, 1977.

_____. Foreign Policy Motivation. Pittsburgh: University of Pittsburgh Press, 1977.

_____ and Gallucci, Gerard. The Rehabilitation of Power in International Relations: A Working Paper. Pittsburgh: University Center for International Studies, 1978.

Craig, Gordon and George, Alexander. Force and Statecraft. New York: Oxford University Press, 1983.

Crow, W.J. "A Study of Strategic Doctrines Using the Inter-Nation Simulation." Journal of Conflict Resolution, 7 (1963): 580-89.

Cusak, Thomas and Ward, Michael. "Military Spending in the U.S., Soviet Union and PRC." Journal of Conflict Resolution (September 1981).

"Detente: An Evaluation." Survey, 20 (Spring-Summer 1974): 1-28.

Deutsch, Morton. "Trust and Suspicion." Journal of Conflict Resolution, 2 (December 1958): 265-79.

_____, et al. "Strategies of Inducing Cooperation: An Experimental Study." Journal of Conflict Resolution, 11 (September 1967): 345-60.

_____. "The Prevention of WW III: A Psychological Perspective." Political Psychology, 4 (March 1983): 3-31.

Downs, Anthony. Inside Bureaucracy. Santa Monica: The Rand Corporation, 1967.

Dunn, Keith. "From Kissinger to Carter." Parameters, 7, No. 4 (1977): 46-55.

Etzioni, Amitai. The Hard Way to Peace: A New Strategy. New York: Collier Books, 1962.

_____ and Winglinsky, M., eds. War and Its Prevention. New York: Harper and Row, 1970.

Frei, Daniel, ed. Definitions and Measurements of Detente. Cambridge: Oelgeschlager, Gunn and Hain Publishers, Inc., 1981.

_____ and Ruloff, Dieter. East-West Relations. 2 Vols. Cambridge: Oelgeschlager, Gunn and Hain Publishers, Inc., 1983. Vol. 1: A Systematic Survey.

Gaddis, John Lewis. Strategies of Containment. New York: Oxford University Press, 1982.

Gamson, William and Modigliani, Andre. Untangling the Cold War. Boston: Little, Brown and Company, 1971.

Gardner, Katherine and Deutsch, Morton. "Cooperative Behavior in Dyads." Journal of Conflict Resolution, 18 (December 1974): 634-45.

Garthoff, Raymond. "American-Soviet Relations in Perspective." Political Science Quarterly, 100 (Winter 1985-86): 541-59.

Gati, Charles, ed. Caging the Bear--Containment and the Cold War. Indianapolis: Bobbs-Merrill Company, Inc., 1974.

_____ and Gati, Toby Trister. <u>The Debate Over Detente</u>. Headline Series, No. 234. New York: Foreign Policy Association, 1977.

Gelman, Harry. <u>The Brezhnev Politburo and the Decline of Detente</u>. Ithaca: Cornell University Press, 1984.

George, Alexander and Smoke, Richard. <u>Deterrence in American Foreign Policy: Theory and Practice</u>. New York: Columbia University Press, 1974.

_____. <u>Presidential Decisionmaking in Foreign Policy: The Effective Use of Information and Advice</u>. Boulder: Westview Press, 1980.

_____. <u>Managing U.S.-Soviet Rivalry: Problems of Crisis Prevention</u>. Boulder: Westview Press, 1983.

Goldmann, Kjell. "Change and Stability in Foreign Policy -- Detente as a Problem of Stabilization." <u>World Politics</u>, 34 (January 1982): 230-66.

Griffiths, Franklin. "The Sources of American Conduct: Soviet Perspectives and Their Policy Implications," <u>International Security</u>, 9 (Fall 1984): 3-50.

Hage, Jerald and Dewar, Robert. "Elite Values Versus Organizational Structure in Predicting Innovation." <u>Administrative Science Quarterly</u> (September 1973): 279-90.

Hammond, Thomas. "Moscow and Communist Takeovers." <u>Problems of Communism</u>, 25 (January-February 1976): 48-67.

Holsti, Ole, Siverson, Randolph and George, Alexander, eds. <u>Change in the International System</u>. Boulder: Westview Press, 1980.

Hulett, Louisa. <u>Decade of Detente</u>. Washington: University Press of America, 1982.

Husband, William. "Soviet Perceptions of U.S. 'Position-of-Strength' Diplomacy in the 1970s," <u>World Politics</u>, 31 (July 1979): 495-517.

Jowitt, Kenneth. <u>Images of Detente and the Soviet Political Order</u>. University of California at Berkeley: Institute of International Studies, 1977.

Kahan, James. <u>How Psychologists Talk About Risk</u>. The Rand Paper Series. Santa Monica: The Rand Corporation, 1979.

Kee, Herbert and Knox, Robert. "The Study of Trust and Suspicion." Journal of Conflict Resolution, 14 (September 1970): 537-66.

Kegley, Jr., Charles and McGowan, Pat, eds. Foreign Policy USA/USSR. Beverly Hills: Sage Publications, 1982.

Kelman, Herbert. International Behavior. New York: Holt, Rinehart and Winston, 1965.

Kennan, George. The Nuclear Delusion - Soviet-American Relations in the Atomic Age. New York: Pantheon Books, 1982.

_____. (X). "The Sources of Soviet Conduct." Foreign Affairs, 25 (July 1947): 566-82.

Kissinger, Henry, ed. American Foreign Policy. New York: W.W. Norton and Company, Inc., 1977.

_____. Years of Upheaval. Boston: Little, Brown and Company, 1982.

Laqueur, Walter. "Detente: Western and Soviet Interpretations." Survey, 19 (Summer 1973): 74-87.

Legvold, Robert. "Containment Without Confrontation." Foreign Policy (Fall 1980): 74-98.

Leng, Russell and Wheeler, Hugh. "Influence Strategies, Success and War." Journal of Conflict Resolution, 23 (December 1979): 655-84.

Linden, Ronald. Bear and Foxes. New York: Columbia University Press, 1979.

Litwak, Robert. Detente and the Nixon Doctrine - American Foreign Policy and the Pursuit of Stability. London: Cambridge University Press, 1984.

Lupfer, Michael, et. al. "Risk-Taking in Cooperative Dyads." Journal of Conflict Resolution, 15 (September 1971): 385-92.

McNeil, Elton, ed. The Nature of Human Conflict. Englewood Cliffs: Prentice-Hall, 1965.

Mason, Richard and Mitroff, Ian. Challenging Strategic Planning Assumptions. New York: John Wiley and Sons, 1981.

Mastny, Vojtech. "Kremlin Politics and the Austrian Settlement." Problems of Communism, 31 (July-August 1982): 37-51.

Matthews, Byron and Shimoff, Eliot. "Expansion of Exchange--Monitoring Trust Levels in Ongoing Exchange Relations." Journal of Conflict Resolution, 23 (September 1979): 538-60.

_____, Kordonski, Byron and Shimoff, Eliot. "Temptation and the Maintenance of Trust." Journal of Conflict Resolution, 27 (June 1983): 255-77.

Mitchell, R. Judson. "A New Brezhnev Doctrine." World Politics. 30 (April 1978): 366-90.

Niezing, Johan. Strategy and Structure -- Studies in Peace Research, II. Amsterdam: Swets and Zeitlinger, 1978.

Nye, Joseph, ed. The Making of America's Soviet Policy. New Haven: Yale University Press, 1984.

Osgood, Charles E. An Alternative to War or Surrender. Urbana: University of Illinois Press, 1962.

Petrov, A. "What Motivates U.S. Stand on Poland." Pravda, 10 January 1982, p. 5.

Petrov, Vladimir. U.S.-Soviet Detente: Past and Future. Washington: American Enterprise Institute for Public Policy Research, 1975.

Piadyshev, B. D. USSR-USA: From Confrontation to Cooperation. Moscow: Knowledge Publishers, 1973.

Pilisuk, M. and Skolnik, P. "Inducing Trust: A Test of the Osgood Proposal." Journal of Personality and Social Psychology, 8 (1968): 121-33.

Pipes, Richard. U.S.-Soviet Relations in the Era of Detente. Boulder: Westview Press, 1981.

Platig, E. Raymond. "Crisis, Pretentious Ideologies, and Superpower Behavior." Orbis, 25 (Fall 1981): 511-24.

Potichnyi, Peter and Shapiro, Jane, eds. From Cold War to Detente. New York: Praeger Publishers, 1976.

Ravenal, Earl. "Nixon's Challenge to Carter." Foreign Policy (Winter 1977-78): 27-42.

_____. "Doing Nothing." Foreign Policy (Summer 1980): 28-39.

Rosenau, James, ed. In Search of Global Patterns. New York: The Free Press, 1976.

_____ and Holsti, Ole. "The Breakdown of Consensuses and the Emergence of Conflicting Belief Systems." World Politics, 35 (April 1983): 368-92.

Rosenberg, Shawn and Wolfsfeld, Gary. "International Conflict and the Problem of Attribution." Journal of Conflict Resolution, 21 (March 1977): 75-103.

Rubinstein, Alvin. "The Elusive Parameters of Detente." Orbis, 19 (Winter 1976): 1344-58.

Rummel, Rudolph. Peace Endangered. Beverly Hills: Sage Publications, Inc., 1976.

Schwab, George and Friedlander, Henry, eds. Detente in Historical Perspective. New York: Cyrco Press, 1975.

Schlenker, Barry and Bonoma, T. V. "Fun and Games: The Validity of Games for the Study of Conflict." Journal of Conflict Resolution, 22 (March 1978): 7-38.

Seabury, Paul. "On Detente." Survey, 19 (Spring 1973): 62-75.

Sheldon, Della, ed. Dimensions of Detente. New York: Praeger Publishers, 1978.

Shulman, Marshall. "Toward a Western Philosophy of Coexistence." Foreign Affairs, 52 (October 1973): 33-58.

_____. "An Overview of U.S.-Soviet Relations." Department of State Bulletin, 79 (December 1979): 40-45.

Shundeyev, V. "To Uphold Detente: A Must of Today." International Affairs (July 1981): 39-46.

Simes, Dimitri. "The Death of Detente." International Security, 5 (Summer 1980): 3-25.

_____. "The New Soviet Challenge." Foreign Policy, (Summer 1984): 113-31.

Smith H. W. Strategies of Social Research. Englewood Cliffs: Prentice-Hall, Inc., 1981.

Sonnenfeldt, Helmut. "Russia, America and Detente." Foreign Affairs, 56 (January 1978): 275-293.

Steinbrunner, John D. The Cybernetic Theory of Decision. Princeton: Princeton University Press, 1974.

Summers, David A. "Conflict, Compromise and Belief Change in a Decision-Making Task." Journal of Conflict Resolution, 12 (June 1968): 215-21.

Tanter, Raymond. Modelling and Managing International Conflicts. Beverly Hills: Sage Publications, Inc., 1974.

Taubman, William. Stalin's American Policy -- From Entente to Detente to Cold War. New York: W. W. Norton and Company, 1982.

Tedeschi, J. T. and Lindskold. "Threateners' Reaction to Prior Announcement of Behavioral Compliance or Defiance." Behavioral Science, 15 (1972): 171-79.

Thompson, James, ed. Approaches to Organizational Design. Pittsburgh: University of Pittsburgh Press, 1969.

Timberlake, Charles. Detente: A Documentary Record. New York: Praeger Publishers, 1978.

Ulam, Adam. Expansion and Coexistence: Soviet Foreign Policy 1917-73, 2nd ed. New York: Praeger Publishers, 1974.

_____. "Unhappy Coexistence." Foreign Affairs, 57, No. 3 (1979).

U.S. Congress. Senate. Commitee on Foreign Relations. Detente, 93rd Cong., 2nd sess., 1974.

Ustinov, D. F. "Defending Peace." Pravda, 22 June 1981, pp. 2-3.

Valenta, Jiri and Potter, William, eds. Soviet Decisionmaking for National Security. London: George Allen and Unwin, 1984.

"Vance Says Moscow Still Seeks Detente," New York Times, 5 March 1977, p. 1.

Weede, Erich. "Threats to Detente: Intuitive Hopes and Counterintuitive Realities." European Journal of Political Research, No. 3 (1977): 407-32.

Weeks, Albert. The Troubled Detente. New York: New York University Press, 1976.

Wessell, Nils. "Issues in Soviet-American Relations." Orbis, 25 (Spring 1981): 209-222.

White, Ralph. Fearful Warriors. New York: Free Press, 1984.

Wiberg, Hakan. "What Have We Learnt About Peace?" Journal of Peace Research, No. 2 (1981): 111-48.

Wolf, Jr., Charles. "Why the Experts Disagree About the Soviets." Washington Post, 25 July 1984, p. A17.

Yanov, Alexander. Detente After Brezhnev: Roots of Soviet Foreign Policy. Berkeley: University of California Institute of International Studies, 1977.

Zaltman, Gerald and Duncan, Robert. Strategies for Planned Change. New York: Wiley, 1977.

Zamyatin, Leonid. "Restore a Climate of Detente and Trust." Literaturnaya Gazeta, 27 February 1980, p. 14.

APPENDIX A

This appendix contains an extended definition of "policy act." The definition allows me to discriminatingly identify and extract an events-oriented population of entries from the historical record spanning the years 1949 to 1981. Following is my definition of "policy act," which pertains to an actor within a dyadic relationship:

> Policy Act: "any purposive action which either states, authorizes or executes an official stance or initiative, and which directly or indirectly affects the other side's domestic and/or international pursuits."

Elaboration

A policy act may therefore be bilateral, as in an agreement, or unilateral, as in, for example, an embargo; it may have either a beneficial or a deleterious effect on the other side. A policy act need not directly specify the other as the target of its action, but it must share a common target or object of focus with the other side -- for example, both the U.S. and USSR worked for a withdrawal of Chinese invasionary forces from Vietnam in 1979, thus affecting each other's policy in a "supportive" manner; or regarding the P.R.C.'s shelling of Quemoy and Matsu in 1958, the USSR's support of the P.R.C. and the U.S.' support of Taiwan affected each other's policy, this time by working at "cross-purposes." A policy act does not necessarily have to be taken by organizations, institutions or firms, as long as it fulfills the conditions of purposiveness and officiality, and is significant enough to perceptibly impact on or affect the other side. Also, occasionally an act committed by a third country may be treated as a U.S. or Soviet policy act if one side/superpower assuredly interprets this third-party act as instigated by, conspired with, or a proxy move for the other side/superpower -- e.g. the Hungarians execute Nagy, the East Germans complicate Western access to Berlin, Iran abrogates its treaty of friendship and cooperation with the USSR in 1959, Cuban exiles land at the Bay of Pigs, etc.

Corollaries

1. Regarding unilateral verbal expressions of policy, these will only count if uttered by an authoritative source:
    for example:
    United States - President, Vice-President, Secretary of State, National Security Advisor, or U.N. Representative.
    USSR - General Secretary, Premier, President/Prime Minister, Foreign Minister, or U.N. Representative.
    Both States - the chief official or delegate assigned to specialized talks or negotiations.

2. Intra-negotiation developments are generally not recorded as policy acts; however, intra-negotiation events of a watershed nature which either cause or prevent the negotiation from stagnating or breaking-up are counted.

3. Regarding policy acts which cover a long stretch of time, e.g. the Korean War, intra-policy events which also qualify for recording as policy acts are those which significantly clarify or depart from the initiatory act of policy, and which warrant significant press coverage.

4. A policy act must be interpretable in and of itself, or be accompanied by an interpretation; for example, the Soviet return of one U.S. World War II lend-lease vessel would not be counted (unless accompanied by an American interpretational pronouncement) -- is this a cooperative act marking the start of a Soviet policy to settle its lend-lease debt, or is it a cynical, conflictual move, highlighting the magnitude of the outstanding debt? (note -- few policy acts suffer from the uninterpretable quality).

5. It must be assumed that all cooperative acts are genuine, and offered in good faith; an assumption of widespread deception would render all policy acts truly uninterpretable.

6. To highlight a point made in the elaboration of my definition of policy act, as found in this appendix, there is no absolute or glorified ideal of detente against which to assess an act's positive or negative impact, only the extent to which it is supportive of, or at cross-purposes with, the other side's approach to the same general area.

1972

Detente Index Scale Score = 2.7

1.   1/2 - Nixon says the Berlin accord of 1971 pointed out the possibility of U.S.-Soviet cooperation in other areas such as the Middle East, arms control, trade, etc.

      risk = .5   magnitude = .05

2.   1/2 - Nixon says he has decided "in principle" to sell more jet fighter bombers to Israel.

      risk = .5   magnitude = -.15

3.   1/2 - Nixon says a U.S. residual force will remain in Vietnam until American POWs are released.

      risk = .5   magnitude = -.15

4.   1/5 - U.S. leases a naval base from Bahrain.

      risk = .5   magnitude = -.15

5.   1/6 - U.S. protests Soviet violation of diplomatic immunity, after an American military attache is attacked.

      risk = .3   magnitude = -.1

6.   1/10 - U.S. Navy leaves the Indian Ocean.

      risk = .5   magnitude = .15

7.   1/12 - Soviet minister of culture opens an exhibit of Soviet arts and crafts in the U.S.

      risk = .2   magnitude = .15

8.   1/13 - After delaying a Soviet exchange student's exit from the U.S. to be sure he was leaving voluntarily, the U.S. strengthens its asylum-granting procedures.

      risk = .3   magnitude = -.15

9. 1/13 - U.S. pact with Israel agrees to set-up production of certain U.S. weaponry in Israel.

   risk = .5   magnitude = -.15

10. 1/13 - Nixon orders 70,000 troops removed from Vietnam over the next three months.

    risk = .5   magnitude = .15

11. 1/14 - USSR expels a visiting U.S. congressman for "improper activites."

    risk = .3   magnitude = -.15

12. 1/25 - Nixon reveals an 8-point program to end the war in Vietnam.

    risk = .5   magnitude = .15

13. 1/25 - (Nixon reveals that) Kissinger has held private talks in Paris with the North Vietnamese over the course of the last year and a half.

    risk = .5   magnitude = .2

14. 1/26 - U.S. and USSR begin talks to ease access to one another's seaports.

    risk = .4   magnitude = .1

15. 1/27 - The USSR and Japan agree to sign a peace treaty in 1972.

    risk = .5   magnitude = .15

16. 2/1 - Tass and a U.S. firm cooperate to begin issuing a bi-monthly newsletter on Soviet economic developments.

    risk = .4   magnitude = .15

17. 2/5 - (State Department reveals that) the U.S. and Greece have reached an agreement on establishing homeport facilities at Piraeus for the U.S. Navy.

    risk = .5   magnitude = -.2

18. 2/5 - U.S. agrees to sell 142 jet fighters to Israel over the next 2-3 years.

    risk = .5   magnitude = =.2

19.   2/9 - Nixon State-of-the-World message hails the emergence of a more constructive U.S.-Soviet relationship.

      risk = .5   magnitude = .05

20.   2/10 - USSR protests American home-port facilities at Piraeus, and warns of a corresponding Soviet action.

      risk = .5   magnitude = -.1

21.   2/11 - Soviet-American Committee for Health Cooperation is formed, for the purpose of fostering joint medical research efforts.

      risk = .3   magnitude = .1

22.   2/15 - U.S. Senate approves the seabed treaty.

      risk = .4   magnitude = .2

23.   2/16 - U.S. approves licenses for another $367 million worth of machine tool exports to the USSR for their Kama River truck plant.

      risk = .4   magnitude = .2

24.   2/17 - U.S. authorizes $70 million worth of arms aid to Greece, citing the Soviet naval build-up in the Mediterranean as justification.

      risk = .5   magnitude = -.15

25.   2/17 - (U.S. announces that) Soviet-American lend-lease repayment talks will reopen.

      risk = .4   magnitude = .15

26.   2/26 - Soviet mission to Syria vows more military and economic aid.

      risk = .5   magnitude = -.15

27.   2/27 - U.S. stresses its support for its 8-point Vietnam peace plan revealed on 1/25.

      risk = .5   magnitude = .1

28. 3/6 - (Laird reports that) the USSR was arming some of its ICBMs with MIRV technology.

    risk = .4   magnitude = -.2

29. 3/6 - A Soviet arms deal with Libya including the provision of MiG-23 aircraft (is reported).

    risk = .5   magnitude = -.15

30. 3/7 - Rogers says he hopes while in Moscow, that Nixon can persuade Brezhnev to a mutual limitation of arms to the Middle East.

    risk = .5   magnitude = .05

31. 3/16 - After a 3/15 attack on a Soviet U.N. envoy, U.S. Ambassador-to-the-U.N. asks Congress to make it a crime to harass foreign diplomats.

    risk = .3   magnitude = .1

32. 3/16 - U.S. says it will violate the nonproliferation treaty by supplying fissionable materials to West Germany, Italy, Belgium and The Netherlands (who are non-adherents to IAEA provisions).

    risk = .4   magnitude = -.15

33. 3/20 - Brezhnev speech queries U.S.-Chinese collusion as implied in their Shanghai communique.

    risk = .5   magnitude = -.05

34. 3/20 - Brezhnev speech welcomes the Nixon visit.

    risk = .5   magnitude = .05

35. 3/23 - U.S. indefinitely suspends the Paris peace talks.

    risk = .5   magnitude = -.15

36. 3/26 - Brezhnev speech accepts the legitimacy of the EEC, and mentions possible EEC-Comecon cooperation.

    risk = .4   magnitude = .15

37. 3/28 - USSR presents a draft treaty at the Geneva disarmament talks to outlaw chemical warfare.

    risk = .3   magnitude = .15

38. 3/28 - U.S. Geneva representative says it is too soon to begin work on a draft treaty to ban chemical warfare, and refers the Committee to its working paper of 3/21.

   risk = .3   magnitude = -.15

39. April - U.S. and Soviet officials indicate a joint U.S.-Soviet manned space mission will take place in late 1975.

   risk = .3   magnitude = .15

40. April = East and West Germany finalize negotiations on a Treaty on Transport Questions.

   risk = .5   magnitude = .15

41. 4/1 - Nixon note says Paris peace talks can resume only when North Vietnam halts its offensive into the South.

   risk = .5   magnitude = -.15

42. 4/4 - State Department says the USSR's provision of tanks and heavy artillery to the North was a new factor in the Vietnam war.

   risk = .5   magnitude = -.1

43. 4/5 - (It is reported that) the USSR offered to finance the referendum campaign of the opponents of Denmark's entry into the EEC.

   risk = .5   magnitude = -.15

44. 4/7-12 - U.S. Secretary of Agriculture Butz visits the USSR, and predicts a big U.S.-Soviet grain sale.

   risk = .4   magnitude = .15

45. 4/7 - (Laird reports that) the USSR had furnished 80% of the equipment being used in North Vietnam's current offensive.

   risk = .5   magnitude = -.2

46. 4/9 - USSR-Iraq treaty of friendship and cooperation is signed.

   risk = .5   magnitude = -.15

47. 4/9 - USSR and Egypt sign a 15-year treaty of friendship and cooperation.

    risk = .5   magnitude = -.15

48. 4/10 - U.N. General Assembly approves the 1971 treaty banning the stockpiling of biological weapons.
    risk = .3   magnitude = .2

49. 4/10 - Nixon condemns Soviet military aid to North Vietnam.

    risk = .5   magnitude = -.1

50. 4/11 - The U.S.-Soviet biennial cultural exchange pact is signed; including new and enhanced program provisions.

    risk = .2   magnitude = .25

51. 4/13 - Lend-lease talks open.

    risk = .4   magnitude = .15

52. 4/14 - Nixon hints at Soviet responsibility for North Vietnam's invasion of the South.

    risk = .5   magnitude = -.05

53. 4/16 - Soviet note protests American air strikes on Haiphong harbor which damaged Soviet ships.

    risk = .5   magnitude = -.1

54. 4/16 - U.S. reply to the Soviet note of the same day says the U.S. strives not to interfere with international shipping, and any damage to Soviet ships had been inadvertent and regrettable.

    risk = .5   magnitude = .1

55. 4/18 - A. U.S. company contracts to publish the 30-volume "Great Soviet Encyclopedia" in English.

    risk = .2   magnitude = .15

56. 4/20 - Soviet Geneva representative says the U.S. working paper on banning chemical warfare was intended to stall such an agreement.

    risk = .3   magnitude = -.1

57. 4/20-24 - Kissinger visits the USSR.

   risk = .5   magnitude = .1

58. 4/20-24 - Kissinger and Brezhnev reportedly work out arrangements to resume the Paris peace talks.

   risk = .5   magnitude = .1

59. 4/26 - Kissinger says Soviet-American negotiations are "on course."

   risk = .5   magnitude = .05

60. 4/26 - Nixon orders 20,000 more troops removed from Vietnam over the next 2 months.

   risk = .5   magnitude = .15

61. 4/27 - Paris peace talks resume.

   risk = .5   magnitude = .1

62. 5/4 - U.S. sends more fighter bombers and a sixth aircraft carrier to Vietnam.

   risk = .5   magnitude = -.15

63. 5/4 - Defense Department releases documentation of Soviet offensive arms being used by North Vietnam.

   risk = .5   magnitude = -.1

64. 5/4 - U.S. again cancels Paris peace talks due to lack of serious North Vietnamese negotiating efforts.

   risk = .5   magnitude = -.1

65. 5/5 - Rogers says the USSR "bears a responsibility" for North Vietnam's invasion of the South.

   risk = .5   magnitude = -.1

66. 5/8 - Nixon orders the mining of North Vietnamese ports, and the interdiction of land and sea supply routes.

   risk = .5   magnitude = -.25

67. 5/8 - Nixon says the U.S. would completely withdraw from Vietnam in exchange for a cease-fire and a release of American POWs.

    risk = .5   magnitude = -.2

68. 5/9 - Kissinger denounces the USSR's attempt to secure better bilateral relations while pressuring the U.S. at the periphery.

    risk = .5   magnitude = -.1

69. 5/9 - Kissinger says the latest U.S. military moves in Vietnam will not affect its pursuance of better East-West relations.

    risk = .5   magnitude = .05

70. 5/11 - Soviet Foreign Trade Minister Patolichev visits Nixon, and implies the U.S.-Soviet summit will take place as planned.

    risk = .5   magnitude = .1

71. 5/11 - Soviet government statement calls on the U.S. to end its "blockade" of North Vietnam.

    risk = .5   magnitude = -.1

72. 5/13 - Soviet-Syrian arms pact signed.

    risk = .5   magnitude = -.15

73. 5/16 - Soviet naval movements occur 200 miles off of Vietnam's coast.

    risk = .5   magnitude = -.15

74. 5/16 - U.S. rejects resumption of the Paris peace talks.

    risk = .5   magnitude = -.1

75. 5/17 - U.S. rejects resumption of the Paris peace talks.

    risk = .5   magnitude = -.1

76. 5/18 - Soviet-Egyptian pact for increased arms deliveries is signed.

    risk = .5   magnitude = -.15

77. 5/18 - USSR again protests damage to Soviet ships from U.S. air attacks on Haiphong.

   risk = .5   magnitude = -.1

78. 5/18 - State Department says it has no confirmation of the damage claimed in a Soviet protest of 5/18.

   risk = .5   magnitude = -.1

79. 5/18 - USSR and China announce their cooperation in providing military aid to North Vietnam by rail.

   risk = .5   magnitude = -.2

80. 5/21 - Kissinger says a SALT pact is likely to result from the Moscow summit.

   risk = .4   magnitude = .05

81. 5/22-27 - Nixon visits the USSR.

   risk = .5   magnitude = .25

82. 5/23 - U.S.-Soviet agreement on health care cooperation is signed.

   risk = .3   magnitude = .2

83. 5/23 - U.S.-Soviet agreement on environmental research is signed.

   risk = .3   magnitude = .2

84. 5/24 - U.S.-Soviet agreement on space cooperation is signed.

   risk = .3   magnitude = .2

85. 5/24 - U.S.-Soviet agreement on cooperation in the field of science and technology is signed.

   risk = .3   magnitude = .2

86. 5/24 - U.S. rejects resumption of the Paris peace talks.

   risk = .5   magnitude = -.1

87. 5/25 - U.S.-Soviet agreement on the prevention of accidents at sea is signed.

   risk = .3   magnitude = .2

88. 5/26 - SALT I and ABM accords are signed.

   risk = .4   magnitude = .25

89. 5/26 - U.S. and USSR set up a joint trade commission to resolve outstanding economic differences.

   risk = .4   magnitude = .2

90. 5/27 - U.S. halts all ABM projects.

   risk = .4   magnitude = .2

91. 5/28 - Nixon makes T.V. address to the Soviet people.

   risk = .3   magnitude = .2

92. 5/29 - U.S.-Soviet declaration of principles is signed.

   risk = .5   magnitude = .2

93. 5/29 - Soviet leaders accept an American invitation to visit the U.S.

   risk = .5   magnitude = .1

94. 5/29 - USSR tells the U.S. it is interested in arranging joint economic ventures.

   risk = .4   magnitude = .05

95. 5/30 - (Rogers reveals that) the USSR has rejected a proposal for former NATO secretary general Brosio to go to Moscow to open preliminary MBFR discussions.

   risk = .4   magnitude = -.1

96. 5/31 - Rogers says the USSR is ready to begin MBFR talks.

   risk = .4   magnitude = .05

97. 6/1 - (Tass reports that) Soviet political and legislative organs have ratified the U.S.-Soviet summit results.

   risk = .5   magnitude = .15

98. 6/1 - Nixon urges Congress to approve the agreements-- especially the SALT accord -- reached at the Moscow summit.

   risk = .5   magnitude = .1

99. 6/2 - A U.S. firm gets a $20 million order for the Kama River project.

    risk = .4   magnitude = .15

100. 6/3 - Big-4 representatives sign the Berlin accords.

    risk = .5   magnitude = .2

101. 6/7 - USSR sets aid to assist in the development of the Iraqi petroleum industry.

    risk = .5   magnitude = -.15

102. 6/13 - Nixon asks for new strategic systems such as a new bomber and long-range submarine.

    risk = .4   magnitude = -.15

103. 6/14 - U.S. rejects resumption of the Paris peace talks.
    risk = .5   magnitude = -.1

104. 6/15 - Podgorny goes to Hanoi, ostensibly to push a solution to the Vietnam war.

    risk = .5   magnitude = .15

105. 6/19 - A U.S. court indicts 3 JDL members in connection with anti-Soviet bombings.

    risk = .3   magnitude = .15

106. 6/19 - Senate o.k.'s the storage of American nuclear weapons abroad without the need of an authorizing treaty.

    risk = .5   magnitude = -.15

107. 6/19 - U.S. firm announces virtual completion of an agreement with the USSR to equip Soviet factories with $55 million worth of machine tools.

    risk = .4   magnitude = .15

108. 6/22 - Nixon urges Congress to ratify the SALT I and ABM accords.

    risk = .4   magnitude = .1

109. 6/24 - Team of U.S. scientists leave for the USSR to exchange information on cancer research.

   risk = .3   magnitude = .15

110. 6/27 - U.S. and Soviet heart specialists set a program of joint research to begin in September.

   risk = .3   magnitude = .15

111. 6/28 - SEATO communique says the Soviet naval force in the Indian Ocean presents no threat to SEATO.

   risk = .5   magnitude = .1

112. 6/28 - Nixon orders 10,000 troops removed from Vietnam by 9/1.

   risk = .5   magnitude = .15

113. 6/29 - Soviet military officials counsel Arabs against starting another war with Israel.

   risk = .5   magnitude = .15

114. 6/30 - U.S.-Soviet pact on the exchange of experimental cancer-treatment drugs is signed.

   risk = .3   magnitude = .15

115. 7/6 - USSR-Cuba communique calls for removal of the U.S. naval base at Guantanamo, and an end to the U.S.' economic and political boycott of Cuba.

   risk - .5   magnitude = -.1

116. 7/6-12/15 - U.S. and Soviet space planners hold a series of meetings in both countries.

   risk = .3   magnitude = .15

117. 7/7 - U.S.-Soviet agreement specifies the concrete program of study to embody the recently signed Soviet-American agreement on science and technology.

   risk = .3   magnitude = .15

118. 7/11 - Rogers calls for face-to-face negotiations between Israel and the Arab states.

   risk = .5   magnitude = .1

119. 7/14 - USSR offers Chile a concessionary $220 million loan, and a willingness to purchase 130,000 tons of copper over the next 3 years.

risk = .5   magnitude = -.15

120. 7/18 - Occidental Petroleum Corp. signs a deal with the USSR to exchange technical information for raw materials.

risk = .4   magnitude = .15

121. 7/20 - U.S.-Soviet negotiations on an overall trade agreement between the two countries begin.

risk = .4   magnitude = .15

122. 8/1 - U.S.-Soviet negotiations on an overall trade agreement end in deadlock.

risk = .4   magnitude = -.15

123. 8/2 - U.S. Senate passes the ABM treaty.

risk = .4   magnitude = .2

124. 8/2 - U.S. Senate passes an amendment mandating the withdrawal of all U.S. forces from Vietnam upon the release of American POWs.

risk = .5   magnitude = .15

125. 8/2 - Senate o.k.'s the largest defense appropriations bill since World War II.

risk = .5   magnitude = -.15

126. 8/10 - House kills the Senate war-end amendment of 8/2.

risk = .5   magnitude = -.15

127. 8/12 - The last U.S. combat troops in Vietnam leave.

risk = .5   magnitude = .2

128. 8/16 - International Harvester Co. will sell $40 million worth of tractors and equipment to the USSR.

risk = .4   magnitude = .15

129. 8/17 - Soviet Geneva representative proposes preparations begin for a world disarmament conference.

risk = .3   magnitude = .1

130. 8/18 - (Rogers announces that) the U.S. has expressed concern to the Soviets over their institution of a new system of exit fees for Jews wishing to emigrate.

risk = .5   magnitude = -.1

131. 8/18 - House approves the SALT I accord (which had been signed as an executive agreement by Nixon).

risk = .4   magnitude = .2

132. 8/23 - Nixon cites his trip to Moscow, and the SALT agreement as reducing the danger of war.

risk = .5   magnitude = .05

133. 8/23 - Suslov warns the U.S. about attempting to amend the SALT I accord.

risk = .4   magnitude = -.1

134. 8/24 - U.S. and USSR sign an accord on the exchange of technological processes.

risk = .3   magnitude = .15

135. 8/29 - Nixon says the bombing of North Vietnam will not end until there is a settlement.

risk = .5   magnitude = -.15

136. September - Soviet arms begin arriving to the Al Fatah Palestinian guerrillas.

risk = .5   magnitude = -.15

137. September - 1972 Pugwash conference held.

risk = .3   magnitude = .15

138. 9/8 - Congress approves funds for a Trident nuclear submarine program.

risk = .5   magnitude = -.15

139. 9/8 - Congress kills funds for a high-accuracy warhead research program.

     risk = .5   magnitude = .15

140. 9/9 - (It is reported that) the U.S. has filed a formal protest with the USSR over the case of two specific persons held in the USSR because of stiff exit fees.

     risk = .5   magnitude = -.1

141. 9/11-13 - Kissinger visits Moscow.

     risk = .5   magnitude = .1

142. 9/13 - (It is reported that) the USSR has arranged to get naval facilities in Syria.

     risk = .5   magnitude = -.2

143. 9/14 - Senate o.k.'s the SALT I accord.
     risk = .4   magnitude = .15

144. 9/14 - U.S.-Soviet communique speculates that SALT talks will resume at an early date.

     risk = .4   magnitude = .1

145. September - U.S.-Soviet communique on trade talks cites "significant progress" toward a comprehensive trade agreement.

     risk = .4   magnitude = .1

146. 9/16 - Kissinger cites "major progress" on various aspects of Soviet-American relations.

     risk = .5   magnitude = .05

147. 9/18 - U.S.-Soviet maritime talks begin.

     risk = .4   magnitude = .1

148. 9/20 - Upjohn Co. announces a multi-million dollar sale of technology to the USSR.

     risk = .4   magnitude = .15

149. 9/20 - Chrysler Corp. agrees to purchase 100,000 troy ounces of palladium from the USSR.

    risk = .4   magnitude = .15

150. 9/21 - A. U.S.-Soviet extension agreement to the recently signed environmental protection agreement arranges for 30 joint projects.

    risk = .3   magnitude = .15

151. 9/21 - House accepts an amendment proposed by Republican Vanik to bar Export-Import Bank loans to any country charging more than $50 in emigration exit fees.

    risk = .5   magnitude = -.2

152. 9/23 - Senate kills the Vanik amendment of 9/21.
    risk = .5   magnitude = .15

153. 9/26 - Nixon tells Jewish leaders he is not going to make an issue out of the USSR's Jewish exit tax.

    risk = .5   magnitude = .15

154. 9/26 - Gromyko U.N. speech proposes a world disarmament conference.

    risk = .3   magnitude = .1

155. 9/27 - State Department tells the Senate it will oppose any legislation linking East-West trade to Communist emigration policy.

    risk = .5   magnitude = .15

156. 9/28 - Nixon cites the U.S.-Soviet medical research pact as a symbol of international cooperation and trust.

    risk = .3   magnitude = .1

157. 9/29 - U.S. and USSR sign an agreement to expand cooperative efforts in the peaceful uses of atomic energy.

    risk = .3   magnitude = .15

158. 9/29 - Supreme Soviet ratifies the SALT and ABM pacts.

    risk = .4   magnitude = .15

159. 9/30 - Nixon signs the SALT I accord.

   risk = .4   magnitude = .15

160. 10/4 - The U.S., USSR and ten other nations set up a "think tank" called the International Institute of Applied Systems Analysis.

   risk = .2   magnitude = .15

161. 10/5 - (Sadat says) the USSR has refused to grant MiG-23 fighter bombers to Egypt, and required that they accept a peaceful settlement with Israel.

   risk = .5   magnitude = .2

162. 10/10 - Nixon hails North Vietnamese good faith.

   risk = .5   magnitude = .1

163. 10/13 - Container Transport International grants a multi-million dollar lease to the USSR for 1,500 containers.

   risk = .4   magnitude = .15

164. 10/14 - U.S.-Soviet maritime accord is signed which sets shipping rates and port access rights.

   risk = .4   magnitude = .2

165. 10/14 - Rogers says the U.S. will use its U.N. Security Council veto more readily, so as to not always be softening its policy stands in order to avoid a Soviet veto.

   risk = .3   magnitude = -.15

166. 10/18 - U.S.-Soviet trade pact is signed, which settles the USSR's lend-lease debt, and promises to seek MFN status for the USSR.

   risk = .4   magnitude = .25

167. 10/19 - U.S. and USSR announce SALT talks will resume in Geneva on 11/21.

   risk = .4   magnitude = .1

168. 10/20 - USSR contracts for $68 million worth of tractors and equipment from the Caterpillar Tractor Co.

   risk = .4   magnitude = .15

169. 10/22 - Nixon says the agreement on ending the Vietnam war is complete.

   risk = .5   magnitude = .15

170. 10/26 - U.S.-North Vietnam 9-point Indochinese peace plan is revealed.

   risk = .5   magnitude = .25

171. 10/27 - Kosygin tells North Vietnamese envoys that he hopes an agreement ending the war will be signed soon.

   risk = .5   magnitude = .1

172. 10/31 - The recent Soviet policy of exempting emigrating Jews from exit fees is reported continuing.

   risk = .5   magnitude = .2

173. 11/2 - U.S. stalls signing an Indochinese peace treaty in order to incorporate Thieu's objections; Nixon bars a hasty accord.

   risk = .5   magnitude = -.15

174. 11/5 - U.S. is confident that there will be an accord on Vietnam.

   risk = .5   magnitude = .05

175. 11/5 - A Big-4 declaration on allied rights in Berlin is completed in order to clarify the situation in the face of anticipated East and West German U.N. membership.

   risk = .5   magnitude = .2

176. 11/5 - Nixon stresses the importance of the second round of SALT talks.

   risk = .4   magnitude = .05

177. 11/8 - South Korea ends its combat role in Vietnam.

   risk = .5   magnitude = .15

178. 11/14 - USSR o.k.'s a Moscow branch of the Chase Bank.

   risk = .4   magnitude = .15

179. 11/16 - An agreement to exchange sales of Pepsi and Soviet wines in the USSR and U.S., respectively, is signed.

   risk = .4   magnitude = .15

180. 11/17 - Nixon speech cites a new era of peace between the superpowers.

   risk = .5   magnitude = .05

181. 11/20 - Kissinger-Tho talks resume.

   risk = .5   magnitude = .1

182. 11/21 - SALT talks resume.

   risk = .4   magnitude = .1
183. November - USSR seeks U.S. loans to finance oil and gas production projects.

   risk = .4   magnitude = .15

184. December - (It is reported that) the USSR had supplied the Irish Republican Army with RPG-7 rockets.

   risk = .5   magnitude = -.15

185. 12/1 - Nixon presses an aide to Thieu to accept the agreement ending the Vietnam war.

   risk = .5   mangitude = .1

186. 12/4 - After 10 years of negotiations, a U.S.-Soviet accord allows each to construct a new embassy in the other's country.

   risk = .3   magnitude = .25

187. 12/7 - State Department begins active contingency planning for a post-war South Vietnam.

   risk = .5   magnitude = .1

188. 12/9 - USSR-North Vietnam agreement promises "large-scale deliveries" of military and economic supplies to North Vietnam in 1973.

risk = .5   magnitude = -.15

189. 12/16 - Kissinger-Tho talks break down; Kissinger says North Vietnam reneged on previously negotiated points.

risk = .5   magnitude = -.15

190. 12/18 - Nixon orders massive bombing north of North Vietnam's 20th parallel.

risk = .5   magnitude = -.15

191. 12/18 - The last Australian military units leave Vietnam.

risk = .5   magnitude = .15

192. 12/20 - Soviet message to the Viet Cong criticizes the U.S. for putting obstacles on the path to peace.

risk = .5   magnitude = -.1

193. 12/21 - A U.S.-Soviet SALT consultative commission is set up to ensure compliance with the signed arms pact.

risk = .4   magnitude = .2

194. 12/21 - Brezhnev says his government "angrily and resolutely condemns" the resumed U.S. bombing of North Vietnam.

risk = .5   magnitude = -.1

195. 12/21 - An East and West German treaty acknowledges the sovereignty of each.

risk = .5   magnitude = .25

196. 12/22 - Nixon sends a congratulatory message to the Soviets on the 50th anniversary of the creation of the USSR.

risk = .3   magnitude = .1

197. 12/30 - Kissinger-Tho talks are to resume on 1/8/73.

risk = .5   magnitude = .1

198. 12/30 - Nixon halts bombing north of North Vietnam's 20th parallel.

risk = .5   magnitude = .15

Detente Index Scale Score = 4.86

1. January-March - U.S. sells Iran more than $2 billion in military equipment.

    risk = .5   magnitude = -.15

2. January-April - USSR ships approximately 40 MiGs, SAM missiles, and other military equipment to Syria.

    risk = .5   magnitude = -.15

3. 1/11 - U.S. and Soviet insurance companies arrange to cover U.S. property in, and to, the USSR.

    risk = .4   magnitude = .2

4. 1/12 - General Electric and the USSR sign an agreement to exchange research and technology.

    risk = .4   magnitude = .15

5. 1/17 - USSR asks for tariff considerations and Export-Import Bank credits.

    risk = .4   magnitude = .15

6. 1/18 - A U.S. firm signs to sell $20 million worth of electric pumps to the USSR.

    risk = .4   magnitude = .15

7. 1/20 - The text of Soviet legislative acts reveals educational exit taxes for emigrants as formally adopted.

    risk = .5   magnitude = -.2

8. 1/22 - USSR offers a draft agenda for a European security conference.

    risk = .5   magnitude = .1

9. 1/23 - U.S. and North Vietnam initial a Vietnamese truce agreement.

    risk = .5   magnitude = .25

10. 1/24 - USSR lauds the Vietnam truce pact.

   risk = .5   magnitude = .1

11. 1/27 - The 4 parties to the Paris peace talks sign the truce pact.

   risk = .5   magnitude = .25

12. 1/29 - U.S.-Soviet talks to regulate fishing practices are begun.

   risk = .4   magnitude = .1

13. 1/30 - Brezhnev says the imminent Vietnam settlement indicates a Middle East settlement can also be found.

14. 1/31 - Preliminary MBFR talks begin in Vienna.

   risk = .4   magnitude = .1

15. 1/31 - U.S.-Soviet Joint Committee on Cooperation in the Field of Environmental Protection slates 22 specific projects.

   risk = .3   magnitude = .2

16. 2/6 - USSR loans American museums 41 paintings by European masters.

   risk = .2   magnitude = .15

17. 2/9 - U.S. and Soviet cardiologists set a research project investigating deaths by heart attack.

   risk = .3   magnitude = .15

18. 2/20 - USSR urges France and China to end nuclear testing in the atmosphere.

   risk = .4   magnitude = .15

19. 2/21 - U.S.-Soviet fishing agreements are signed, which regulate fishing off the U.S. Pacific coast, and establish fisheries review boards in each other's capital.

   risk = .3   magnitude = .15

20. 2/21 - Brezhnev lauds the Vietnam peace pact.

   risk = .5   magnitude = .1

21. 2/22 - Preliminary MBFR talks stall over the identity of appropriate participants in the formal talks.

    risk = .4   magnitude = -.15

22. 2/27 - U.S. stresses it will work to foster an Egyptian/Israeli dialogue.

    risk = .5   magnitude = .1

23. 3/9 - USSR says that regarding international copyright obligations, U.S. authors would receive part of their royalties in dollars.

    risk = .2   magnitude = .15

24. 3/11-14 - U.S. Treasury Secretary Shultz engages in trade talks with Moscow.

    risk = .4   magnitude = .15

25. 3/12 - U.S.-Soviet SALT talks resume.

    risk = .4   magnitude = .1

26. 3/12 - U.S. Export-Import Bank delays granting $225 million worth of credit to the USSR for its Kama River project.

    risk = .4   magnitude = -.1

27. 3/20 - U.S. Export-Import Bank loans the USSR $203 million.

    risk = .4   magnitude = .2

28. 3/23 - U.S. and USSR sign an agreement to conduct joint studies on water pollution.

    risk = .3   magnitude = .15

29. 3/28 - U.S. opens a trade office in Moscow.

    risk = .4   magnitude = .15

30. 3/29 - State Department says it is still interested in promoting an interim Middle East settlement.

    risk = .5   magnitude = .1

31.   3/29 - All U.S. troops are gone from Vietnam.

       risk = .5   magnitude = .15

32.   April - Soviet ships ferry Moroccan troops to Syria to fight
       against Israel.

       risk = .5   magnitude = -.2

33.   4/6 - (It is reported that) recent Soviet tank deployments in WTO
       countries puts the East's tank total at 3 times that of Western
       Europe.

       risk = .5   magnitude = -.2

34.   4/8 - (It is reported that) the USSR has built a naval base in
       Somalia, and that the number of its military advisors there has
       risen sharply.

       risk = .5   magnitude = -.2

35.   4/10 - Nixon opposes any Congressional attempt to legislate
       Jewish emigration levels for the USSR.

       risk = .5   magnitude = .15

36.   4/12 - Occidental Petroleum and the USSR sign a multi-billion
       dollar barter arrangement involving the production of fertilizer.

       risk = .4   magnitude = .15

37.   4/12-14 - USSR rejects Mexican President Echeverria's request
       that the USSR abide by the protocol banning the export of
       nuclear weapons to Latin America.

       risk = .4   magnitude = -.15

38.   4/13 - USSR institutes multiple visas for U.S. businessmen, rather
       than having them apply for a new one every time they enter or
       leave the country.

       risk = .4   magnitude = .15

39.   4/13 - (It is announced that) the U.S. Navy is planning a $30
       billion building and conversion program covering 271 ships.

       risk = .5   magnitude = -.2

40. 4/19 - Pepsi Co. signs a deal with the USSR to exchange the sale of Pepsi for vodka and wine.

    risk = .4   magnitude = .15

41. 4/23 - Brezhnev tells visiting U.S. Senators he is looking forward to a major expansion of U.S.-Soviet trade.

    risk = .4   magnitude = .05

42. 4/23 - Brezhnev announces that the exit fee for emigrants has been suspended.

    risk = .5   magnitude = .2

43. 4/26 - AFL-CIO attacks Nixon's policy of granting trade credits to the USSR.

    risk = .4   magnitude = -.1

44. 4/27 - A Central Committee declaration supports East-West political summitry, and trade.

    risk = .5   magnitude = .1

45. 4/30 - Rogers supports American bombing in Cambodia to enforce North Vietnamese compliance with the Cambodian cease fire.

    risk = .5   magnitude = -.1

46. 4/30 - (Nixon says) his Administration is already preparing for the 1973 U.S.-Soviet summit talks.

    risk = .5   magnitude = .1

47. May - (It is reported that) the number of Soviet Jews allowed to emigrate rose by 17,000 in 1972 over 1971.

    risk = .5   magnitude = .2

48. 5/1 - Brezhnev speech stresses a policy of improved ties with the U.S., Japan and West Europe.

    risk = .5   magnitude = .1

49. 5/3 - Nixon says MBFR negotiations will have to entail asymmetrical reductions, with the larger Soviet bloc forces making the bigger cut.

   risk = .4   magnitude = -.15

50. 5/6-7 - Kissinger visits the USSR.

   risk = .5   magnitude = .1

51. 5/7 - West Germany and Czechoslovakia begin talks to restore diplomatic ties severed since World War II.

   risk = .5   magnitude = .15

52. 5/9 - (It is reported that) the U.S. refuses to discuss their European-based nuclear bombers in the SALT talks.

   risk = .4   magnitude = -.15

53. 5/10 - House cuts off defense funds for military operations in Cambodia.

   risk = .5   magnitude = .2

54. 5/11 - Bonn ratifies the treaty establishing formal relations with East Germany, and approves the entry of both East and West Germany into the U.N.

   risk = .5   magnitude = .25

55. 5/12 - White House announces that June 18-26 will be the dates for Brezhnev's visit to the U.S.

   risk = .5   magnitude = .1

56. 5/16 - Nixon criticizes Congressional actions aimed at cutting off funds for military operations in Indochina.

   risk = .5   magnitude = -.1

57. 5/17 - Kissinger-Tho talks begin on implementing the Vietnam truce.

   risk = .5   magnitude = .1

58. 5/18-23 - Brezhnev visits West Germany.

   risk = .5   magnitude = .15

59. 5/19 - USSR and West Germany sign 3 agreements on economic and cultural cooperation.

   risk = .5   magnitude = .15

60. 5/19 - Nixon warns that a diminution in the defense budget could reduce his bargaining power with Brezhnev.

   risk = .5   magnitude = -.05

61. 5/19 - Nixon speaks approvingly of upcoming U.S.-Soviet SALT, MBFR, and trade talks.

   risk = .4   magnitude = .05

62. 5/21 - Brezhnev speech cites improved U.S.-Soviet relations as an example of international cooperation.

   risk = .5   magnitude = .05

63. 5/21 - USSR and West Germany declare that both countries will work for the success of the Vienna MBFR talks and the preliminary European security conference talks.

   risk = .5   magnitude = .1

64. 5/28 - U.S. asks the USSR and West Europe to assist in forcing Libya to alter its cumbersome passport regulations.

   risk = .5   magnitude = .1

65. 5/29 - The Bank of America opens a Moscow branch.

   risk = .4   magnitude = .15

66. 5/31 - NBC television network and the USSR sign an agreement to exchange news broadcasts and personnel.

   risk = .2   magnitude = .2

67. 5/31 - U.S. Export-Import Bank preliminarily approves $180 million worth of credit to help finance the fertilizer deal signed with Occidental Petroleum on 4/12.

   risk = .4   magnitude = .15

68. 5/31 - Senate cuts off all funds for military activities in Laos and Cambodia.

   risk = .5   magnitude = .2

69. 6/1 - (It is reported that) while in Moscow, Kissinger received assurances from Brezhnev that levels of Jewish emigration will remain high (36,000-40,000 per year) and that the education exit tax will remain suspended.

risk = .5   magnitude = .2

70. 6/1 - U.S. and USSR government letters endorse recent Soviet fertilizer deals with private U.S. firms.

risk = .4   magnitude = .2

71. 6/5 - Rogers claims MiGs are being sent to Iraq.

risk = .5   magnitude = -.1

72. 6/8 - USSR and two U.S. companies sign a $10 billion agreement on a long-term project to bring Soviet natural gas to the U.S.

risk = .4   magnitude = .15

73. 6/8 - An agenda for a European Security Conference is approved.

risk = .5   magnitude = .15

74. 6/11 - Rogers criticizes Soviet arms sales to Iraq.

risk = .5   magnitude = -.1

75. 6/12 - A leading U.S. accounting firm signs a cooperative agreement with the USSR to exchange information on accounting practices and international finance.

risk = .4   magnitude = .15

76. 6/13 - The First National City Bank of New York opens a branch in Moscow.

risk = .4   magnitude = .15

77. 6/13 - The original 4 parties to the Paris peace talks sign a new 14-point agreement aimed at strengthening the 1/27 Vietnam cease fire.

risk = .5   magnitude = .2

78. 6/14 - Brezhnev assures that Soviet Jews, except those connected with national security work, are free to emigrate.

risk = .5   magnitude = .15

79. 6/14 - Brezhnev calls for "large-scale" U.S.-Soviet trade.

    risk = .4   magnitude = .1

80. 6/14 - ITT signs an agreement with the USSR to exchange research and technology.

    risk = .4   magnitude = .15

81. 6/14 - Brezhnev hosts U.S. newsmen in Moscow; says he hopes the upcoming summit will further improve Soviet-American relations.

    risk = .5   magnitude = .1

82. 6/15 - NATO ministers back the upcoming European security conference.

    risk = .5   magnitude = .1

83. 6/16-21 - Brezhnev is in the U.S. for summit talks.

    risk = .5   magnitude = .25

84. 6/19 - U.S.-Soviet agreement on oceanographic research is signed.

    risk = .3   magnitude = .2

85. 6/19 - U.S.-Soviet agreement on cooperation in the field of transportation is signed.

    risk = .3   magnitude = .2

86. 6/19 - U.S.-Soviet agreement on agricultrual research is signed.

    risk = .3   magnitude = .2

87. 6/19 - U.S.-Soviet biennial cultural exchange agreement, with expanded provisions, is signed.

    risk = .2   magnitude = .25

88. 6/19 - Brezhnev lobbies U.S. Congressmen regarding MFN status for the USSR.

    risk = .4   magnitude = .1

89. 6/20 - U.S.-Soviet statement of principles pledges to speed up the SALT process.

    risk = .4   magnitude = .1

90. 6/20 - U.S.-Soviet agreement on peaceful uses of nuclear energy research is signed.

    risk = .3   magnitude = .2

91. 6/20 - U.S.-Soviet agreement is signed which eliminates double taxation for each side's nationals working in the other's country.

    risk = .4   magnitude = .2

92. 6/21 - Nixon accepts an invitation to visit the USSR in 1974.

    risk = .5   magnitude = .15

93. 6/22 - U.S.-Soviet agreement to control fishing off the U.S. Atlantic coast is signed.

    risk = .4   magnitude = .2

94. 6/22 - U.S.-Soviet agreement on the prevention of nuclear war is signed.

    risk = .5   magnitude = .25

95. 6/22 - U.S.-Soviet Chamber of Commerce is created.

    risk = .4   magnitude = .2

96. 6/22 - U.S. and USSR agree to establish trade centers in each other's capital.

    risk = .4   magnitude = .2

97. 6/23 - An agreement is signed to expand U.S.-Soviet air passenger service.

    risk = 2.   magnitude = .15

98. 6/23 - Soviet consulate opens in San Francisco.

    risk = .3   magnitude = .2

99.   6/24 - Brezhnev's 47-minute taped address to the American people airs on nationwide T.V.

risk = .3   magnitude = .15

100.   6/25 - U.S.-Soviet communique asks for further talks on limiting chemical weapons, and says a world disarmament conference could be convened at an appropriate time.

risk = .4   magnitude = .1

101.   6/25 - U.S.-Soviet communique foresees a permanent SALT accord in 1974.

risk = .4   magnitude = .1

102.   6/25 - U.S.-Soviet communique lauds the Vietnam truce.

risk = .5   magnitude = .1

103.   6/25 - U.S.-USSR communique says MBFR talks will begin in Vienna on 10/30.

risk = .4   magnitude = .15

104.   6/25 - House accepts a Senate supplemental funding bill which cuts off funds for military activities in Laos and Cambodia.

risk = .5   magnitude = .15

105.   6/27 - Nixon vetoes the supplemental funding bill of 6/25 due to its war curbs.

risk = .5   magnitude = -.15

106.   6/27 - U.S. firms sign a preliminary agreement to assist the USSR in the exploitation of Siberian natural gas.

risk = .4   magnitude = .15

107.   6/29-30 - A Nixon-Congress compromise is worked out to allow Cambodian bombings to continue until 8/15.

risk = .5   magnitude = -.15

108.   7/2 - Bechtel Corp. signs an agreement with the USSR to exchange engineering and construction information.

risk = .4   magnitude = .15

109. 7/3 - The 35-nation Conference on Security and Cooperation (CSCE) opens in Helsinki.

risk = .5   magnitude = .25

110. 7/6 - U.S. consulate opens in Leningrad.

risk = .3   magnitude = .2

111. 7/16 - The plea of Western newsmen to attend the trial of Soviet dissident Pyotr Yakir is rejected.

risk = .2   magnitude = -.15

112. 7/18 - House passes a bill limiting Presidential power to commit U.S. forces to future hostilities without Congressional approval.
risk = .5   magnitude = .15

113. 7/19 - (Kissinger reports that) Brezhnev has promised to allow a large number of Jews on a U.S.-submitted list of hardship cases to emigrate.

risk = .5   magnitude = .15

114. 7/20 - Senate passes a bill similar to the one in the House on 7/18, which limits the President's war powers.

risk = .5   magnitude = .15

115. 7/31 - (It is reported that) U.S. exports to the USSR during the first half of 1973 have already exceeded total two-way trade during 1972.

risk = .4   magnitude = .25

116. 8/3 - Nixon speculates that a Congressional cut-off of war funds for Indochina may have ominous consequences.

risk = .5   magnitude = -.05

117. 8/6 - U.S. urges Israel and Egypt to propose some new ideas which might break the Middle East stalemate.

risk = .5   magnitude = .1

118. 8/15 - North Korean pilots are detected in Egypt, presumably flying air defense missions.

risk = .5   magnitude = -.2

119.   8/15 - U.S. bombing in Indochina ends.

risk = .5   magnitude = .2

120.   8/15 - Nixon denounces Congress for bringing about the bombing halt, asserting it would harm prospects for world peace.

risk = .5   magnitude = -.1

121.   8/20 - Given recent Soviet successes with MIRV technology, Rogers says a comprehensive SALT treaty is urgent.

risk = .4   magnitude = .05

122.   9/7 - Kissinger testifies before Congress that American foreign policy cannot be "dependent upon the domestic structure of the USSR."

risk = .5   magnitude = .1

123.   9/9 - (It is reported that) the U.S. protests to the USSR over their provision of surface-to-air missiles to Palestinian commandos.

risk = .5   magnitude = -.1

124.   9/10 - USSR stops jamming VOA and other Western broadcasts for the first time in 5 years.

risk = .2   magnitude = .15

125.   9/10 - General Motors and Soviet officials begin preliminary talks on a possible second truck plant to be built in Siberia.

risk = .4   magnitude = .1

126.   9/12 - Final approval is given for a $180 million U.S. loan to the USSR for a fertilizer project.

risk = .4   magnitude = .15

127.   9/13 - USSR denounces the Chilean coup.

risk = .5   magnitude = -.1

128.   9/13-16 - Numerous U.S. groups, such as the Academy of Sciences, appeal to the USSR for the freedom and safety of Soviet dissidents, such as Andrei Sakharov.

risk = .5   magnitude = -.1

129. 9/17 - Senate resolution calls on Nixon to try to end Soviet domestic repression, asking this as a Soviet concession to be considered in trade and disarmament talks.

    risk = .5   magnitude = -.2

130. 9/19 - Brezhnev blasts the U.S. Senate resolution of 9/17.

    risk = .5   magnitude = -.1

131. 9/19 - U.S. firms contract to build a $110 million International Trade Center in Moscow.

    risk = .4   magnitude = .15

132. 9/21 - USSR severs diplomatic ties with Chile.

    risk = .5   magnitude = -.2

133. 9/21 - Senate imposes a permanent fund cut-off for U.S. combat forces in Indochina, unless authorized by Congress.

    risk = .5   magnitude = .15

134. 9/24 - U.S. protests the assault and arrest of an American newsman filming a Jewish protest in Moscow.

    risk = .2   magnitude = -.1

135. 9/24 - U.S. recognizes the Chilean junta.

    risk = .5   magnitude = -.15

136. 9/25 - Gromyko warns the West in a U.N. speech not to interfere in the USSR's conduct of its emigration policy.

    risk = .3   magnitude = -.1

137. 9/25 - Gromyko U.N. address proposes that U.N. Security Council permanent members cut their defense budgets by 10% and spend the savings on foreign aid.

    risk = .3   magnitude = .15

138. 9/26 - (USSR announces) it has ratified two 1966 U.N. human rights covenants.

    risk = .3   magnitude = .2

139. 9/26 - Nixon disfavors U.S. trade restrictions with the USSR concerning its emigration policy; sees them as jeopardizing improving relations.

    risk = .5   magnitude = .15

140. 9/26 - General Dynamics Corp. and the USSR sign an agreement for broad scientific and technical cooperation.

    risk = .4   magnitude = .15

141. 9/27 - Citing a Soviet MIRV threat, the Senate votes to accelerate development of the Trident submarine.

    risk = .5   magnitude = -.15

142. 9/27 - Senate amendment necessitates a 23% cutback in the number of U.S. troops stationed abroad.
    risk = .5   magnitude = .15

143. October - A record number of Jews are allowed to emigrate from the USSR.

    risk = .5   magnitude = .15

144. October - 189 U.S. oil companies display oil exploration and production equipment in Moscow.

    risk = .4   magnitude = .15

145. October - Dresser Industries signs a technology transfer agreement to assist in Soviet offshore oil exploration.

    risk = .4   magnitude = .15

146. October - USSR pulls back its advisors and dependents from potential areas of conflict prior to the outbreak of war in the Middle East.

    risk = .5   magnitude = -.15

147. October - USSR begins a major airlift of military supplies to Egypt and Syria.

    risk = .5   magnitude = -.25

148. October - Soviet fleets mass in the Mediterranean and east Atlantic.

    risk = .5   magnitude = -.2

149. October - (U.S. claims) the USSR refused to cooperate with the U.S. in restraining arms shipments to the Middle East during the first week of the Arab-Israeli crisis.

    risk = .5   magnitude = -.25

150. October - USSR sends Scud missiles to Egypt.

    risk = .5   magnitude = -.2

151. 10/3 - Nixon opposes the amendment to the Trade Reform Act of 1973 which links MFN status for the USSR to eased emigration regulations.

    risk = .5   magnitude = .15

152. 10/3 - U.S. opens a commercial office in Moscow.
    risk = .4   magnitude = .15

153. 10/4 - Nixon asks Congress for authority to grant MFN status to the USSR.

    risk = .4   magnitude = .15

154. 10/6 - Kissinger telephones Dobrynin and urges Soviet restraint during the Middle East crisis.

    risk = .5   magnitude = .1

155. 10/6 - Kissinger pleads with Israel and Egypt to stop their fighting.

    risk = .5   magnitude = .1

156. 10/7 - Nixon proposes U.S.-Soviet consultation on the Middle East to Brezhnev.

    risk = .5   magnitude = .1

157. 10/7 - USSR blames Israel for the current fighting in the Middle East.

    risk = .5   magnitude = -.1

158. 10/8 - Brezhnev says he hopes the Arab-Israeli war will not interfere with Soviet-American detente.

    risk = .5   magnitude = .05

159. 10/8 - Senate resolution calls for an immediate Middle East cease fire and return to the status quo ante.

    risk = .5   magnitude = .15

160. 10/10 - (It is reported that) the USSR sent messages to all Arab governments, assuring maximum Soviet arms aid, and beseeching these governments to give Egypt and Syria every means of support.

    risk = .5   magnitude = -.2

161. 10/12 - Kissinger says Soviet arms shipments to Egypt and Syria were not irresponsible enough to endanger detente.

    risk = .5   magnitude = .05

162. 10/13 - Kissinger reveals a U.S.-Soviet plan to seek a cease-fire in place on the Syrian and Egyptian fronts.

    risk = .5   magnitude = .25

163. 10/14 - USSR accuses the U.S. of sending Israel large quantities of military aid, and using American pilots to fly missions for Israel.

    risk = .5   magnitude = -.1

164. 10/14 - U.S. launches a massive airlift of arms to Israel.

    risk = .5   magnitude = -.25

165. 10/15 - USSR-Algeria communique includes a Soviet pledge of every type of assistance to recover lost Arab lands.

    risk = .5   magnitude = -.1

166. 10/15 - Kosygin stresses that the USSR is interested in settling the Arab-Israeli war.

    risk = .5   magnitude = .1

167. 10/16 - The U.S. fleet is massing in the Mediterranean and east Atlantic.

    risk = .5   magnitude = -.2

168. 10/17-18 - Kosygin meets with Sadat, reportedly to find a way to end the Arab-Israeli war.

    risk = .5   magnitude = .15

169. 10/17 - U.S. Defense Department will ask Congress for a $2 billion supplemental bill to replace U.S. arms being sent to Israel.

    risk = .5   magnitude = -.15

170. 10/19 - Nixon asks Congress for $2.2 billion in military aid for Israel.

    risk = .5   magnitude = -.2

171. 10/20-21 - Kissinger and Brezhnev work out a Middle East cease-fire plan in Moscow.

    risk = .5   magnitude = .2

172. 10/21 - Sadat receives assurances from Brezhnev regarding the Security Council cease-fire resolution.

    risk = .5   magnitude = .1

173. 10/22 - U.N. Security Council adopts a U.S.-Soviet-sponsored resolution calling for a Middle East cease fire.

    risk = .3   magnitude = .2

174. 10/22 - U.S. rejects the idea of Soviet and American peace-keeping troops in the Middle East.

    risk = .5   magnitude = -.15

175. 10/22-23 - Egypt and Israel agree to a Middle East cease fire.

    risk = .5   magnitude = .2

176. 10/24 - The Control Data Corp. and the Soviet government sign a 10-year agreement on the cooperative development of computer technology and services.

    risk = .4   magnitude = .2

177. 10/24 - Brezhnev note to Nixon warns of the "destruction of the state of Israel" if Israel did not halt its advance.

    risk = .5   magnitude = -.15

178. 10/24 - USSR approves the idea of superpower peacekeeping troops in the Middle East.

   risk = .5   magnitude = -.05

179. 10/25 - USSR approves the establishment of a Middle East peace-keeping force, excluding the Security Council's permanent members.

   risk = .3   magnitude = .2

180. 10/25 - American military forces at key bases are put on "precautionary alert."

   risk = .5   magnitude = -.25

181. 10/25 - Brezhnev cancels a major foreign policy speech due to concern over the American military alert.

   risk = .5   magnitude = -.15

182. 10/25 - U.S. and Soviet lawyers begin meeting to establish a legal framework for trade practices.

   risk = .4   magnitude = .15

183. 10/26 - Brezhnev reaffirms the USSR's policy of detente with the U.S.

   risk = .5   magnitude = .1

184. 10/26 - Brezhnev accuses the U.S. of artificially drumming up a Middle East crisis to justify its world-wide military alert.

   risk = .5   magnitude = -.1

185. 10/26 - Nixon says his personal relationship with Brezhnev was instrumental in defusing the Middle East crisis.

   risk = .5   magnitude = .05

186. 10/26 - Kissinger advances a plan to provide relief aid to the trapped Egyptian III Corps.

   risk = .5   magnitude = .15

187. 10/29 - Nixon asks Congress to delay decision on MFN status for the USSR, in light of the tense Middle East situation.

   risk = .4   magnitude = -.15

188. 10/29 - Kissinger expresses disgust at NATO passivity in the current Middle East fighting.

   risk = .5   magnitude = -.05

189. 10/31 - USSR sounds out the PLO about a possible negotiated Middle East settlement.

   risk = .5   magnitude = .15

190. 10/31 - Senate passes a measure mandating a cut in U.S. NATO-assigned troops in any European country not financially contributing to their maintenance.

   risk = .5   magnitude = .15

191. November - USSR continues to probe the PLO on their requirements for a homeland.

   risk = .5   magnitude = .15

192. 11/1 - U.S. and USSR have reportedly secured arrangements for direct Arab-Israeli negotiations.

   risk = .5   magnitude = .15

193. 11/7 - Soviets display a new ICBM, described by Tass as having "unique power and accuracy."

   risk = .5   magnitude = -.15

194. 11/9 - Egypt and Israel accept a U.S.-sponsored 6-point agreement aimed at strengthening the Middle East cease-fire.

   risk = .5   magnitude = .15

195. 11/14 - U.S. and Soviet science officials slate 5 conferences on cancer research in 1974 and 1975.

   risk = .3   magnitude = .15

196. 11/20 - USSR insists that the PLO participate in any Middle East peace conference.

   risk = .5   magnitude = -.15

197. 11/21 - U.S. officials muse the possibility that the USSR sent nuclear weapons to Egypt during the recent Arab-Israeli crisis.

   risk = .5   magnitude = -.05

198. 11/23 - A leading U.S. industrial design firm gets a contract with the USSR to design a number of manufactured goods.

risk = .4   magnitude = .15

199. 11/29 - USSR and India sign a 15-year economic, technological, scientific and trade agreement.

risk = .4   magnitude = -.15

200. 11/30 - U.S. and USSR sign a protocol on the first major exchange of scientists and engineers (as many as 500) between the two countries.

risk = .3   magnitude = .2

201. 12/3 - Soviet and Turkish officials sign protocols defining their common border.

risk = .5   magnitude = .15

202. 12/4 - House foreign aid bill grants $25 million to assist Soviet refugees.

risk = .5   magnitude = -.15

203. 12/4 - USSR-U.K. communique supports implementation of the Paris cease-fire agreements on Indochina.

risk = .5   magnitude = .1

204. 12/4 - USSR-U.K. communique agrees on the need for a Middle East peace conference.

risk = .5   magnitude = .1

205. 12/5 - (It is reported that) the USSR has begun using Guinea as a base for its reconnaissance flights.

risk = .5   magnitude = -.2

206. 12/6 - Kissinger expresses doubts about a joint U.S.-Soviet Middle East peace-keeping force.

risk = .5   magnitude = -.05

207. 12/6 - Kissinger admits that the USSR had been instrumental in arranging an upcoming Egyptian-Israeli Geneva peace conference.

risk = .5   magnitude = .05

208. 12/11 - House passes a comprehensive foreign trade bill, including trade curbs with the USSR due to its emigration restrictions.

risk = .5   magnitude = 0 (mixed)

209. 12/18 - Kissinger says the U.S. could not allow Soviet-supplied arms to defeat U.S.-supplied arms at any time in any setting.

risk = .5   magnitude = -.15

210. 12/18-19 - Soviet bloc leaders meet in Moscow to discuss ways to counteract Western demands for freer movement of persons and ideas in Europe.

risk = .5   magnitude = -.15

211. 12/21 - USSR grants economic aid to the Provisional Revolutionary Government in South Vietnam.

risk = .5   magnitude = -.15

212. 12/21 - Geneva Middle East peace conference opens; Groymko and Kissinger are co-chairmen.

risk = .5   magnitude = .2

213. 12/23 - USSR warns Western publishers not to print the works of Soviet dissidents.

risk = .2   magnitude = -.15

214. 12/27 - Kissinger calls Soviet Geneva conference conduct "constructive."

risk = .5   magnitude = .05

Traditional intercoder reliability tests focus on the number of errors (differing value assignments) across coders. Such a demanding standard will not be applied to the recoding of the Detente Index's events data due to three conditions which disadvantage highly similar scores: these conditions are -- 1) no training session(s) was held for the recorders; 2) recoding was done from the author's synopses of events (such as those found in Appendix B) rather than from the much richer original descriptions in <u>Facts on File</u>; and, 3) data for contiguous years were not used, thus penalizing the recoders' ability to get a feel for the flavor of a stream of events (a stream which does not necessarily respect New Year's Eve as a natural stopping or starting point). The approach used here will simply be to gauge the closeness or similarity of the summated Detente Index scale scores.

The difference between two coder's scores cannot be evaluated in relation to the scores themselves, as even a very small difference between two scores which are near zero will seem vast. For example, two hypothetical Detente Index scores -- .05 and .1 -- with an absolute difference of .05, are extremely similar or close to one another, even though they differ by 50%. This would mean that scores of 2.0 and 4.0 would fare just as well by the above standard of a percentaged difference (even though in absolute terms, the two are far apart). What we must do is to compare the difference between two coder's annual scores in relation to the total amount of cooperative/conflictive potential in the system of Soviet-American relations. For practical purposes, we can consider the amount of cooperative potential to be 4.9 (the Detente Index scale score for 1973, the highest one of the post-war period) and the amount of conflictive potential to be -6.5 (the Detente Index scale score for 1981, the lowest one). Theoretically, the cooperative and conflictive potentials would be at least slightly greater than those which have been demonstrated by history. Theoretically extending these potentials would narrow the percentaged differences between coders' Detente Index scores; therefore, the empirical ceiling and floor used give us a worst-case assessment of the variation in our scale scores. To summarize the technique outlined here for evaluating intercoder reliability for the three years tested*, each Detente Index score produced by the two coders is subtracted from the corresponding score calculated by the author; the difference between each pair is then divided by 4.9 (if the author's score is positive) or 6.5 (if the author's score is negative). The results are presented in the table below.

----

*Arbitrarily selected as the middle year of each decade in our post-war sample: 1955, 1965 and 1975.

	Author		Coder 1		Coder 2	
	Score	% dif-ference	Score	% dif-ference	Score	% dif-ference
Year						
1955	1.2	-	1.1	2%	1.0	5%
1965	-3.1	-	-2.7	6%	-2.0	17%
1975	-.28	-	.05	5%	.02	4.5%

The fact that the six recoded years -- with one exception (Coder #2: 1965) -- vary from the author's original calculations by approximately 5% or below is most encouraging. This is a level of accuracy I would have stipulated only with training sessions, expanded descriptions of events, and a set of continuous rather than separate years. The Detente Index therefore shows itself to be sufficiently replicable as a measuring instrument.

APPENDIX D

Soviet Criticisms of the U.S.

I. Coding Rules

1. For the years examined -- 1949, 1953, 1956, 1958, 1963, 1964, 1969, 1971, 1973, 1976, 1981 -- all criticisms of American foreign policy printed in either <u>Pravda</u> or <u>Izvestia</u>, as provided by the <u>Current Digest of the Soviet Press</u> were scored. The intent of using only these two newspaper sources was to increase confidence that something of a "main" or "official" line was being monitored.

2. We were coding "themes" rather than specific words. The purpose was to record specific attributions to the other, rather than to count words, or to distil vague overall impressions. Counted themes usually occurred as statements; occasionally (but not often) it would take two or more sentences to present a specific criticism. The somewhat loose content of the specific coding categories was intentional, in the hope of avoiding slavish adherence to a rigid codebook, and thus allowing the coder to pick up on the all important nuances of each specific text examined. Only the specific context of an article can tell us exactly how to score a criticism: for example, criticisms of American positions of strength diplomacy could be " no. XV, Refusal to admit mutual equality ..." or "no. IV, Militarism," depending entirely on the context and supporting arguments.

3. A single sentence may contain more than one criticism; for example, the following hypothetical sentence would be scored on three counts: namely, "militarism," "imperialism," and "aggressive military intent." The U.S., as part of its overall plans of militarization, refuses to remove their troops from Korea where they serve the functions of enslaving South Korea, and establishing a springboard for military aggression against the USSR." However, each expressed point of criticism only received one coding classification; for example, you would not have the criticism-types "militarism" and "general interest foreign policy malevolence" being simultaneously scored or recorded for the same point or assertion.

4. Perjorative words which are pro forma or unconnected with a specific criticism are not scored; e.g. a sentence which begins, "The American imperialists ..." is not scored for imperialism, unless the rest of the sentence explicitly makes this charge.

5. Criticisms by non-Soviets (even Americans) which are printed in <u>Pravda</u> or <u>Izvestia</u> are counted, since we can infer that the Soviets subscribe to these positions.

6. If the terms "United States" or "America" do not appear in an article's (1) title, (2) lead paragraph, or (3) second paragraph if the lead paragraph is only one sentence long, or if it simply lists participants in a meeting, then any criticisms found in this text will be treated as "references" to U.S. policy (therefore coefficient values per each criticism-type are reduced by one-half), rather than "articles" dealing with U.S. policy. The reason behind doing this is that, for example, a criticism of American imperialism in the Third World which was the sole message of an article, and discussed at length differs in degree of impact or stridency from an article which analyses the situation in the Middle East, but contains a reference to American Third World imperialism embedded somewhere in the body of the article. Therefore, I employ this article/reference distinction to reflect the difference in stridency. The reader can see for himself how the article/reference distinction manifests itself by consulting the actual HOC coding sheets provided in Appendix E.

7. "Certain Circles," as found at the bottom of the Hierarchy of Criticisms Scheme: Soviet Criticisms, are usually identified by the terms "certain" or "some" circles, per se; also, any one person (excluding the President, Secretary of State, or National Security Advisor) or any one newspaper (without attributing the U.S. official line to its position) are also counted as certain circles.

Note: The Current Digest of the Soviet Press (CDSP) is notable for the consistency of its format over the years, which helps to remove some of the doubt that the volume of criticisms recorded per year is an artifact of CDSP reporting practices; however, there have been slight variations in format which must be acknowledged. In general, I have read all foreign-policy relevant articles in each of the surveyed years, despite slight changes in the indexing format (e.g., subheadings) over time. 1949, which recorded the heaviest volume of criticisms, accomplished this in part due to a CDSP practice of extensively using attendant references (e.g., "See Also _____"). 1949 was the only year I surveyed which was strongly affected by this practice, and since the year was a mainstream cold-war period, rather than one of mixed tendencies, the distortion was minimized. Also, as press translations from New Times (Vol. 1, 1943) and International Affairs (Vol. 1, 1955) become increasingly represented in the CDSP, it is conceivable that reportage on articles from Pravda and Izvestia covering the same or similar topics might have diminished somewhat. CDSP volumes have slimmed down in recent years, but this appears to have taken place at the expense of New Times and International Affairs (which I do not monitor anyway), as well as due to shorter digested versions of lengthy articles and speeches.

II. Explanation of Certain Coding Designations

A. Criticisms

1. Regarding the distinction between "international law" (criticism-type XVI) and "bilateral agreements" (criticism-types XI and XII), I treat post-war Big-4 activities, and East-West multilateral fora (e.g., CSCE) as bilateral, rather than international.

2. With no self-evident category present to accommodate it, I have treated the criticism "diplomatic exclusion" as the equivalent of no. XV -- "Refusal to admit mutual equality and the need for reciprocity in bilateral agreements."

3. There is a fine, almost subjective line between "subversion (criticism-type II) and "meddling" (criticism-type X). The difference is really a matter of degree; an attempt to spell out the difference follows:

   - subversion: (a) physical act perpetrated on the other's terrain which is cited as injurious; (b) incitement of an indigenous group in the other's country; (c) the weakening or overthrow of the other's political system is implicit in such an action.

   - meddling: (a) verbal suggestion or demand for the other to act in a certain way; (b) an attempt to impact on the other's decisions; (c) the effect is seen as inconvenient or insulting, rather than threatening.

Note: President Carter's human rights campaign can be treated as both, depending on the context.

4. A couple of significant criticism-types emerged during the coding which had not been identified in the pretests, and therefore were not included in the HOC schemes. Accommodating these criticisms has led to some distortion which was not discerned during coding. The two unforeseen criticisms are: (1) quest for hegemony/world domination (not quite criticism-type II or III), and (2) direct support of an insurgency (not quite analogous to criticism-type VIII). The first of these two unforeseen criticisms was scored by logging two marks ("imperialism" plus "domination") and the second similarly ("imperialism" plus "militarism"). This in essence endowed these two criticisms with the influence of a coefficient value equal to .866. This would mean that each of these two criticism-types reflects a perceived enemy image much more salient than that reflected by, for example, "aggressive military intent against oneself"; this is not true for "supporting insurgents," and whereas it might be for "hegemony/world domination," it would not be so to the great extent implied by the equivalent of a .866 coefficient value. Therefore, although this situation interjects a bit of distortion into the logic of my method for ranking criticism-types, the distortion is consistent for all years examined.

Explanation of Certain Coding Designations

B. Countries

1. The People's Republic of China is treated as a member of the USSR's attendant bloc until the year 1969.

2. In the Soviet press, the Korean War was almost exclusively depicted as a case of imperialist aggression against the people of South Korea, rather than as a war against socialist North Korea.

3. The Vietnamese War was treated alternately by the Soviet press as imperialist aggression against the people of South Vietnam or as a war against socialist North Vietnam, depending on the thrust of the article.

III. Hierarchy of Criticisms: Example Themes (asterisk connotes "usually stated as such")

1. "Aggressive military intent."*

2. "Political or economic subversion: sabotage." -- especially espionage; also economic blockade/boycott.

3. "General interest in the outbreak of war." -- this goes beyond militarism (a general orientation), and implies that war is a feasible immediate contingency for the other side.

4. "Aggressive Third World imperialism or domination of allies: militarism" -- (a) imperialism - controlling other states' government structure and functioning; directly siphoning benefits via one's own monopolies abroad; (b) domination - foisting decisions (usually onerous) on allies without considering their point of view or soliciting their input; (c) militarism - an orientation towards military solutions of international problems; fostering the arms race; transferring weapons needlessly or provocatively to other states.

5. "General malevolence or intransigence of the other's foreign policy or foreign policy leadership." -- (a) malevolence - interest in whipping up tensions and fostering international problems; the dictation of U.S. foreign policy by monopolies; association with fascists, racists, Hitlerites, etc.; prone to committing acts which are criminal, inhuman, barbaric, etc.: (b) intransigence - consciously prolonging negotiations, or avoiding needed negotiations altogether.

6. "General misinformation, propaganda or slander."*

7. "Perpetration of a provocative act." -- this is a sort of catch-all category which refers to a discrete act; e.g. a naval vessel is

bumped by a battleship belonging to the other side, a peaceful installation is buzzed by aircraft belonging to the other side, a child is kidnapped and granted political asylum by the other side, etc. This category is similar to no. II "subversion," but provocative acts usually do not take place on Soviet terrain, and the outcomes are usually perceptual (e.g., produce indignation) rather than tangible (e.g., produce loss or difficulty).

8. "Aggression by proxy: support of an aggressor."* -- usually Israel or South Africa.

9. "Neocolonialism" -- indirect subjugation via economic terms of trade; fostering dependency via aid monies, etc.

10. "Meddling in the other's internal affairs" -- see Explanation of Certain Coding Designations, Part A, No. 3.

11. "Breaking bilateral agreements."*

12. "A bilateral agreements terms are not carried out sufficiently due to, e.g., stinginess, tardiness."*

13. "Official foreign policy seeks to reverse improving bilateral relations." -- includes the charge of undermining detente.

14. "A tacit bilateral understanding is construed or miscomprehended."*

15. "Refusal to admit mutual equality and the need for reciprocity in bilateral agreements."*

16. "Breaking or inadequate adherence to international law or norms."* -- may also include perversion of international institutions, e.g., the U.N., (unless explicitly couched as proof of general malevolence of U.S. foreign policy).

17. "An act or policy is anachronistic given an improved bilateral relationship/international environment."*

18. "Detente policy is subject to loss of central direction due to the influence of irresponsible domestic or international third parties." -- careful not to confuse this with "some circles" criticisms; e.g., is the criticism of the central government for its vulnerability and instability, or of a group for trying to influence the central government.

19. "Failure to foresee the negative connotation which would be attached to certain actions."*

20. "Some Circles: Major Malevolence"/"Some Circles: Malevolence." -- the term "some circles" simply means that a criticism is ascribed

202

to a political grouping(s) in the other state, but not to those who are responsible for a state's official foreign policy. "Major malevolence" simply means any criticism which receives a coefficient value greater than .290 on the HOC scheme-- "malevolence" meaning those criticisms ranking below this .290 mark.

U.S. Criticisms of the USSR

Due to the close similarly of the Hierarchy of Criticisms (HOC) scheme as voiced by both the U.S. and Soviet sides, resulting in a strong overlap of coding rules, definitions, and criticism-types, this section of Appendix D will be much shorter than the first. By comparing Tables 4 and 5 in the text, one will find that I have dropped four criticism types germane to the Soviet press from the HOC scheme: U.S. criticisms (Table 5), as well as added eight new ones to Table 5; both the deletions and additions were due to the differing styles and points of attack favored by the two sides. As the reader identifies the specific additions and deletions, the motivating logic for such alterations should be quite clear.

Due to the inordinate amount of time that was consumed reading "all" Soviet criticisms of American foreign policy per annum, I decided to "sample" articles from the Index to the New York Times. I used a systematic sampling technique to ensure avoidance of cyclical reporting biases, and drew exactly forty articles per year. The sampling of articles reduced the meaningfulness, if not validity, of the article/reference distinction which I employed for Soviet criticisms of American foreign policy, so it was dropped.

Although the example themes I provided in the first section of this appendix for each criticism-type are still basically valid, the emphases of American, as opposed to Soviet, criticisms will, of course, be somewhat different. Due to the slightly expanded length of the American HOC scheme, as well as my previous experience in working with the Soviet HOC scheme, these twnety-five criticism-types accommodated the empirical world nicely. There did occur, however, a few unforeseen types of criticisms, which I had to map to their closest analogues in the scheme; for example:

1.   General expansionism = no. III, "Imperialism."

2.   The professed Soviet policy of detente has involved words but no deeds = no. XII, "A bilateral agreement's terms are not carried out sufficiently."

3.   It is too soon to relax our vigilance because a Soviet policy of cooperation may not last long = no. XXI, "Detente policy is subject to loss of central direction...."

203

APPENDIX E

SOVIET CRITICISMS OF THE U.S.

YEAR: 1949 articles		SCALE SCORE = 296.4 references
I.	37	1
II.	44	4
III.	33	1
IV.	383	21
V.	73	1
VI.	65	3
VII.	1	-
VIII.	-	1
IX.	1	-
X.	2	-
XI.	50	-
XII.	-	-
XIII.	-	-

NOTE: Numbers in each box represent the incidence or frequency of that criticism type.

SOVIET CRITICISMS OF THE U.S.

references

XIV.	-	-
XV.	-	-
XVI.	16	-
XVII.	-	-
XVIII.	-	-
XIX.	-	-
XX.	5	-
XXI.	-	1

SOVIET CRITICISMS OF THE U.S.

SCALE SCORE = 301.0

	articles	references
I.	15	6
II.	51	22
III.	11	6
IV.	290	100
V.	133	28
VI.	53	8
VII.	5	-
VIII.	22	8
IX.	8	1
X.	1	-
XI.	20	5
XII.	1	-
XIII.	-	-

NOTE: Numbers in each box represent the incidence or frequency of each criticism-type.

SOVIET CRITICISMS OF THE U.S.

YEAR: 1953		references
XIV.	2	-
XV.	5	2
XVI.	13	3
XVII.	5	-
XVIII.	-	-
XIX.	-	-
XX.	31	12
XXI.	2	1

SOVIET CRITICISMS OF THE U.S.

SCALE SCORE = 55.8

	articles	references
I.	-	3
II.	15	15
III.	1	-
IV.	34	27
V.	19	13
VI.	18	7
VII.	1	-
VIII.	4	4
IX.	-	4
X.	1	1
XI.	1	1
XII.	2	-
XIII.	1	1

NOTE: Numbers in each box represent the incidence or frequency of each criticism-type.

SOVIET CRITICISMS OF THE U.S.

         references

	1956	references
XIV.	-	-
XV.	2	-
XVI.	5	2
XVII.	4	2
XVIII.	-	-
XIX.	-	-
XX.	10	7
XXI.	3	-

SOVIET CRITICISMS OF THE U.S.

YEAR: 1958   SCALE SCORE: 129.7

	articles	references
I.	7	7
II.	11	10
III.	7	2
IV.	94	91
V.	40	28
VI.	38	16
VII.	18	1
VIII.	1	1
IX.	-	-
X.	1	-
XI.	-	-
XII.	4	3
XIII.	-	-

NOTE: Numbers in each box represent the incidence or frequency of each criticism-type.

SOVIET CRITICISMS OF THE U.S.

references

XIV.	-	-
XV.	7	4
XVI.	8	2
XVII.	2	2
XVIII.	1	-
XIX.	-	-
XX.	12	10
XXI.	-	-

SOVIET CRITICISMS OF THE U.S.

	articles	references
I.	7	13
II.	17	15
III.	-	3
IV.	72	70
V.	28	22
VI.	21	13
VII.	3	4
VIII.	3	6
IX.	7	3
X.	1	-
XI.	1	-
XII.	2	-
XIII.	-	-

NOTE: Numbers in each box represent the incidence or frequency of each criticism-type.

SOVIET CRITICISMS OF THE U.S.

references

XIV.	-	-
XV.	-	1
XVI.	13	3
XVII.	4	2
XVIII.	1	1
XIX.	-	-
XX.	33	33
XXI.	5	4

SOVIET CRITICISMS OF THE U.S.

<u>YEAR: 1964</u>   <u>SCALE SCORE = 155.0</u>

	articles	references
I.	7	7
II.	16	19
III.	-	-
IV.	135	105
V.	44	15
VI.	21	8
VII.	19	8
VIII.	4	9
IX.	5	2
X.	-	-
XI.	-	-
XII.	-	-
XIII.	1	-

NOTE: Numbers in each box represent the incidence or frequency of each criticism-type.

214

SOVIET CRITICISMS OF THE U.S.

	YEAR: 1964	references
XIV.	1	-
XV.	-	-
XVI.	18	5
XVII.	10	-
XVIII.	4	-
XIX.	-	1
XX.	54	11
XXI.	2	2

SOVIET CRITICISMS OF THE U.S.

	YEAR: 1969 articles	SCALE SCORE = 156.4 references
I.	11	6
II.	16	9
III.	-	-
IV.	135	156
V.	45	20
VI.	20	8
VII.	3	1
VIII.	8	18
IX.	7	3
X.	1	-
XI.	2	-
XII.	-	-
XIII.	-	-

NOTE: Numbers in each box represent the incidence or frequency of each criticism-type.

SOVIET CRITICISMS OF THE U.S.

YEAR: 1969		references
XIV.	-	1
XV.	-	-
XVI.	6	5
XVII.	1	-
XVIII.	1	-
XIX.	-	1
XX.	39	11
XXI.	4	-

SOVIET CRITICISMS OF THE U.S.

<u>YEAR: 1971</u>
articles

<u>SCALE SCORE = 250.2</u>
references

	articles	references
I.	21	7
II.	7	6
III.	-	-
IV.	245	217
V.	88	42
VI.	30	15
VII.	3	1
VIII.	23	34
IX.	2	2
X.	1	1
XI.	-	-
XII.	-	-
XIII.	2	-

NOTE: Numbers in each box represent the incidence or frequency of each criticism-type.

SOVIET CRITICISMS OF THE U.S.

YEAR: 1971		references
XIV.	-	-
XV.	3	3
XVI.	7	3
XVII.	2	1
XVIII.	-	-
XIX.	-	-
XX.	24	-
XXI.	4	2

SOVIET CRITICISMS OF THE U.S.

YEAR: 1973   SCALE SCORE = 26.0
         articles   references

	articles	references
I.	-	-
II.	1	-
III.	-	-
IV.	19	41
V.	4	2
VI.	2	1
VII.	1	-
VIII.	2	6
IX.	-	-
X.	-	-
XI.	1	-
XII.	1	1
XIII.	-	-

NOTE: Numbers in each box represent the incidence or frequency of each criticism-type.

SOVIET CRITICISMS OF THE U.S.

YEAR: 1973		references
XIV.	-	-
XV.	-	-
XVI.	-	1
XVII.	3	2
XVIII.	2	-
XIX.	-	-
XX.	21	2
XXI.	5	3

SOVIET CRITICISMS OF THE U.S.

	YEAR: 1976 articles	SCALE SCORE = 83.1 references
I.	-	-
II.	6	4
III.	-	-
IV.	72	16
V.	45	8
VI.	19	4
VII.	7	-
VIII.	4	1
IX.	5	-
X.	5	-
XI.	2	-
XII.	2	-
XIII.	2	-

NOTE: Numbers in each box represent the incidence or frequency of each criticism-type.

SOVIET CRITICISMS OF THE U.S.

references

XIV.	1	-
XV.	1	-
XVI.	4	1
XVII.	4	-
XVIII.	11	-
XIX.	-	-
XX.	35	6
XXI.	22	1

SOVIET CRITICISMS OF THE U.S.

	YEAR: 1981 articles	SCALE SCORE = 280.8 references
I.	12	5
II.	24	17
III.	-	-
IV.	284	99
V.	108	39
VI.	70	9
VII.	22	-
VIII.	21	12
IX.	1	1
X.	4	-
XI.	2	3
XII.	-	-
XIII.	19	6

NOTE: Numbers in each box represent the incidence or frequency of each criticism-type.

SOVIET CRITICISMS OF THE U.S.

YEAR: 1981		references
XIV.	-	-
XV.	8	4
XVI.	12	-
XVII.	10	1
XVIII.	-	-
XIX.	1	-
XX.	28	4
XXI.	4	-

policy change), 71-72, 94. See
also Organizational learning

Empathy, 121

Enemy image, 25-26, 95, 107-8, 122.
See also Imagery (of another
state); Relational-type (between
countries)

Equity, 6-7

Etzioni, Amitai, 5

Evoked set, collective, 136-37.
See also Psychological factors
in detente

Exchange theory, 5

Expectations, realization/non-
realization of, 7, 77. See
also Probe, retrodictive
strategic

Exposure (as risk), 13-14

Facts on File, 12

Falkland Islands war, British-
Argentine, 119

Foreign policy, inter-Superpower,
36-37, 41-42, 111. See also
Foreign policy, Soviet; Foreign
policy, U.S.

Foreign policy, Soviet, xvii, 93,
128, 130

Foreign policy, U.S.: 111-12, 128,
138; control of, 71, 80-81, 84;
receptivity to academic inputs,
108; susceptibility to single-
interest groups, 74, 122, 130.
See also, Elections, U.S.
Presidential; Detente, policymaking problem

Foreign Policy Motivation, 25

Foreign policy strategy. See
political strategy

Gamson, William and Andre Modigliani,
128

Garthoff, Raymond, 86

Geopolitical competition, 127-29

George, Alexander, xiv, 138

Germany, Hitler's, 93

Goldmann, Kjell, 6

Gorbachev, Mikhail, 132

Graduated Reciprocation in
Tension-reduction (GRIT),

5, 111

Hage, Jerald and Robert Dewar,
71

Hierarchy of Criticisms
Scheme, 17-37, 97

Horn, Robert, 128

Ideologies, role of Soviet and
American, 127, 129-30

Imagery: of another state,
25-28, 80; relationship to
policy behavior of, 33-37.
See also Relational-type;
Enemy Image

Implementation, policy, 83, 84

Incentives, material (role in
fostering policy change),
71, 72-73, 84, 117-18. See
also Organizational learning

Inequity. See Equity

Institutionalization. See
Detente, institutionalization
of

Instrumental learning, 72, 73

Irrationality. See rationality

Issue-area, 11-12, 96

Jackson-Vanik amendment
(Trade Reform Bill), xv

Jewish emigration from the
USSR, 134. See also
Linkage, policy.

Kennan, George, 134

Kissinger, Henry, 7, 73, 86,
94, 95

Khrushchev, Nikita, 94, 129

Legitimation, policy, 122. See
also Detente, domestic requirements; Detente, in-
stitutionalization of

Liberalization of the Soviet
political system, 133-35

Military build-up, Soviet, 86-
87

Military funding (and detente
enhancement), 73

228

ABOUT THE AUTHOR

Paul F. Herman, Jr., a Phi Beta Kappa at the University of Florida, earned Bachelor and Master of Arts degrees there in political science. He spent 1978-79 abroad, studying and conducting research in Poland. As a graduate assistant, he did his doctoral work in international affairs/Soviet studies at the University of Pittsburgh's Graduate School of Public and International Affairs. While at the University of Pittsburgh, Dr. Herman was awarded a Foreign Language and Area Studies fellowship from the U.S. Department of Education, as well as the university's Samuel T. Owens Graduate Fellowship. He was able during this time to co-author or contribute to several publications, including "Forecasting Energy Futures: A Comparative Assessment" with Michael Brenner, and "Target Tokyo: The Story of the Sorge Spy Ring" by Gordon Prange with Donald Goldstein and Katherine Dillon. Dr. Herman has presented papers at various academic conferences on such topics as content analysis, academic exchanges, and U.S.-Soviet detente. He currently works as an analyst for the United States Department of Defense.